CHILDREN'S HOMES

LIVING AWAY FROM HOME: STUDIES IN RESIDENTIAL CARE

Other titles in the series

CHILDREN'S HOMES

A Study in Diversity

Ian Sinclair and Ian Gibbs

JOHN WILEY & SONS

Chichester · New York · Weinheim · Brisbane · Singapore · Toronto

Copyright © 1998 by John Wiley & Sons Ltd,
Baffins Lane, Chichester,
West Sussex PO19 1UD, England

National   01243 779777
International   (+44) 1243 779777
e-mail (for orders and customer service enquiries):
cs-books@wiley.co.uk
Visit our Home Page on http://www.wiley.co.uk
or http://www.wiley.com

Other Wiley Editorial Offices

John Wiley & Sons, Inc., 605 Third Avenue,
New York, NY 10158-0012, USA

WILEY-VCH Verlag GmbH, Pappelallee 3,
D-69469 Weinheim, Germany

Jacaranda Wiley Ltd, 33 Park Road, Milton,
Queensland 4064, Australia

John Wiley & Sons (Asia) Pte Ltd, 2 Clementi Loop #02-01,
Jin Xing Distripark, Singapore 129809

John Wiley & Sons (Canada) Ltd, 22 Worcester Road,
Rexdale, Ontario M9W 1L1, Canada

Library of Congress Cataloging-in-Publication Data

Sinclair, Ian, 1938–
    Children's homes : a study in diversity / Ian Sinclair and Ian
  Gibbs.
        p.   cm. — (Living away from home)
    Includes bibliographical references and index.
    ISBN 0-471-98456-6 (pbk.)
    1. Children—Institutional care—Great Britain.   I. Gibbs, Ian.
  II. Title.   III. Series.
  HV866.G7S56   1998
  362.73'2'0941—dc21   98–18632
                                                       CIP

British Library Cataloguing in Publication Data

A catalogue record for this book is available from the British Library

ISBN 0-471-98456-6

Typeset in 10/12pt Palatino by Dorwyn Ltd, Rowlands Castle, Hants
Printed and bound in Great Britain by Bookcraft (Bath) Ltd, Midsomer Norton, Somerset
This book is printed on acid-free paper responsibly manufactured from sustainable
forestry, in which at least two trees are planted for each one used for paper production.

CONTENTS

LIST OF TABLES

ABOUT THE AUTHORS

Ian Sinclair has a background in teaching, operational research, social work and social work research. He is currently a professor of social work at York and was previously director of research at the National Institute of Social Work. In 1971 he helped pioneer the cross-institutional approach to research in residential care with a study of probation hostels, and in 1975 he co-edited a book bringing together examples of the approach with Ron Clarke and the late Jack Tizard. He has published widely both in journals and in books.

Ian Gibbs has been involved in social and economic research for 25 years, the last 11 at the University of York. During his time as a full-time researcher his work has included research on teacher education and social work education, skill mix in nursing, the financial resources available to older people and quality issues in both old people's and children's homes. He is currently working with Ian Sinclair on research which looks at supporting foster placements.

FOREWORD

We are pleased to have the opportunity to provide the foreword to this book, which is one of a series of publications which, we are sure, will prove to be a significant contribution to thinking in both the practice and management of the care of children who need to live away from home.

The group of studies about residential care was commissioned to address key concerns arising from public inquiries, such as the Utting (Children in the Public Care) and Pindown Inquiries, and to provide a balanced account of what life is like for children and staff in the majority of children's homes in the UK in the 1990s.

Twelve linked research studies were commissioned by the Department of Health in the period 1990–94: (a thirteenth—that of David Berridge and Isabelle Brodie—was not commissioned by the Department). These research studies came in the wake of the implementation of the Children Act 1989 and its Regulations and Guidance, which provided significant new safeguards for children living away from home. Additional government action to protect these children was taken following the publication of the reports 'Children in the Public Care', 'Accommodating Children', 'Another Kind of Home' and 'Choosing with Care', notably through the publications of the Support Force for Children's Residential Care and circulars issued by the relevant Departments of State. However, as Sir William Utting tells us in his second report 'People Like Us', published in 1997, providing safe and caring settings for children looked after away from home remains a significant challenge for the nineties.

This book, taken together with the overview publication, and the others in the series contains lessons for all those concerned with children and young people living away from home, who are the responsibility of all of us.

Carolyn Davies, *Department of Health*
Lesley Archer, *University of York*
Leslie Hicks, *University of York*
Mike Little, *Dartington Social Research Unit*
—Editors

ACKNOWLEDGEMENTS

This research was a team effort. A key member of this team was Carol Stimson. She helped in the development of the interviews with the heads of homes, piloted the interview, trained the interviewers and rated the tapes. Her skill, wit, enthusiasm and style played a great part in making the project both highly enjoyable and intellectually stimulating for other members of the team. Carol died in a car crash not long after this project finished. We would like this book to be one of the ways in which her gifted life is remembered.

The main interviewers on the project were Gerard Szary, Madeleine Leech, Penny Williams, Philip Raws and Hilary Cole. They explained the project to the staff and young people: carried out all the main interviews with parents, young people and heads of homes, and generally managed the project in the local authorities. Dianne Wilson helped in developing the codes, coded the open-ended questions in all the main interview schedules, collected the quotations and generally prepared the data. Dot Taylor and her colleagues in Data Preparation prepared and entered the data for analysis. Sarah Clark helped with the typing of the final draft. Janet Moore maintained secretarial oversight of the project, helped to set up and run the procedure of receiving and checking the postal question-naires, and sending reminders and thank you letters. All these very dif-ferent individuals gave their help with good humour, efficiency and with dedication way beyond the call of duty. The project could not have been completed on time and in all the main practical parts successfully without them.

This project benefited from advice and support from Peter Lee of the University of York Mathematics Department, who not only instructed us in the finer points of logistic regression but made sure we got this right by doing the analysis himself. Finally, one of us received informal but very helpful advice from David Shaw, who happened to be in his home and had deep insight into children's homes, and his own wife Elma Sinclair, a former residential social worker.

Our advisory committee, composed of Dr Pat Cawson, Dr Carolyn Davies, Mr Ted Hillier, Mr John Rowlands, Mr Graham Jarvis and Ms Lynda Fean, read drafts of instruments, commented on the design of the study and warned us when our thoughts became confused. Even though they had been selected for their professional rather than their research skills, their expertise in both fields proved invaluable. After the project was finished, John Rowlands continued to read drafts, helping to iron out mistakes even when the result would be the clearer presentation of a point with which he disagreed. Carolyn Davies, our research liaison officer, provided her usual patience, constructive criticism, encouragement and support.

Our main thanks must go to those who, for reasons of confidentiality, we cannot name: the managers and the liaison officers in the authorities who were prepared to participate in, and support, a project which took up a lot of their and their department's time; and the heads of homes, staff, young people, parents and social workers who agreed to talk to us or filled in the sometimes lengthy questionnaires. Children's homes are complex exercises in the management of human pain. They are also a testimony to the collaboration of very diverse people and to their wit, courage, experience and skills. By giving us insights into these complex matters, our respondents are largely responsible for whatever success this project may have had.

Ian Sinclair and Ian Gibbs

1

INTRODUCTION TO THE STUDY

Local authorities . . . were faced with a situation in the 1980s that was very difficult to manage. Residential care lost half its population in five years and two-thirds in ten. It now cries out for a planned structure in which it can be seen as a positive resource within the range of children's services . . . Staff need to be assured that what they are doing is important, is valued and will endure (Utting 1991).

[Children's homes are] still contracting under the pressures of financial retrenchment and ideological prejudice. . . . It is safer to err on the side of generosity of provision, even with an expensive service like residential care. Choice is safety (Utting 1997).

AIMS

This book is about 48 local authority children's homes. The central aim is to measure and explain the different outcomes achieved by the homes—to see, for example, if smaller homes or homes with higher staffing ratios did 'better' than others. By the end of the book we will have given answers to these questions and to other related ones about the way the homes were run and the resources devoted to them.

The search to explain outcomes in terms of home characteristics clearly requires us to describe both. Description, however, has a value of its own. There are few academic studies of children's homes and two of the most important (Berridge 1985; Colton 1989) may no longer apply. Three further studies have now provided detailed qualitative information on small samples of homes (Berridge and Brodie 1998; Brown *et al.* 1996) and on the staff world (Whitaker, Archer and Hicks 1998). This book complements these studies by providing systematic information on a large sample of homes, and on the staff, residents, parents and social workers associated with them. Such information does not in itself provide an evaluation of the homes. Without this background, however, evaluation cannot begin.

THE BACKGROUND TO THE RESEARCH

The research was commissioned against a background of anxiety about children's homes and an associated flurry of reports (e.g. Audit Commission 1994; Kirkwood 1993; Levy and Kahan 1991; Skinner 1992; Social Services Inspectorate 1994; Social Services Inspectorate for Wales 1991; Wagner 1988; Warner 1992; Utting 1991). Overtly these anxieties were concerned with cost and scandal. More fundamentally, perhaps, they arose from changes in society and in the homes themselves and from uncertainty over the moral and theoretical basis for residential care. Change and uncertainty led to pragmatic difficulties in running, staffing and financing the homes, which nevertheless still seemed to play an essential role in the care system in most authorities. So there was a conflict between the problems presented by the homes and the apparent need to have them. This conflict led to the reports.

The crisis which faces residential homes arises in part from changes in the labour market. In 1969 care might have been seen as a helping hand for those who were in danger of falling off a ladder that led from school to the employment which would, in time, allow young people to pay for accommodation and set up a family. Families were (by current standards) stable, and the divorce rate was comparatively low. Such certainties are gone. Secure employment does not await the 16 year-old school leaver, the period of launching is protracted and more difficult, the proportion who leave school at 16 is less than half what it was and those who do so are most unlikely to get a job. For those cast on to the job market at 16 without skills and family support, the ladder seems to lack numerous rungs (see, for example, Coles 1995 for a summary). The residents of children's homes are typically in this position. Descriptive studies of residential care suggest that it neither mounts a determined attack on their educational problems nor keeps them until they are properly launched (Stein 1994, 1997).

Economic change has been accompanied by ethical uncertainty. A strong value base was considered essential to the well-being of residential care in the 1970s (Wolins 1974). Values which gave a social group a high importance relative to the family justified the exchange of a family for a group upbringing and were the foundation for establishments as diverse as the Israeli kibbutzim, Russian boarding schools, and public schools for the British upper classes. These values are no longer widely held. Boarding schools for the upper classes have to make greater allowance for family allegiance if they are to recruit (Gooch, 1996). The Children Act (1989) reinforces the value of families. Delinquency and poor school attendance are no longer in themselves grounds for removing children so that their 'moral standards' can be improved. The religious beliefs which underpinned so much residential care are declining. They can hardly be espoused by authorities which pride themselves on providing equal treatment irrespective of a person's faith or lack of it.

Theoretical uncertainty has accompanied ethical unease. Traditionally, one class of residential establishment was intended to change its residents. The theoretical basis for this treatment was always disputed, with competing philosophies variously urging the virtues of training, of therapeutic communities providing challenge and confrontation, and of nurturing environments within which the 'frozen' child could grow. Even where there was an official theory, staff and residents often did not share it or were hostile to it (Ackland 1982; Polsky 1965; Walter 1977); the goals of the institution (e.g. the maintenance of good order) often had little to do with the residents' problems on release (Millham, Bullock and Cherrett 1975; Petrie 1980; Walter 1977); and changes in the residents that did take place were often nullified by the environments to which they were discharged (Allerhand, Weber and Haug 1966; Coates, Miller and Ohlin 1978; Lewis 1982; Petrie 1980; Sinclair 1971; Taylor and Alpert 1973).

Doubts over treatment were married to outright disapproval of homes as damaging and unnatural places in which to bring up children. This disapproval lacked a research basis. It relied heavily for its research support from the swingeing attack by Goffman (1961) on institutions and from Bowlby's (1953) equally devastating critique of residential care for very young children. Goffman's work was heavily influenced by one study of a psychiatric institution and Bowlby's by studies of the kind of orphanage which England no longer has. Children's homes are now small establishments, which cater, as Berridge (1985) first emphasised, almost entirely for adolescents. Nevertheless, social workers and even residential staff in the 1980s saw residential care as second best to other forms of substitute care, and very much a last resort (Fisher et al. 1986; Millham et al. 1986; Packman 1986). At best, researchers have tended to see residential care as providing a benign but irrelevant interlude which leaves children ill-equipped for their future lives and cut off from their parents and backgrounds (Department of Health 1991; Parker 1988; Stein and Carey 1986).

Professional disapproval has provided the context for auditors' concerns (Audit Commission 1994). The financial resources devoted to the homes are very large (a total of £550 million, at an average gross cost per client per year of £41,483 in 1993–4 in England and Wales, according to the Chartered Institute of Public Finance and Accountancy [CIPFA 1996]). Costs since then have risen and are now estimated to average £61,000 per place per year (Carr-Hill et al. 1997)—an increase which easily maintains the position of residential care as the branch of children's social services which makes the greatest call on resources. There are considerable differences between authorities in the relative proportions of children who are looked after in children's homes and in foster care. This index is in some respects misleading, since it ignores variations in 'throughput' (Rowe, Hundleby and Garnett 1989) but has been widely used. Variations in the index suggested to the Audit Commission that authorities with high numbers in residential care could both save money and improve standards by substituting other services.

Against this background the number of places in children's homes has, not surprisingly, declined. In 1979 the 29,000 residents in community homes constituted 31% of those in care. By 1990 the comparable numbers had shrunk to 11,000 and 17%. By March 31 1996 there were only 5500 children and young people in community homes in England, as opposed to 33,000 in foster placements (Department of Health 1997). A small number of authorities—most famously Warwickshire, but also others—have no community homes of their own. More significantly, perhaps, the overall reduction in children's home places conforms to a trend that applies to all sectors of boarding and residential care for children in the UK (Gooch 1996) and on the continent of Europe as well (Colton and Hellinckx 1994; Madge 1994).

In England these reductions have applied particularly to certain sectors of residential care. Therapeutic communities, community homes with education, and residential nurseries have gone or all but gone. Arguably, remand homes, reception centres and family group homes have either gone or have changed into something so different that they are hardly recognisable. The remaining establishments (largely small, local children's homes) may be suspected of catering for the clientele formerly served by these other kinds of establishment.

This shift poses staff in the homes with awkward problems. The staff themselves are known to be largely untrained (Barr 1987; Utting 1991, 1997; Warner 1992). Theories which relied on the creation of a 'special world' separate from that in which the residents normally moved are dubiously relevant in open establishments where the young people are placed as close as possible to their families. Yet these theories have in the past provided the rationale for much residential care and, it may be suspected, a means of control. So untrained staff in establishments which have their ancestry in the small orphanage are faced with a clientele much of which might once have been served by the Approved Schools. Questions connected with the purpose of the establishment and with establishing order inevitably arise.

Evidence of these 'pragmatic' problems is seen in research, official statistics and reports. Reduction in the number of homes has led to reorganisation and uncertainty for the remaining institutions (Utting 1991), a more difficult clientele (Berridge and Brodie 1998), a greater difficulty in defining roles as establishments strive to fulfil a wider range of functions (e.g. Rowe, Hundleby and Garnett 1989), and additional costs as the number of residents is reduced more rapidly than the number of staff (see, for example, Utting 1991 on unit costs). The homes themselves are prone to scandals associated with sexual abuse or outbreaks of serious disorder (Stein 1993). The theoretical vacuum is reflected in two of the most notorious of these (Kirkwood 1993; Levy and Kahan 1991). What was striking about these events was not merely the malign influence of particular individuals, but the ease with which extraordinary practices, widely known in the authority, were seen as having an acceptable rationale.

The combination of cost and scandal suggests that residential care may not survive. That it has survived so far reflects the difficulty of doing without it. The homes deal with young people whose activities are of particular interest to the media and who are particularly hard to place. 'Rat boy', 'blip boy', safari boy' and other 'looked after' young people who make the headlines for reasons connected with their treatment or delinquency most commonly come from the residential sector. Fat files bulging with information on 'hard-to-place' children occupy the time of the senior managers of Social Services Departments. Even Warwickshire, which cut out its own children's homes, continued to use some out-of-county placements, had to contain a number of children who disrupted a large number of foster placements, and found considerable difficulty in allowing adequate choice within its foster care system (Cliffe with Berridge 1991).

In the face of such pragmatic problems residential care continues to be frequently used, if increasingly for shorter periods (Department of Health 1997). Rowe, Hundleby and Garnett (1989) in their study of substitute care in six authorities found that nearly half the placements of teenagers involved residential care. Both Biehal and her colleagues (1992) and Garnett (1992) found that almost all the care leavers in their study had spent time in residential care and many left from it. Residents placed in children's homes have more behaviour problems than those of a similar age who are placed in foster care (Rowe, Hundleby and Garnett 1989) and, as we have already mentioned, their problems are on average more serious than they were 10 years ago (Berridge and Brodie 1998).

So residential care continues—a dilemma for those who provide it, a matter of concern to politicians and the public, and a fertile source of enquiries and media reports. What is apparent is that if it is to be provided it should be of as high a quality as possible.

POTENTIAL CONTRIBUTION OF THIS RESEARCH

These problems relate to the changing role of residential care for young people, its alleged unsatisfactory state, and the lack of a theory which would link the methods employed to outcomes. In this situation research can help by describing both the general features of this care, its diversity and the way in which this diversity leads to different outcomes. Changes have led to uncertainty about the role of homes. It is sensible to look carefully at what they are doing, and at whether different homes are playing different roles. There are problems connected with costs, disorder and staff training in residential care. It is sensible to see how widespread these problems are, and whether some homes avoid them and might have lessons for others. By describing diversity in provision and outcomes, research can provide the building blocks for evaluation. Thus we are able to examine the consequences of difference. In this way we can begin to provide an empirical basis for a theory of residential care.

In developing this research we are able to build on the analysis in official reports. These have emphasised the importance of clarifying the role of residential care in general and individual homes in particular (Audit Commission 1994; Department of Health 1993; Utting 1991; Warner 1992). This clarification is seen, among other things, as avoiding an unsuitable mix of young people (Social Services Inspectorate for Wales 1992). It is to be reinforced by strong management, including particularly procedures for handling complaints, care planning and inspection and, by appropriate staff selection, training, support and development (Audit Commission 1994; Levy and Kahan 1991; Social Services Committee 1984; Utting 1991; Warner 1992). The importance of providing an adequate number of staff is given particular emphasis. Implicitly or explicitly this is expected to reduce the risk of abuse (notably by enabling more than one member of staff to be on duty at any one time) (Levy and Kahan 1991; Utting 1997). Overall these recommendations suggest a hierarchy of cause and effect—the role of the home implies staffing and management arrangements, which in turn will determine the reactions of the residents and hence outcomes.

In keeping with this analysis, this book will examine *the roles the homes play*—the kinds of young people admitted, the reasons for their admission, the purposes for which they are admitted, the length of time for which they stay, and their proposed destinations. In evaluating these roles it is important to get the views of residents, their parents and their social workers, and to examine what, if any, alternative provision they would have liked. In examining these issues we have built on earlier work by Rowe and her colleagues (1989) and on consumer studies, particularly those by Fisher and his colleagues (1986) and Packman (1986). We have, however, tested their conclusions in the new conditions of residential care. We have also provided more information than was previously available on the kind of provision (e.g. foster care or supported lodgings) that parents, young people and social workers would ideally like.

The book will also examine the way the *homes as units* are resourced, managed and run. The homes have been said to be expensive, to have untrained staff, to be seeking to fulfil too many purposes, and to have no clear theoretical rationale. So we will examine how far the staffing ratio and proportion of qualified staff varies between homes, whether they are in fact classified in terms of the purposes they serve and whether some of the heads of homes have a clear rationale for what they are doing. We will also examine whether these variations matter—for example, whether homes with multiple aims or heads with unclear philosophies tend to 'do worse' than other homes.

A final set of problems has to do with the *resident world*. There is a suspicion that residents are out of control, and that the delinquent and disorderly activities that undoubtedly characterise a minority of homes are equally characteristic of all. Here again, our aim is partly descriptive—to describe the world of the residents and the way they behave within it. However, we also want to see whether this world varies with the way the homes are run and resourced. So we aim to set up measures which describe this world and the behaviour of residents on leaving it and see whether variations are related in a sensible way to the characteristics of the homes themselves. For if we can achieve this, we will have made a small inroad into the lack of a proven theoretical base which is one of the basic problems of residential care.

In pursuing this agenda, we look back to a stream of British research in the 1960s and 1970s which challenged the view that residential care for children was uniformly bad. Studies of different establishments showed wide variations in their ideologies, organisation and staffing and in the attitudes and behaviour of children. Among apparently similar institutions, there were massive variations in absconding, criminal behaviour, bullying, the quality of talk between staff and young children, and the degree to which children felt supported (Tizard, Sinclair and Clarke 1975). Links were found between variables connected with the organisation of the establishment (e.g. the autonomy given to staff), the characteristics and attitudes of the staff and the reactions of the residents.

These findings on the variety of residential care suggest that the latter could have a long-term beneficial effect. Some work (Sinclair 1971, 1975) suggests that any effect is likely to be short-term, with young people responding to the immediate impact of the institutions but proving equally malleable to the environments to which they return. These studies, however, leave open the possibility that long-term change may be achieved if the changes produced in care 'fit' the demands of the environment to which a child returns (e.g. if a child learns a skill which is marketable in the 'outside world'). These ideas on the importance of 'fit' and on the 'sequence of cause and effect' in child care were emphasised by Parker and his colleagues (1991). They believed that *the notion of sequential outcomes should occupy a more prominent place in thinking about child care evaluation*, and quoted with approval Quinton and Rutter's (1984) concept of 'causal chains' and Maluccio's ideas on the interplay between motivation, skills and environment.

The research we have just discussed was carried out prior to 1985 (Parker and his colleagues provided a synthesis rather than a fresh study). The results may no longer apply to establishments which are, for example, much smaller and much more locally based than was formerly the case. So we need to know whether the findings on delinquent sub-cultures, variation between establishments and difficulties in ensuring long-term change apply now as in the past. And if these problems do remain, is it inevitable that the homes should operate as they do or could a higher standard of performance be achieved by learning from the best?

RESEARCH DESIGN

Our research questions called for a design which was both comparative and longitudinal. It had to be comparative in order to compare the effects of different ways of resourcing and running homes. It had to be longitudinal in order to explore ideas on 'fit' and 'causal chains'. So in style our research combined the cross-institutional research pioneered in England in the mid-1960s with the longitudinal studies of substitute care which became popular in the 1980s (Bullock, Little and Millham 1993a). The research was also eclectic in another sense—we have tried to get and present the views of professionals and young people but we have, somewhat unusually, combined this approach with the collection of large sets of data and quite heavy statistical analysis.

The selection of authorities is described in more detail below but, briefly, it was designed to provide variety and depended on willingness to participate and ease of access for the researchers. We were not able to include a London authority, mainly because the few that had enough residential care felt unable to participate.

Our data collection was focused on a sample of 48 homes and a sample of 223 residents in them. We wished to collect data on the homes, the residents' experience in the homes, and the residents' subsequent experience in such a way that we could interrelate these three major areas. We give below a quick overview of the size and the nature of the various samples. Those who wish to skip these details should nevertheless find the book intelligible.

The main sources of data were:

1. Mainly about the home and its staff:
   - *Head of Home Interview*—guided interview with the heads of homes on their aims, the way they tried to implement them, the difficulties they experienced and the success they thought they had had. Information was available from 47 heads of home.
   - *Details of Home Questionnaire*—data on the regime and structure of the home collected by postal questionnaire from 44 heads of home.
   - *Staff Log*—details on current staffing (e.g. posts, ages, length of time in post and qualifications) collected by post from 44 heads of home and on 540 staff.
   - *Resident Log*—brief details on all residents in the home over the last year which could be used, for example, to calculate turnover, sex ratios, etc. Data were available from 44 homes. Unless otherwise reported, sample size is 1090.
   - *Staff Questionnaire*—postal questionnaire to all staff covering their experience in the home, views (e.g. on training) and morale. This yielded data from 304 staff.
   - *Interviewer Rating Schedule*—a brief schedule completed by the interviewers which rated the home.
2. Mainly about the residents:
   - *Resident Interview Schedule*—structured interviews with 223 residents covering their views on the reasons for which they entered 'care', their current lives outside the home, what they liked and did not like about the home, their perception of its 'social climate' and their hopes for the future.
   - *Parent Interview Schedule*—structured interviews with 99 of the parents of young people in the above sample. Whilst much of the focus was on their child, the interview also covered the parents' experiences of and views on social workers and the children's home.
   - *Social Worker Questionnaire*—postal questionnaire to social workers, seeking their views on the same residents and covering the residents' backgrounds, problems and development, and the plans which the social worker had made and would like to have made. It was available on 176 residents.
   - *Keyworker Questionnaire*—postal questionnaire covering much the same ground from the point of view of the keyworker. The response rate was low and we have not used it in this book.
3. Resident follow-up
   - *Social Worker Follow-up Questionnaire*—postal questionnaire to social workers seeking information on what had happened to a resident, their evaluation of the outcome, and progress and problems in selected areas of the resident's life. It was completed on 141 young people, six to nine months after the first interview.

- *Resident Follow-up Questionnaire*—a brief questionnaire to the young people involved in the first interview, asking where they were, whether they were glad they had been to the home, how happy they were and how they thought things had turned out. We had replies from 141 young people six to nine months after the first interview.

Each of these instruments is introduced in more detail where appropriate in the report. Appendix A considers issues of response rates and sampling bias. It will probably not surprise those used to reading research reports that we do not consider these issues to be serious. In our view we managed to obtain both representative samples and good response rates. The study itself is very large and it complements other more qualitative research by providing description based on sizeable samples and through statistical exploration of cause and effect.

THE PARTICIPATING AUTHORITIES

Four of our five authorities were in the Midlands or the North, and in the past their economies have been heavily based on iron and steel. These four authorities all had pockets of high unemployment, largely reflecting the collapse of these industries, but they differed widely in other ways. There were difficult inner and outer city estates in Areas 1 and 4 and parts of Area 2, wide tracts of unspoilt country in Area 2, and districts of considerable wealth, particularly in Area 4. Area 3, by contrast, was a home county, with unemployment about two-thirds the national average, incomes per person much above average, and an association with green belts, new towns and garden cities. Table 1.1 gives some basic information on the five authorities, with numbers rounded so that they cannot be easily identified from published data.

Table 1.1 The five areas

Referred to in report as:	Status	Population	Population per hectare	Lone parents (%)	Income support (%)
Area 1	County	555,000	9	7	21
Area 2	Shire	950,000	3	4	12
Area 3	Shire	1,000,000	6	4	10
Area 4	Metropolitan District	700,000	12	6	14
Area 5	Metropolitan District	300,000	9	5	14

Source: 1991 Census County Reports; Regional Trends.

Generally (and even in the prosperous Area 3, which had pockets of deprivation) the authorities illustrated the dilemmas facing under-skilled youth, for whom traditional jobs were no longer available, and whose delayed entry into the job market might be complicated by lack of support from family and social security. Child care policy, however, appeared not to be driven by these dilemmas, but by a common desire to lower the numbers 'in care', particularly in 'residential care'.

The authorities aimed to reduce the numbers in residential care in two ways. They sought to collaborate with other agencies in preventing admissions to the care system. They sought to support to develop better-supported foster care and after-care services, so that young people who were looked after could be contained by these systems rather than by residential care. The methods chosen to pursue these aims differed in detail, including, for example, schemes which allowed for overnight stays for adolescents, bail support schemes, special family support teams, and enhanced payment, support and training for foster carers dealing with difficult adolescents. All these provisions, however, were seen as supporting rather than replacing a smaller, more specialised, high quality residential service, mostly (except in one authority) provided on a localised basis.

These policies were reflected in local trends which ran parallel with those we have described at a national level. All the authorities had dramatically reduced their numbers in residential care over the previous 10 years. The rate at which this had been done varied between authorities and some had started on 'cuts' more recently than others. Generally, however, authorities seemed to be converging in terms of their rates of young people 'in care' in general and the proportion of them in residential care in particular. Taken together, our five authorities had almost identical admission, 'in care' and 'in residential care' rates to those found in England as a whole.

As in England as a whole, these developments contained within them three difficult dilemmas. First, the reduction in numbers in residential care had been accompanied in all authorities by a large increase in the reported costs of residential care in 1983–4 and 1993–4. After allowing for inflation, costs per place per week had increased at current prices by amounts varying from £107 (£284 to £391) in one authority to £701 (£450 to £1151) in another. As a result, the diversion of resources from residential care needed to fund prevention and foster care was taking place more slowly than might have been expected. In all authorities a very small minority of adolescents in residential care were still absorbing a highly disproportionate proportion of resources. Second, the emphasis on small, locally-based residential care conflicted with a coexisting desire to give each unit a specialised role and purpose. As the numbers of homes fell, the likelihood increased that each home would have to accommodate a highly diverse set of young people. Third, the emphasis on family support and returning young people to the community as soon as possible coincided with the evidence from national studies that families, the main source of community support, were under increasing pressure; that schools had incentives not to retain difficult young people; and that support for adolescents from the social security and housing systems had diminished. Unskilled young people who did not stay on at school but had difficulty in getting work face a prolonged and hard transition to adulthood. The financial pressure on the care system, however, was to have done with them as soon as possible.

THE BOOK

This book follows the logic of the research study and builds from description to evaluation. We suggested earlier that official reports contain an implicit analysis which leads from the role of the homes to the implications for the homes as units, and thence to the impact of these arrangements on the resident world and to outcomes. This analysis defines the main sections of the book.

The next four chapters deal with *the role of residential care* as viewed, respectively, by social workers, parents and young people when we first contacted them, and also (in the case of social workers and young people) six to nine months later when we followed them up.

Chapters 6 to 9 deal with the *homes as units*. They cover the basic details (e.g. size, staffing, occupancy and purpose), regimes, the views and philosophies of the heads, and the experience and morale of the staff.

Chapters 10 to 12 deal with *the resident world*, including the residents' lives outside the home, their view of life within it, their behaviour and the degree to which they are happy or miserable.

Chapters 13 and 14 deal with *evaluation*. These chapters are the culmination of the book. They use the material previously presented to develop measures of outcome in the immediate and medium term, they seek to explain these measures in terms of the structure of the homes and the way they were run, and they draw together the findings.

Chapter 15 considers the bearing of this material on three basic questions:

- Why, if at all, is residential care needed?
- What kinds of residential homes should there be?
- What will ensure that these homes are as good as they can be?

PRESENTATION

This book is the descendant of a research report. In turning it into a book we have faced a number of difficulties. By describing the solutions we may make it easier for the reader to get the most out of the book with the least inconvenience.

First, we have had some difficulties with *language*. Children and young people in the care system are now said to be 'looked after'. The word 'care' is now correctly reserved for an order (i.e. for indicating that the child is subject to some legal requirement and is not simply 'accommodated' on a voluntary basis). This situation creates the problem of finding an appropriate synonym for the old word 'care' (as in 'received into care'). The state of 'being looked after' seemed clumsy. We have used the word 'care' instead (where 'care' is being used in its technically correct sense, as in 'Care Order', we make this clear). We have also used the word 'convicted' when 'cautioned or convicted' would have been more accurate. Occasionally we have used a name for a resident or home. All such names are pseudonyms.

Second, we are conscious that much of the *statistical material* is not easy to read. Some readers will be unfamiliar with the statistical techniques used. Others may fear being overwhelmed by the quantity of information. To counter these dangers the conclusions to most chapters contain a summary of key findings. So it is possible to skim over the more factual sections of the chapters and return later to any part which is of particular interest.

Third, each chapter is written on a small section of the overall data. The sources of data are numerous. So it is easy to lose sight of the degree to which the results in one chapter seem to complement, confirm or contradict those of another. To overcome this problem, we have provided four sections which summarise the issues arising in the four major sections of the book. These sections will be found at the end of Chapters 5, 9, 12 and 15.

These various devices bring with them the disadvantage of repetition. We hope the reader will forgive this inelegance. The book is intended for administrators, practitioners from different professions, academics, research specialists, students and interested members of the general public. It is not possible to write a book which will please all these audiences all the time. We have aimed to provide one from which all can take something that suits their needs.

2

THE ROLES OF RESIDENTIAL CARE— THE SOCIAL WORKERS' VIEWS

INTRODUCTION

To understand the role of children's homes we need to know about their clientele: why these young people enter the homes, what their problems are, and what their plans are for the future. These issues may be differently seen by social workers, parents and young people. The next chapters are based on these various points of view.

This chapter presents the most 'official' version—that of the social workers. The chapter covers three main areas of the residents' lives:

- The basic details (sex, age, care career and reasons for placement).
- Problems and areas for development.
- Future plans.

The data are drawn from the 176 questionnaires returned by social workers on the 223 residents interviewed in the main study—a response rate of 79%. Appendix A compares the respondents with non-respondents in terms of a number of key variables. Briefly, the only major difference was by area. The lack of any other differences between responders and non-responders suggest that the variation by area is not a serious source of bias.

It is important to remember that we are sampling residents who were in the homes at a particular point in time. These will inevitably contain a higher proportion of long-stay residents than would a sample based on admissions or discharges. This weighting in favour of those who stay longer is entirely appropriate if the focus is on the use of resources. However, it will tend to underplay the role of the homes with short-stay residents, and this will need to be kept in mind when we come to the conclusions.

THE BASIC DETAILS

Table 2.1 describes the sample in terms of the sex, age, ethnicity and the composition of their family home. As can be seen, male residents outnumbered female ones by six to four, comparatively few residents were under 12 or over 17, and 90% were white. Out of the remaining 18 on whom we had information, only two were described as African-Caribbean and one as Asian, while 15 were described as African-Caribbean/white (9), Asian/white (5) or other (1). The over-representation of dual-heritage young people is in keeping with other research (Bebbington and Miles 1989; Rowe, Hundleby and Garnett 1989), although their overwhelming predominance in this study may reflect a sampling error or the particular authorities involved. Appendix C brings together our data on this small group of residents and compares them with the remainder of the sample.

The figures for family composition are striking. Accuracy in this area is notoriously difficult, since the families re-configure themselves frequently

Table 2.1 Age, sex, ethnic background and composition of family home

	(*n*)	(%)
Age		
12 and under	22	12.5
13, 14	63	35.8
15	40	22.7
16 and over	41	29.0
Sex		
Females	72	40.9
Males	104	59.1
Ethnic origin		
White British/White other	158	89.7
African-Caribbean	2	1.1
Asian	1	0.6
Mixed	14	7.9
Other	1	0.6
Composition of family		
Lone parents	65	36.9
Birth parents	28	15.9
1 Birth, 1 other	62	35.2
Other	21	11.9
Total	176	100.0

Source: Questionnaire to social workers.

and it is often hard to know when, for example, a parent should be described as 'lone' or as in some permanent relationship. Nevertheless, the proportion living with both natural parents, at around one in six, was very low by national standards. Overall, only a quarter of the sample were said to have families involving their natural father. The comparable figures for mothers was higher at just over three-quarters (79%). Nevertheless the great majority of these young people had had to face the sadness, clashes of loyalty and confusions that arise from separation and divorce.

Reasons for Care

In exploring the reasons for which these young people became 'looked after', we asked the social workers to describe briefly the circumstances in which this had occurred. Their replies stressed four things.

First, there was the behaviour of the young people:

He is remanded into care of the local authority, therefore no decision was made as such. However, if he was not remanded an agreement for accommodation would have been sought because of a serious assault that meant he could not go back home or live with young children.

Second, there was the abuse or neglect that the young people had suffered.

Physical abuse by step-father precipitated coming into care. Previous concerns about physical abuse by mother and sexual abuse by step-father.

Mother found to be living with a S.I. offender. Cohab. had not been assessed for level of risk and had not received treatment for offending behaviour.

Third, there was the breakdown of relationships which either accompanied these situations or took place independently of them:

Believed to be a child in need but debatable in the circumstances. Requested own accommodation as didn't want to be at home any more—threatened to take tablets/get in trouble with police if he was not accommodated.

Following illness and subsequent death of younger brother, he was accommodated at his and his mother's request. Long-standing relationship problems with step-father (brother's natural father) and mother finding it difficult to 'keep the peace' between them—emotions naturally high.

Fourth, there was sometimes a set of accompanying circumstances which made it difficult for young persons to be fostered or to remain at home—

for example, there were no suitable foster placements, their parents would not have them back or their offences were so grave or so unacceptable to the local community that they required secure accommodation.

We followed this open-ended question by asking the social workers to choose a primary and secondary reason for 'care' from a set of options we gave them. Our list was developed from work by Packman *et al.* (1986) and others (e.g. Vernon and Fruin 1986; Millham *et al.* 1986) in the 1980s. This earlier research had suggested that children and young people who were looked after could be broadly classified as 'victims' (i.e. abused or neglected), 'villains' (e.g. delinquent or 'beyond control') and 'volunteers' (e.g. the victims of circumstances such as family ill-health). The classification was broadly derived from the legal framework of the time. Moreover, the victims and volunteers were on average much younger than the sample with which we were dealing. Nevertheless, we expected that this classification would be a useful way of ordering our data.

Table 2.2 confirms the overall picture provided by the social workers accounts. In around seven out of 10 cases there had been a breakdown of relationships, but this was something to which the young person's behaviour had frequently contributed. Abuse and neglect were less common reasons, as were 'other' reasons, which often had to do with delinquency or remands.

Care Careers

A rather different way of classifying residents is in respect of their 'care careers' (cf. Garnett 1992). In this respect the homes were sheltering both the long-term casualties of the care system and the casualties of

Table 2.2   Main and second reason why young persons 'looked after'

	Main reason		Second reason	
	(*n*)	(%)	(*n*)	(%)
Family illness/housing problem	3	1.7	9	5.1
Breakdown of relationship between young person and family	93	52.8	29	16.5
Young person's behaviour	37	21.0	64	36.4
Potential/actual abuse of young person	18	10.2	14	8.0
Neglect of young person	7	4.0	13	7.4
Other	6	3.4	3	1.7
Not answered	12	6.9	44	25.0
Totals	176	100.0	176	100.0

Source: Questionnaire to social workers.

adolescence. Overall, nearly a third of the sample were said to have first been 'looked after' before the age of 11. One in eight were under five at first admission. Around half (52%) had first been admitted when they were aged between 11 and 14 and a further 15% when they were 15 or over and perhaps looking to start a life on their own.

Age at first admission was related to reasons for admission. The majority of those who had first been admitted before the age of 11 were classified as victims. The most common reasons for those admitted between 11 and 15 was the breakdown of relationships (44%), closely followed by the young person's own behaviour (32%). Breakdown of relationships was also the major reason for those first admitted when 15 or over.

Variations in age at first admission suggested interesting differences in authority policy. Approximately half those first admitted before the age of 11 came from Area 4, which provided slightly less than a quarter of the sample. Conversely, no resident from Area 4 was first admitted after the age of 15. The reasons for Area 4's concentration on younger residents are not clear. One possibility is that it reflects a difficulty in recruiting foster carers capable of containing difficult younger children. Another possibility is that it reflects priorities. Whereas most areas seem to have been prepared to consider 15 year-olds whose relationships with their parents had broken down, Area 4 did not.

As might be expected given the official emphasis on rehabilitation, most (60%) of the sample had been looked after on more than one occasion. Approximately three-quarters of those first admitted before the age of 11 had had more than one care episode, as did six out of 10 of those first admitted between 11 and 15. Only for those first admitted when 15 or over was it rare for rehabilitation to have been tried. Even then it had been attempted for a fifth of the cases.

Despite these efforts to return the residents to their families, most had already passed the six months 'milestone' in 'care' (Rowe, Hundleby and Garnett 1989). For around a quarter of the sample, their most recent admission to 'care' had occurred within the last six months. For a further quarter it had been within the year, for just over a third between one and three years, and for between a sixth and a seventh it had lasted for three years or more. The longer periods were very largely accounted for by those who had entered 'care' for some reason connected with abuse (19 out of 25 residents whose episode had lasted for three years or more), and were also much more common in Area 4 than elsewhere.

The Lead-up to Care in the Current Home

About 80% of young people had lived somewhere else between leaving their parental home and entering their current children's home. Of those who had lived elsewhere, 60% had been in foster care at some stage or another during this interim period, a similar percentage had lived in another children's home, and about 40% had lived with relatives or adults other than foster or adoptive parents. Many in fact lived in more than one setting—for example, one clearly identifiable pattern included foster care combined with residence in at least one other children's home.

Significantly more young men than young women came direct to their present children's home from their parental home; conversely, significantly more young women than young men had lived in more than two other settings during this interim period—findings which may suggest that children's homes are seen as more suitable for young men. Most (83%) of the admissions were emergencies, either from the community (45%) or as a result of placement breakdown (38%). Emergencies seemed equally common in all authorities, but they did not entirely pre-empt other reasons for placement. To examine the latter we used a question from a study by Rowe and her colleagues (1989). As can be seen from Table 2.3, the purposes were varied and none of them applied to more than a fifth of the sample. For around one in five, the aim was a long-term placement and, for one in 10, it was to 'treat behaviour'. Apart from the small 'other' category, the remaining placements involved children's homes as a stop-gap or a conscious step on the road to somewhere else. Young people were given a roof over their heads; distraught families were given a break (all relief breaks were emergency placements); there was to be a short placement for assessment while everyone thought what to do; or, for roughly a sixth of the sample in each case, the young people were prepared for long-term care or independence.

The variety of these aims meant that we had to group them for statistical purposes and we did so under three headings: 'long-term'; 'treatment' (treat behaviour, prepare for long-term placement and prepare for independence); and 'short-term' (the remainder apart from 'other').

Table 2.3   Main purpose of placement

Main purpose	(n)	(%)
Roof over head	17	10.1
Relief care	13	7.7
Assessment	10	5.9
Other short-term	11	6.5
Prepare for long-term place	27	16.0
Treat behaviour	17	10.1
Long-term placement	34	20.1
Prepare for independence	31	18.3
Other	9	5.3
Total	169	100.0

Source: Questionnaire to social workers.

The three groups differed in a variety of ways. Unsurprisingly, those admitted for long-term purposes were more likely to have stayed more than a year in the home than those admitted for 'treatment', who in turn had stayed longer than those admitted for short-term reasons. 'Short-term' cases usually came in as the result of an emergency in the community and for these, as we will see, the aim was often rapid rehabilitation home. The others were apparently more embedded in the care system and more likely to have had a placement breakdown. Nearly half the long-stay cases had entered the care system before the age of 11, whereas the others predominantly entered in their teens.

Thus, children's homes were operating, often simultaneously, as first aid posts designed to classify the casualties and return the walking wounded to the frontline of family warfare, as casualty clearing stations providing the treatment necessary to enable the patient to move elsewhere, and as long-stay base hospitals designed for those who were too severely wounded to be managed in any other way.

PROBLEMS AND AREAS FOR DEVELOPMENT

So much for the basic characteristics of the sample—what of their problems, strengths and developmental needs? To cover these we adapted material from the *Looking After Children* project (Parker *et al.* 1991), and developed our own list of 'difficult behaviour'.

The completion rate for the 'problem behaviour' was not as good as we expected. We therefore decided to omit 36 cases where the social worker was unable to make any response to at least six of the nine questions posed. Comparison of these cases with the others in respect of those items relevant to behaviour which had been filled in suggested that the two groups did not differ. Thus, the reasons for non-completion probably had to do with factors extraneous to the young person (e.g. the fact that a social worker had only recently taken over a case and did not feel that the extraction of detailed factual information from the file was either justified or practical). Other recent work, e.g. by Farmer and Pollock (1998) and Biehal and Wade (personal communication), has also pointed to the difficulties which social workers have in extracting accurate information from files.

The information on the remaining respondents illustrated their difficulties. More than four out of 10 had run away from their family home at least once, nearly two-thirds were said to be occasionally or persistently delinquent, and more than four out of 10 had sometimes been violent towards their parents. In addition, around half had been violent to other children, approximately a third had made a suicide attempt or harmed themselves, around half at least sometimes engaged in sexual behaviour which put themselves or others at risk, four in 10 were persistent truants or had been excluded from school, the great majority had 'other' difficult behaviour. Seven out of 10 exhibited at least one of these problems persistently (see Table D1 in Appendix D for further details).

Some of these problems were particularly common in males or in females. Persistent violence towards parents was a male phenomenon. Nearly one in five of the young males were said to have exhibited it. Persistent truancy or school exclusion was also more common among young men and was reported in nearly 60% of them. By contrast, persistently placing oneself or others at sexual risk was apparently more common among females, for whom it was reported in over a quarter of the cases.

Age was less frequently associated with particular problems than was the case with sex, but there was one exception. Violence towards other children was far commoner among younger residents and was reported for 90% of those under 12 as against only 27% among those aged 16 or over. It is possible that younger residents were carrying the blame for violence subtly provoked by more sophisticated older ones. However, residential placement was rare for those under 12 and it is likely that such young people were only placed in homes when their behaviour made it impossible for them to be contained elsewhere.

Our coverage of the dimensions suggested by the *Looking After Children* project painted a somewhat more encouraging picture. The young people were predominantly seen as healthy, as able to look after themselves to the level appropriate for their age, and as having a reasonable knowledge of their origins. Socially they fared somewhat less well, but a majority were described as being able to present themselves reasonably and to be acceptable to other adults and children. The main problems appeared to arise in the areas of self-esteem, education, close friendships (or rather the lack of them) and emotional and behavioural problems (see Tables D2 and D3 in Appendix for further details).

In order to simplify our analytic task, we analysed much of this data using four summary scores, concerned respectively with health, adjustment, educational involvement and relationships (see Appendix D for further details).

Among young people of school age, involvement in school dropped sharply with age. Female residents were also more involved in school and its activities than male ones. The strongest relationship was between age and adjustment. On our measure, the younger residents were rated as far more disturbed than older ones. As with violence towards other children, the explanation is probably that it is very unusual for young children to be placed in a children's home. Those that are, are considered by their social workers to be very disturbed.

PLANS AND TREATMENT

We have considered the problems and characteristics of the young people—what were the long-term plans?

The first question we asked was why the young people could not be fostered or returned home immediately. There were basically five answers. Return home was officially discouraged or forbidden; the young person's parents would not have him/her (a reason which applied in seven out of 10 cases); the young person him/herself was unwilling to go home or (if this was offered) be fostered; the young person's behaviour was such that no foster parent would have him/her or that it would be unfair to place him/her with foster parents; or there were no suitable foster parents available. In a few cases there were 'other' reasons, for example, the young person had mended fences with his/her family and it was thought that a return home would disrupt this.

Given that the residents were not returning home immediately, we wanted to know what the future plans were. Table 2.4 sets out the data on where, according to the social worker, the residents were expected to go. As can be seen, the future destinations were varied. The most popular was 'independent living', accounting for around a third of the sample. Return home or rehabilitation to relatives accounted for around a fifth of the sample and foster care for between a sixth and a seventh. Nearly one in five of the sample had no definite destination as yet.

Where plans existed, a date had not necessarily been fixed. Indeed, in around a third of the sample (34%) the social worker could not say when

Table 2.4   Where young person was expected to go on leaving placement

Destination	(n)	(%)
No plans made as yet	31	17.9
Return to birth parents	34	19.7
Return to other relatives	2	1.2
Long-term foster care	27	15.6
Hostel	5	2.9
Flat	36	20.8
Lodgings with landlady	13	7.5
Somewhere else	25	14.4
Totals	173	100.0

Source: Questionnaire to social workers.

the young person was due to leave. Around four out of 10 did not have plans which included both a definite destination and an expected period within which they would leave.

A relatively low proportion (20%) were definitely expected to return home. This seems out of keeping with the spirit of the Children Act 1989, with its emphasis on rehabilitation and family life. Two points should be made. First, those returning home often did so quickly. A study of admissions and discharges would therefore show a higher proportion of young people destined for rehabilitation than a study of current residents. Second, we will see that most residents, while wanting to maintain contact with their families, do not want to go back to them. So plans which take serious account of the residents' views will typically not aim at rehabilitation.

The residents' planned destinations were related to their past care careers and to the length of time they were expected to stay in the home in the future. Seventy per cent of those for whom the plan was a *return to their families* were being looked after as the result of an emergency admission from the community. Relatively few of them were placed in the hope that they would change their behaviour or acquire new skills; the great majority (85%) had been looked after on their most recent episode for less than a year, and two-thirds were expected to return home within six months. Thus, for those being rehabilitated, the home was essentially a stop-gap—it did not treat, it did not shelter long-term and speed of return was of the essence.

Those for whom *fostering* was planned were also expected to leave quickly—always provided that a place could be found, since nearly half of them had no leaving period planned. They were also likely to have begun their period of being looked after in the last year. Their major differences from those returning home were that they were over twice as likely to have entered the home as a result of an emergency occurring while they were being looked after, and over three times as likely to be there for the purpose of 'treatment' (i.e. to learn skills or change their ways of behaving).

The third main group were those destined for *independent living*. Only a third of them had entered the homes within the last year (roughly half the percentage of those destined for foster care and just off a third of that for those returning home). Their admissions were the most likely to have been planned (although at 22%, the percentage was not great), six out of 10 were there for treatment (i.e. to learn the skills of independent living) and they had the highest proportion of residents placed long-term of any group, except those for whom no plans existed. They were also, for obvious reasons, on average older than the other two groups.

These findings confirm the picture derived from the discussion of the purposes of placement. The homes provide brief emergency placements for those at odds with their parents, a role analogous perhaps to the one sometimes played by the friends and relatives. They act as a decompression chamber and coaching establishment for those suffering from breakdowns in care—allowing them to reflect before choosing another placement (if one is available) and to modify their ways. They provide longer-stay care for those who are not going to return home or be fostered and a crash course for some in the skills of independent living.

CONCLUSION

The young people were described by their social workers as troubled and troublesome. Their family situations were highly disrupted; less than one in six had families where both their natural parents were living together. Their behaviour was problematic. Seven out of 10 had been excluded from school or frequently truanted, six out of 10 had at least some involvement in delinquency, sizeable proportions (four out of 10 or more) had been violent to adults, violent to other children, run away from care, run away from their own homes and put themselves or others at risk through sexual behaviour; and more than a third had attempted to commit suicide or harmed themselves. These difficulties were complemented by a number of strengths. Generally they were healthy, could look after themselves, and knew about their origins. However, they were also seen as having low self-esteem and poor educational attainments, and as lacking friends.

These characteristics had influenced their care careers. Generally, they had entered care for the first time as teenagers—only a third had done so before the age of 11—and because they could not get on with their families. Minorities had been abused or had got into trouble outside their own homes. They were seen as too difficult to be fostered or as unwilling to be fostered, and few of them had entered their current placement as part of a planned move. For around a third, the purposes of the placement were essentially short-term—to allow assessment or a breathing space while plans were sorted out, or to provide the young person and his/her family with a break from each other. For nearly half, there was some more ambitious but finite end in view—to treat behaviour, prepare for a long-term placement, or prepare for independence. A sizeable minority were there to live until such time as they ceased to be looked after.

The young people's proposed destinations were logically related to the purposes and length of placement. Only a minority (around a fifth) were definitely expected to return home, and the remainder were destined for foster care or—more commonly—independent living. Generally, the plans for those returning home were that they should do so as soon as possible. Those who were to be fostered were commonly expected to stay somewhat longer, partly to allow time for reflection, partly to help them to become more 'fosterable' and partly because foster placements were difficult to lay on. Those destined for independent living included some who were being prepared for discharge in the reasonably near future and others whose discharge was still some time ahead.

So residential homes need to be evaluated against four very different criteria. The first is their success in responding to short-term emergencies, where young people need to be contained and assessed and, in many cases, returned to their parents as soon as possible. The second is their capacity to provide a time for reflection and perhaps for treatment, so that the young people have time to come to terms with any placement break-down and are better able to cope with their next placement. The third is their capacity to provide a realistic preparation for living independently in the community. The fourth is their success in providing a stable, homely environment in which young people can live for some time. A key issue concerns the degree to which these purposes can be handled successfully in the same home. In our conclusion we will argue that more than three types of home are required.

3

THE ROLES OF RESIDENTIAL CARE: THE VIEWS OF PARENTS

INTRODUCTION

So far we have given the social workers' view on what the home was about. How far did this coincide with that of the parents? The Children Act has emphasised the importance of parental views. Paradoxically, research (Packman *et al.* 1986) has suggested that parents often welcome a child's removal from home, at least on a temporary basis—something which the Act is popularly interpreted as discouraging. Fisher and his colleagues (1986) found, like Packman and her colleagues, that parents were often relieved when their child went into care but also that the experience commonly disappointed them. In the case of adolescents, parents often hoped that residential homes would provide the authoritative control which their child needed but which they were unable to provide. In practice, however, a number felt that control was lacking and that their child was led astray.

Against this background we were interested in seeing how far a more recent sample of parents corroborated the views expressed in the earlier studies. Our interview with parents covered, among other things, why the child entered 'care', how they thought their child was getting on in the home, their thoughts on the plans for their child's future, how they thought the home should be run and their response to contact with social workers. Most of these questions bear implicitly or explicitly on the roles of residential care. However, this is the only chapter to report parental views, and we have sometimes digressed, thinking it more important to give the parents a say than to stick rigidly to our topic.

The interviews with parents proved difficult to obtain, as many simply refused and others, despite telephone calls and up to three visits to their address, could not be contacted. In addition, we were requested by the authorities not to contact certain parents if the case was at a particularly delicate stage; in a small number of cases the young person had no parent to interview. A total of 99 interviews were obtained and available for analysis. Appendix A considers how far these interviews can be considered representative.

REASONS FOR ADMISSION

The vast majority of parents confirmed that the social worker had explained the reasons why their child was going into care. The three most common reasons given were that the young person was 'not getting on with people at home' (25%), that they were 'getting into trouble' (21%) or that they were 'in some kind of danger' (14%). Table 3.1 compares the explanations offered by parents and those given by the young people interviewed.

It would seem that, whereas parents tended to play down 'not getting on with people at home', their children placed greater emphasis on this as a reason why they were taken into care. Parents were also more likely than their children to opt for the less specific item 'other reasons'.

One reason for the differences between parents and children could be that parents would be less likely to take part in an interview where their child had been removed for reasons connected with abuse. In order to check this possibility, we developed a classification based on all the information we had available. We had asked parents, young people and social workers about the reasons why the young people had gone into care. We used information from all three sources to classify the problems behind the reasons for 'care' according to the following rules:

Table 3.1   Reasons given by social worker for care—parents and young people

Reason given	Parents (n = 99) (%)	Young people* (n = 99) (%)	Young people# (n = 223) (%)
Not getting on at home	24.7	51.5	44.8
In some kind of danger	14.4	15.5	13.0
Getting into trouble	20.6	13.4	13.0
Not looked after/neglect	2.1	3.1	7.2
Without a home	2.1	3.1	2.7
Other	35.1	13.4	14.3
No explanation/not answered	1.0	—	4.9

* Children of parents interviewed.
# All young people interviewed.
Source: Interview with parents; interview with residents.

- *Abuse*—any mention that the young person was in any danger or abused.
- *Behaviour*—no evidence of abuse but some mention of the young person's behaviour.
- *Relationships*—no abuse or a behaviour problem but some mention of relationships.
- *Other*—none of the above.

The reasons for this ordering were partly our perception of the relative seriousness of abuse, behaviour and relationship problems. We also thought that abuse would be more likely to be concealed than other problems and that any mention of it would imply a serious reason for 'care'.

This classification enabled us to compare the three samples in terms of the apparent reason for care and we found no significant differences between them. The differences shown in Table 3.1 therefore seem to reflect differences in the way the parents chose to present the situations, rather than an underlying difference in the situations themselves.

Knowing the reason why your child was placed in care does not necessarily imply acceptance of that outcome. However, in this study over 70% of parents agreed that the move was a good idea. Many reasons were offered in support of this conclusion. These included a sense of rejection on one side or the other or the need of the family for a rest:

I wanted him to go—he was getting me down—the situation was getting worse. He kept going off for days at a time—seven days once. It had been building up slowly but it got to the point where I suggested we had a break.

This was often coupled with the feeling that they could no longer cope:

There was nowhere else for her to go. I needed a break or something terrible would have happened. I was at breaking point.

I put her in care as I was hitting her. There was so much shouting and arguing. I was taking it all out on her—what had happened was I was knocking her about— I know it's wrong but I couldn't handle it any more.

Commonly there were complaints about the young people's behaviour:

I had to think about the other children living at home. He was taking things from home, even the TV and video on one occasion. You can't have that with other kids around—they will think they can do it as well.

As we have seen, the great majority of the placements were in response to an 'emergency'. So it was not surprising that less than a quarter of the parents had been able to see the children's home before their child was placed there. Moreover, less than a third felt that they had been given a chance to say whether they wanted their child to go there in the first place. A similar minority (31%) felt that they had been given sufficient time to think about the placement and talk it over. Whilst a majority of parents (71%) were clear about the legal position over the return home of their child, if this were what both child and parents wanted, greater uncertainty was felt about the legal position over who was, and who was not, allowed to see the young person.

Just over a quarter of parents said that, if the choice had been in their hands, they would have preferred for their child to have remained with them.

I wanted him to stay with us as we're a close family. He was in quite a state and needed moral support and security that I could have given him at home.

Almost three in four, however, indicated a preference for their child to have gone elsewhere—37% to a children's home, 7% to relatives, 16% to foster parents and 13% to some form of independent living or somewhere else. The reasons were those which previous research (Fisher *et al.* 1986; Packman 1986) would lead one to expect—a sense that they could no longer cope and the hope, if the choice was a children's home, that this would provide a measure of control.

I knew she would be safe in the home and not roaming the streets. I would like to have her back but I couldn't handle it just yet.

I thought the home would make her see sense. I thought she needed a shock to realise what she was doing to herself, and foster parents would be too like being at home.

CARE PLANS

Most parents lacked a clear understanding of the care plan and only a handful were prepared to say where their child was supposed to go on leaving their present children's home or, for that matter, when this transition should take place. Nevertheless, they were certain in their own minds where they would ideally want their child to go on leaving the present placement. Table 3.2 sets out the results for the parents' wishes and demonstrates how these vary according to the age of their child.

Given the uncertainty over the intentions of the care plan, as opposed to their ideal wishes, it was not surprising that few parents were able to say whether they wanted to keep in touch with their child after the

Table 3.2 Parents' wishes for their child on leaving present home

	Age of young person		
Location	Under 15 ($n = 50$) (%)	15 and over ($n = 49$) (%)	All ages ($n = 99$) (%)
Home with parents	68.0	20.8	44.9
Other relatives	4.0	2.1	3.1
Foster parents	10.0	6.3	8.2
Another children's home or Community Home with Action (CHE)	2.0	—	1.0
Independent living	4.0	50.1	26.5
Other	12.0	20.8	16.3

Differences significant at .0001 level.
Source: Interview with parents.

present placement ended or how often any contact should be. Despite the uncertainty surrounding the details of the care plan, many parents accepted that leaving the children's home depended very much on their child's behaviour. On the other hand, few parents were willing to accept that the move depended on them at all:

It depends on how well he gets on at home during the home visits. He's got to stop offending and stick to the rules of the family home.

Well, I need to see a change in her. At the moment she still has the same attitude when she comes home—telling lies and causing trouble.

Although the fine detail in the care plan was often missing, or, perhaps more generously, could not be recalled by parents, it was clear that plans of one kind or another had been discussed. Table 3.3 sets out whether parents had been able to discuss the plans with various key people.

Where parents had spoken to a social worker about the plans for their child, the minority who had found the discussion 'unhelpful' (30%) was

Table 3.3 Whether care plan discussed with various people

Key person	Yes (%)	No (%)	Not applicable (%)
The young person	60.6	39.4	—
Other parent	24.2	37.4	38.4
Social worker	56.6	43.4	—
Staff in home	41.4	58.6	—
Other key person	17.2	31.3	51.5

Source: Interview with parents.

more than counterbalanced by those who had found it 'helpful' (28%) and 'very helpful' (42%). Although fewer parents had talked to staff in the homes than social workers, where this did occur the discussion was invariably viewed as positive—'helpful' 33%; 'very helpful' 62%.

Although vague when pressed earlier in the interview about the details of the care plan, most parents were nonetheless ready to pronounce on them:

I'm reasonably happy really—they've consulted me and listened to what I have to say. If anything happens they write to me or ring me up.

I just hope it all works, but it's the best plan anyone has come up with so far. If the plans for college work out I'll be very pleased.

Well, I've got mixed feelings—I'm down that he won't be coming home to me but appreciate that the plans seem sensible.

Overall, six in 10 parents were either happy or very happy with the plans made for their child, especially if the child was in the younger or older age groups (see Table 3.4).

CONTACT WITH AND EXPERIENCE OF THE HOME

All but eight of the parents had visited the home in which their child was currently living and, for the majority, the task of visiting was not a difficult one. The main problem for the minority of parents experiencing difficulty was travel and transport which, in some cases, involved a long journey and changing buses or an expensive taxi fare. As might be expected, parents in some authorities found travel much easier than they did in others—a difference that probably reflected distance and transport systems.

Table 3.4 Feelings about the care plan by age of young person

Age of young person	(*n*)	Very unhappy/ unhappy (%)	Happy/ very happy (%)
12 and under	13	23.1	76.9
13–15	61	51.9	48.1
16 and over	24	18.2	81.8
Totals	98	39.1	60.9

Differences significant at .01 level.
Source: Interview with parents.

Once at the home, the vast majority of parents (87%) reported that they were made to feel welcome. The small minority who found otherwise commented on the way they were spoken to by staff or the attitudes of staff:

I dislike the way some talk to me—as if I'm stupid.

Staff don't really talk to us about our worries for Lee; they just provide a room. We always feel as though we're intruding.

Two-thirds of the parents said they had contact with their child at least once a week, either by visiting the children's home or their child returning home for brief visit.

We asked the parents whether the home gave them as much information about their child as they would have liked. This question identified some differences between local authorities. Three-quarters of the parents in Areas 1 and 2 felt that they had as much information about their child from the home as they wanted, but only a third thought this in Area 4.

Over three-quarters of the parents felt that the home had encouraged them to maintain contact with their children. For the few who did not ($n = 21$) the results suggest a 'home effect'—that is, the 'no' results tended to cluster in a small minority of homes in three of the five authorities, rather than in a particular authority. Most parents in this minority group also felt that the home had not given them as much information about their child as they would have liked.

Overall, three-quarters of the parents felt that they had as much contact as they wanted. For the rest it was largely a matter of less, rather than more, contact than they would have liked.

During the interview parents were invited to say what they thought were the best and the worst bits for their child about being in the home, and their open-ended responses were subsequently grouped into categories. The following quotes are examples of the comments that parents offered about the best bits:

● Activities, amenities and outings
He's taken for days out and given pocket money and bought new clothes—things we can't afford because we don't have the money.

Holidays and lots of activities.

● Staff
Having contact with grown up men, men to talk to and a father figure which he doesn't have at home.

Key worker is amazing—excellent support, brilliant, James has a lot of respect for him.

He's getting lots of attention even though he shits on them.

- Time and space to think
  A chance for her to appreciate what she had with her mum and appreciate me a bit more.

  They encourage her to sort her life out and she tends to listen to them. She realises it's an opportunity to make a break.

- Supervision and discipline
  She's under supervision there, which is what she needs; she needs someone to tell her what to do.

  Someone to control him as I can't cope with him here.

- Secure and looked after
  I know where he is and that he'll be looked after.

  I know she's well looked after and off the streets.

- Removed from sources of danger
  Away from his step-father and not aggravating him.

  Out of danger from others and herself.

Other parents also made positive comments of more general nature about the home. In total, three-quarters of the parents mentioned one or more 'best bits'; the remaining quarter were adamant that there were no redeeming features. Most parents who had identified positive aspects of their child being in the home were also aware of the 'down side', for which three categories were dominant:

- Influence of other children
  The boys are always hassling and annoying her and destroying her property and the staff do nothing.

  She is a monster now. She has picked up all kinds of bad behaviour and attitudes.

  She's picked up a lot of bad behaviour and has been involved in stealing, drinking and drugs.

  Getting dragged into trouble—the home seems unable to restrain him and impose discipline.

- Strains on relationship
  Not being with her dad.

  Being away from her family, she misses them desperately.

  Although we see her about once a week we seem to be drifting apart.

- Laxity of regime
  Complete lack of control over his behaviour because of the law.

  There is no discipline, she does just what she likes.

  The staff haven't got enough power to stop bad behaviour.

  They don't discipline her enough. I know that they have disciplined her but then they go and give her £20 to go to school.

About 10% of the parents said they were unaware of any 'worst bits'.

Parents were also asked to consider whether their child had been changed for better or worse by living in the children's home. Almost half (43%) though their child had changed for the better:

She seems less short-tempered—and is cleaner and takes more care of herself.

He's calmed down a lot—before he was angry and loud and violent to his brothers and sisters.

She thinks before she lets things go. She would swear like a trooper but now she's a better girl.

Twelve per cent thought that no change was apparent and 18% that the effects had been mixed:

The good thing is that they have stopped him from stealing and made him attend school. The bad thing is that he doesn't want to come home now.

I thought he had improved up to two weeks ago but we've had trouble since then, so I'm not sure now.

Twenty-seven per cent thought that living in the home had made their child worse, variously attributing this to lax discipline and the influence of other young people:

She's not the same—it could be to do with why she is in care but it could be the other kids' influence on her. She didn't do these things before, that she does now (self-harm).

He used to be bullied but bullies others now. His language and attitude are worse now. No one tells them off for swearing or anything.

Since he's been there he's been arrested for shoplifting and for being drunk—he gets into bad company and is easily led.

These judgements varied significantly by area. However, on inspection this was explained by the fact that a small number of homes were consistently seen by parents as having either favourable or unfavourable effects on their children.

At this point in the interview, parents were asked about other aspects of their dealings with the home, most notably their involvement with decisions concerning their child's day-to-day life in the home (e.g. schooling and health) and with decisions involving their future (e.g. training, employment or accommodation). In general, parents were involved more by the home in decisions about their child's future than they were in decisions about their day-to-day life in the home. Parents in Area 3, parents of boys, and parents of children under 12 were all significantly more likely than others to think that they had been involved in the decisions regarding their child's future. In part these differences may reflect the practice in different areas, but it seems likely that older children and young women were seen as better able to cope on their own and that parents were therefore less likely to be consulted.

Towards the end of the interview we asked the parents whether they felt strongly enough to have cause to complain about the home. One in three said 'yes'. The vast majority of those with a grievance had in fact made a formal complaint. Of these, 40% were satisfied with the response they had received, the rest were left dissatisfied for different reasons:

My complaint was about the lack of discipline but I was told that I'm her legal guardian and they couldn't punish her. I feel they let them do what they like just for a quiet life.

I felt there wasn't enough security but my complaining didn't change a thing—he's still able to commit crimes.

Only one of the staff responded properly to my complaint, the rest let the kids do what they want.

Concern over the lack of discipline, behaviour of young people and sanctions in the home was a recurring theme throughout the interview. The results in Table 3.5 reflect particular concern among the parents of young people under the age of 16, and conversely, perhaps, the wearied

Table 3.5 Reaction of parents to discipline, behaviour and sanctions in the home—by age of their child

	(n)	Unfavourable (%)	Favourable (%)
Discipline			
12 and under	13	84.6	15.4
13–15	61	75.4	24.6
16 and over	24	45.8	54.2
Totals	98	69.4	30.6
Behaviour			
12 and under	13	84.6	15.4
13–15	61	70.5	29.5
16 and over	24	33.3	66.7
Totals	98	63.3	36.7
Sanctions			
12 and under	13	84.6	15.4
13–15	61	86.9	13.1
16 and over	24	50.0	50.0
Totals	98	77.6	22.4

All differences significant at .01 level or more.
Source: Interview with parents.

acceptance among parents of young people aged 16 and over that this was the norm and there was little they could do about it.

FAMILY RELATIONSHIPS

One of the major justifications for placing young people in residential care is to provide 'breathing space' for parents and families under stress, so that relationships among those left behind can recover and those between the parents and child can be re-established. So much for the rationale, but did it work in practice? According to the parents, the answer was often 'yes'. Forty per cent of parents said that relationships in the family had changed for the better, 33% that the result was mixed or about the same and 12% that relationships in the family had worsened.

Mechanisms for producing this improvement could include the break itself, and the quality of the contacts between parent and child that did occur. The extent to which parents found the contacts with their child useful varied. Just over half said they were helpful:

We're both certainly pleasant enough to one another, which is very different from before—yes, I would say things are improving.

It was a chance to sit down and talk about things—discuss why he had behaved so badly and how I had treated him.

A third found the contacts a mixed blessing and just over 10% said they were definitely unhelpful:

It depends on what mood she's in. Sometimes she is lovely, and we get on well when I visit her, but if she wants something and I can't give it to her, she plays up something rotten.

I found it upsetting because you go there and you feel like you are just visiting someone a long way away. It just underlined the fact that he was in care and not at home.

Three analyses in the area of family relationships found significant differences by local authority and all three favoured the same authority. The first concerned the relationship between the parent and the child in 'care'. Over three-quarters of the parents interviewed in Area 3, but no more than four out of ten in any other area, thought that their relationship with their child was better now than before; few parents thought that the relationship had worsened, although a large minority thought that there had been no effect at all. Area 3 was also far more likely than the other areas to be praised for having produced an improvement by providing a break from the child and, conversely, for enabling contact with the child on his/her own when parents visited.

CONTACT WITH SOCIAL WORKERS

We asked parents about the frequency, nature and usefulness of the contact they had with their social worker.

Overall, about a sixth of parents saw their social worker on a regular weekly basis, just under a quarter about once or twice a month and the remaining 60% less often than this. It is possible that these figures are an underestimate. In just over half the cases, parents and social workers were in agreement about frequency of contact; in just over a third, the social worker said the contact was more frequent, and in one in 10 cases, less frequent than that remembered by parents.

We were interested in the respective roles of social workers and staff in the home and asked the parents about the help they had received from each source. Table 3.6 sets out the results. Four in 10 parents said they had received practical help from a social worker for one or more of the items in the table, but staff in homes were not apparently involved in this kind

Table 3.6 Help given by social workers and staff in homes

	Social workers (Yes) (%)	Staff in home (Yes) (%)
Housing	18.1	0.0
Money/finance	17.0	2.4
Alcohol/drugs	7.6	2.4
Family relationships	25.5	13.6
Other	20.0	3.7

Source: Interview with parents.

of work apart from one or two isolated instances. Appendix B gives further information on the relative roles of field and residential social workers.

Parents were also asked whether the social worker had visited them to talk about various aspects of their child's welfare. In all, just over half the parents had received a visit from a social worker to talk about one or more aspects of their child's welfare. Of those that had, half found the contact helpful or expected it to prove so in the future:

Knowing that they are there all the time has been helpful. They're always willing to help—24 hours a day someone will be there. They've listened to me about Jack's behaviour and also let me know about his behaviour. If he needs to be spoken to about something we work it out with the social worker who will speak to him.

We know we'll get some help when my son comes home. We need support and so does he to help him settle in again and not go back to his old ways.

The rest were equally divided, viewing social workers as either a mixed blessing or unhelpful, although sometimes acknowledging that the social worker did his/her best:

When I came out of hospital with my youngest daughter, I had to get the social worker involved—she took Jim off for a few hours until he calmed down (he was smashing up the house). She's also tried to keep the family together, but it couldn't work because Jim couldn't get on with his step-father and it broke down again. At the moment, she's trying to get us a bigger house.

The final question in this part of the interview asked parents to rate how well they got on with the social worker and to say why this was so. Overall, nearly three-quarters said they got on well or very well and only in a quarter of cases was this not so. Parents were most likely to see the social worker favourably when the fault was apparently in the young person's behaviour and least likely to do so when the young person was seen as being in some danger. To put it another way, the more the fault was likely to be seen as with the parent, the less acceptable to the parent the social worker was likely to be.

The qualities that the parents liked in their social workers were those that have already been identified in other research (e.g. Packman *et al.* 1986; Triseliotis *et al.* 1995). They liked honesty and straight-forwardness, a willingness to listen and understand:

She's honest, she doesn't promise anything—she does what she can and is straight with you. She doesn't let you down—I don't know what I would have done without her.

We just hit it off. She's very good at listening and keen to do things right—she's learning all the time and takes me seriously. She takes notice of everything I say.

They also valued reliability and an ability to get things done:

He's always there if I have a question that needs answering. He has a child himself the same age as mine, so he knows the problems.

The social worker was good at explaining the procedures step by step with me so that I was able to understand what was likely to happen to my daughter.

They did not like those who showed the converse of these qualities or who appeared to look down on them or patronise them:

She's got an attitude problem! She says we're responsible for the ills of the world—it's our fault Jane isn't here . . .

I'd rather not be involved with the social worker. I see her for Muriel's benefit, not mine. She interfered too much in my personal life and made me feel guilty.

CONCLUSION

Two-thirds of parents would have preferred that their child was fostered, stayed with them or went somewhere else than residential care. Nevertheless, most parents welcomed the break produced by their child's removal to care, seeing it as the resolution of an intolerable family situation. On the whole they saw the effects as positive, feeling that the young people calmed down and that absence made the heart grow fonder. Drawbacks, if any, were the sadness of separation and the corrupting influence of delinquent peers. Worries about the effect of the young people's contemporaries and the perceived lax discipline in the homes were a recurring theme in many of the interviews.

Parental attitudes were strongly related to the age of the young person. They wanted younger children to return home in due course and felt that the homes provided them with too little discipline. They were more likely to accept that older children would be unlikely to return and were also of an age which required a relaxed regime.

A potentially important finding was that 'care' in one area was seen as having a much more positive effect on family relationships than 'care' in another. This area had only three children's homes and so the average distance between the young people and their parents was greater than elsewhere. In keeping with this difference, this area was much more likely to be perceived as having provided a helpful break from the child. It was also more likely to be seen as having helped by providing time for parent and child to be alone on visits.

What, if anything, produced this finding we cannot say. It is possible that it reflects 'idealisation'—because the young people were not always around the house, they were seen in a rosier light. On the face of it, however, it does not suggest that very close geographical proximity is necessary for the resolution of family difficulties. In the conclusion to the book we will argue that if residential care is to survive, it needs to specialise more. If this is to happen, it will need to be less dominated by the need for homes to be close to the residents' families.

Overall, our findings fit with the suggestion of Fisher and his colleagues (1986). In their study, the parents see the role of residential care as exercising the kind of parental control that the parents themselves were unable to provide. In our study the parents also wanted their child controlled and safe. If the child was too young to cope on her/his own, they foresaw a return home with relationships restored on both sides and an improvement in behaviour. Where the young person was older they were prepared to accept a more relaxed regime followed by a transition to independence.

4

THE ROLES OF RESIDENTIAL CARE: THE RESIDENTS' VIEWS

INTRODUCTION

So much for the outsiders to the placement. What were the views of the residents who must undergo it? Curiously, there is very little systematic information on what young people in care want. Qualitative studies have established the criteria against which they evaluate care—for example, that the adults involved should listen to them (e.g. Kahan 1979; Whitaker *et al.* 1985). However, much less is known about whether they want to be looked after at all; if so, whether they would prefer this to be in foster care, residential care or some other form of provision, how they feel about the plans that are made for them and where they want to go next. All these questions are relevant to the role of residential care. The study gave us a chance to pursue them with a large sample of young people.

This chapter derives from the responses to the questionnaire given to our main sample of 223 residents. It therefore represents the views of those who were to be found in the homes at a particular point—as we have noted before, a rather different population to that which passes through them. We have related the residents' replies to a standard set of variables—authority, sex, age, household composition, reason for entry to care, and purpose of placement as reported by the social worker. Where the results vary by these variables in a statistically significant and striking way, we report them. As usual, the representativeness of the sample is considered in Appendix A.

REASONS FOR BEING LOOKED AFTER

We approached the question of the reason for 'entry in to the children's home' by asking the young people to think back to the last time that they 'went into care'. We wanted to know what explanation the social worker had given them for this, whether they thought it was a good or bad idea and why.

In asking about the social worker's explanations for these events, we gave the residents a card with a standard set of possible responses. Table 4.1 sets out their replies. The most common, which applied to around half the sample, was that they were not getting on with people at home. Minorities (just under one in seven in each case) said that they were in some kind of danger or that they were getting into trouble. Around half that number said that they were not being properly looked after (our euphemism for neglect). Examination of other sources of data suggested that just under half the remaining 'other' and 'no explanation' categories could also have been grouped under 'not getting on at home'. This seemed to be a primary or secondary reason for around two-thirds of the residents, a proportion comparable to that suggested by the social workers in Chapter 2.

In general, the reasons given were similar between authorities. However, there was an interesting difference in the relative frequency with which residents used the most common explanation of 'breakdown of family relationships'. Residents in Area 3 were nearly twice as likely to do this as residents in Area 4. Area 3 has, in fact, an impressive system for responding to family breakdown and attempting to ensure that accommodation is not needed. By contrast, Area 4 is impressive for the determination of its 'gatekeeping' system. So Area 4's method of preventing admissions—saying they were of too low a priority to justify a place—may have been more effective in lowering the number admitted than Area 3's (attempting to deal with the need in other ways). As a result, Area 3 may have had a higher proportion of residents who were in homes because they wanted to be than Area 4. As we will see below, there was evidence that this was so.

Table 4.1 Main and second reason why young persons 'looked after'

| | Main reason | | Second reason | |
	(n)	(%)	(n)	(%)
Family illness/housing problem	6	2.7	4	1.8
Breakdown of relationship between young person and family	100	44.8	34	15.2
Young person's behaviour	29	13.0	43	19.3
Potential/actual abuse of young person	29	13.0	13	5.8
Neglect of young person	16	7.2	13	5.8
Other	32	14.3	16	7.2
Not answered	11	4.9	97	43.5
Totals	223	100.0	223	100.0

Source: Interview with residents.

We approached this question of whether residents came into 'care' because of want or need by asking whether at the time they thought that 'coming into care' was a good idea. In general they displayed mixed feelings. Four out of 10 said that it was a good idea, nearly as many (one in three) said it was a bad idea and nearly as many again gave mixed responses or said that they were not sure.

There was a striking variation in the proportion of residents who said that 'care' had been a good idea in the different areas. This proportion was over three times as great in Areas 2 and 3 as it was in Area 4. Conversely the proportion thinking it was a bad idea was three times as great in Area 4 as in Area 3.

On first discovering this difference we were worried that it might be accounted for by the way the young people were interviewed. For it was a weakness of our design that—for practical reasons—we had in most cases one interviewer per area. We decided, however, that this explanation was implausible. The question did not seem more obviously loaded than others (e.g. on whether the young person liked their social worker) on which the answers did not differ by area. It was the first question in its section and there was no obvious way in which the interviewer could have conveyed to the resident what the answer should be. Moreover, in the two areas which shared interviewers the distribution of answers did not vary by interviewer but varied—almost significantly—by area ($p < .1$).

In considering possible explanations for this difference we need to examine what other variables were associated with thinking that the decision had been a good one (Table 4.2). In terms of our 'standard' variables it was associated with age, and the purpose of 'care'. Residents under the age of 12 usually thought it was a bad idea. With age they became increasingly likely to think it was a good one until the age of 16, when perhaps a flat became more attractive.

In terms of the purposes of placement, those whose social workers had some short-term aim in mind were the most likely to see 'care' as a bad

Table 4.2 Whether resident thought 'going into care' was a good thing—by age

Age	(n)	Good idea (%)	Mixed (%)	Bad idea (%)
12 years and under	29	24.1	27.6	48.3
13–14 years	74	36.5	29.7	33.8
15 years	56	57.1	14.3	28.6
16 years and over	61	39.3	23.1	29.5
Totals	220	40.9	25.9	25.9

Differences significant at .05 level.
Source: Interview with residents.

idea (44%), although a third thought it was a good one. Those who were there for some treatment purpose were the most likely to approve the idea (53%) and the least likely to say that it was a bad one (21%). Those who were there for a long-term purpose were the most ambivalent. Nearly half expressed mixed views and the remainder were equally split between those for and those against.

Explanations for these last two findings must be tentative. It seems to us most likely that 'care' is acceptable when it 'goes with the grain'. Young children are least likely to want to leave home and therefore do not want 'care'. With age, the attractions of leaving home increase until around the age of 16, when the idea of total independence in a flat may be somewhat less daunting. At any age a placement that appears to have a structure, a purpose and an end seems to be more acceptable than a short-term emergency measure on the one hand or long-term 'care' on the other. The latter, however, is only likely to be proposed where the situation at home is untenable. It may therefore be accepted as 'Hobson's choice' and with mixed feelings.

So, how far does all this account for the unpopularity of the decision to admit in Area 4? Not very much, it seems. We analysed the relationship between area and attitude to admission, taking into account age and purpose of placement. The results (from hierarchical log-linear analysis) showed that area and attitude were still very significantly associated, even when these other variables were taken into account. Within Area 4 there was no association between length of stay and attitude, so the changes of policy which have characterized it recently are unlikely to be the cause. Perhaps the explanation again has to do with motivation. Area 4 was probably under the greatest 'pressure' of all those in our study and guarded its resources with corresponding care. As mentioned earlier, its 'gatekeeping' measures gave greater priority to 'need' as judged by professionals and less to 'want' as expressed by young people. A consequence would have been that in that area those who might have seen 'care' as a positive solution were least likely to get it.

THE NATURE OF THE CHOICE

We asked those in homes who had been somewhere else since leaving home whether they had wanted to go to their current placement. Six out of 10 said they had, a quarter that they had not, and the remaining one in eight gave mixed responses. Age, once again, appeared influential. Only 42% of those under the age of 12 as against 56% of 13 and 14 year-olds and 77% of 15 year-olds agreed to the change.

To our surprise, there was no significantly greater agreement to the change among this group if the social worker said the placement had been planned. So we were interested in how far the choice could have been said to have been a considered one about which the young people felt they had been consulted.

We asked first whether the residents had had a chance to see the home before they came. Forty six per cent had. We then asked whether they knew their legal position—for example, whether they could decide to go home if their parents agreed. Half (53%) said 'yes', a small number (7%) thought they did but were not sure, and the remaining four out of 10 said they did not. This percentage varied significantly by the purposes of placement. Sixty per cent of those placed for long-term purposes, as against 50% of those whose placement was only for short-term ones and 33% of those whose placement was for treatment were sure they did not know. The percentage of those who did not know or were uncertain also fell steadily from 62% of those at the age of 12 to 40% of those at the age of 16 or over. So those whose youth or proposed length of placement puts them most 'in the power' of the care system may have been least likely to understand the legal basis on which they were there.

Asked whether they had been given a choice over whether to go into the home, 40% said they had. Almost the same proportion said that they had enough time to think things over. Neither of these proportions varied significantly by any of our standard variables.

We then asked them where, if the choice had been in their hands, they would have most preferred to live, and if they could not have had their first choice, where they would have preferred next. Table 4.3 gives the percentage choosing each of a standard list of options.

As can be seen, the most popular first choice (by 29% of the sample) was with the resident's own family. The next most popular choice was the current children's home (25%), followed a long way down by a flat (11%), foster parents and other relatives (9% each) and then the 'also-rans'. Overall, 38% of the sample would have made their present children's home their first or second choice and nearly half (48%) would have chosen some residential home first or second.

An important question is whether those who got their first or second choices differed from the others in the way the choice was made. In this respect, the apparently 'harder' variables turned out not to distinguish. Those who had visited the home and those who knew their legal position were no more likely than others to say that they would have chosen it. Residents were more likely to say that they had got what they wanted if they said that they had been given a choice and if they felt that they had had adequate time to consider it, but this was hardly surprising.

Table 4.3   Where residents would have liked to have gone if choice was theirs

	First choice		Second choice	
Preference	(*n*)	(%)	(*n*)	(%)
Birth parents	66	29.9	16	7.8
Other relatives	20	9.0	36	17.6
Foster parents	19	8.6	40	19.5
Adoptive parents	5	2.3	3	1.5
This home	55	24.9	26	12.7
Another home	17	7.7	34	16.6
Hostel	—	—	2	1.0
Flat	25	11.3	18	8.8
Lodgings	4	1.8	7	3.4
Other	10	4.5	23	11.2
Totals	221	100.0	205	100.0

Source: Interview with residents.

An equally important question concerns the differences there may be between those who do and do not make some form of residential care a first or second choice. The proportions choosing residential care in this way varied by the purpose of placement and sex. More female than male residents would have chosen it (a consequence perhaps of the fact that the option is less likely to be considered for females). The proportion who would have chosen a residential option rose from 38% among those there only short-term, to 45% for those there for medium-term purposes and to over 70% for those there for long-term placement.

The residents who chose residential care did not necessarily want to be in their current home. In this respect there was considerable variation by age. Half the young people aged 12 and under who were prepared to consider residential care would have chosen another home as their first choice, but this was true for only one in 27 of those aged 16 and over.

So the upshot seems to be that although most residents do not want to be in a children's home, they are more likely to chose it than any other form of 'care'. It could be argued that this preference reflects a choice of the devil they know, or the difficulty of making a choice in a vacuum, or even that they are in no real position to make a choice at all. However, even those with experience of foster care chose residential care in preference to it by a ratio of three to one. Quite different figures could well have been found if we had been interviewing a sample in foster care—indeed, Colton (1988) provides evidence that they would be. However, if we are to take seriously the preferences of those who have been in the system we would be wary about closing down all residential care.

PLANS

As Whitaker and her colleagues (1985) have shown, residents tend to be preoccupied with their future. Their expectations of what it will be are likely to shape their current experience of the home.

In explaining this issue we asked the residents whether they knew where they were supposed to go when they left the home. Sixty per cent said that they did and 40% that they did not. Apparent certainty was strongly linked to age ($p < .00001$). Eighty-six per cent of those aged 16 or over but less than half that proportion (42%) of those aged 13 or 14 said that they knew where they were going. The 12 year-olds and under and the 15 year-olds were somewhat better informed, as they thought. Just over half of each group said they knew.

As hinted above, this certainty may have been more apparent than real. Forty-six per cent of those for whom the social worker said plans did not exist, nevertheless said they knew where they were going. By contrast, a third of those for whom plans did exist said they did not know what their destination was to be.

Comparison of the actual destinations proposed revealed a similar extent of disagreement. Where the social worker said there was a planned destination, 41% of the residents agreed about what it was. In calculating this figure we grouped our possible destinations into larger categories (own home, 'care', independent living and other). The disagreement, therefore, was not just about whether the young person may, for example, be living in a hostel or in lodgings (a level of detail at which disagreement was much greater), but over much larger questions, such as whether they were going home at all.

This situation could have three possible explanations. First, the respondents may in some way have interpreted our lists differently—this is possible, but is unlikely to account for the extreme nature of the disagreements (e.g. over whether the resident was going home). Second, the information was gathered at different points in time, so that the plans may have changed from one point to another. The difference in time was not great, generally a matter of a month or two, but this is a likely explanation for some of the difference. Third, there may simply have been a lack of communication between social worker and resident and this is also likely to be part of the explanation.

More detailed examination showed that disagreements were most likely to arise when the young person believed that there were no plans but the social worker had made some. Other areas of relatively high disagreement occurred where the young persons believed that they were going to move within the care system (55% disagreement) or when they thought that they were going to some 'other' destination (66% disagreement). Relatively high agreement occurred where the young persons expected to go home (65% agreement) or into independent living (66% agreement).

The degree of agreement varied significantly by authority. There was 66% agreement in both Areas 1 and 2 but the proportion in the remaining authorities varied between 29% and 35%. This suggests that some aspect of practice or procedures may affect it considerably, although we are unable to say what this is. It is certainly not the frequency with which social workers visit or the quality of their relationship as reported by the young people. We examined these variables and found no relevant associations. It will be remembered, however, that Areas 1 and 2 were also seen as doing well on providing information to the parents, so perhaps an emphasis on communication is one of their hallmarks.

Undoubtedly, however, the main factor in explaining these misunderstandings was the degree to which the social workers' plans matched the young person's wishes. As described below, we asked the young people where, ideally, they would like to live when they left the home. When their answer coincided with what the social worker was planning there was 68% agreement on what the actual destination was going to be. Where it did not, there was 29% agreement.

Similar issues were raised by our next question, when we asked the young people when they expected to leave the home. Forty-five per cent could not say and most of the remainder expected to leave within six months. High agreement between social worker and young person on this question was not to be expected, as they were not answering at exactly the same time. Moreover, the degree of agreement found was far greater than would be expected by chance. Nevertheless there was still a surprising amount of misunderstanding apparent. In the 38 cases where the young person expected to leave within three months and where we had the social worker's plans, the social worker predicted a stay of more than six months in three cases, a stay of more than a year in another and could not predict the length of stay in a further 10.

We were interested in how far the young people felt they could influence the date of their discharge and asked whether it depended on anything they did. Around half the sample said that it did. Pressed further on what they needed to do, almost a third of the sample (31%) said that they had to learn to control their temper:

My behaviour really: I put my foot through a door and smashed a mirror so I've got to control my temper.

Well, I've got to be less bad tempered, less loud—my general behaviour needs to be better, i.e. my attitude.

One in 20 said that they needed to acquire the skills needed for independent living, and in some cases show that they could manage by 'doing independent living whilst I'm here'.

I've got to learn to cope on my own in terms of skills and finances.

I'm not very good at looking after myself, so I suppose I've got to learn how to do this—you know, shopping and cleaning and those sort of things.

A further one in 10 gave a wide variety of answers (e.g. that they needed to get on with parents):

Whether parents agree to me going home.

Sixty per cent of the sample were also prepared to list other factors—perhaps less under their control. These included the age at which they left school (7%), their relatives' situation (6%), the efforts of social services (16%) and a wide variety of other factors:

My age, no housing trust will take me on yet.

Whether local housing department can find me a flat.

Depends on when you leave school. If you leave school and get a job you have to leave. I'm not sure whether I can stay 'cos of wanting to go to college.

The young people, therefore, were in a situation where they were in some difficulty over controlling their lives. They saw themselves as having tempers which might disrupt their plans, and the plans themselves were often dependent on factors such as the efforts of social services, which they could not control.

To judge from the evidence of Bullock and his colleagues (1993b) and Biehal and hers (1995) the residents were likely to be at least equally vulnerable when they got to their new destinations. We therefore asked them whether on leaving the home there would be any reliable person whom they could trust and to whom they could turn. In answering this question, 11% said there would be no-one, but the remainder were more optimistic. A quarter mentioned friends, a fifth relatives, and around one in eight a social worker. Interestingly, the most popular answer (just, and given by 26% of the sample) mentioned the staff in the home. Unless our authorities are very different from those examined in other research, the staff were likely to prove disappointing in this respect. Homes close, staff move, and in some authorities there is a policy of actively discouraging contact between staff and residents (partly perhaps because of fears of the 'corrupting' influence of former residents). Yet our data also suggest that these things could change. There were very large and highly statistically significant differences between our five areas in the degree to which residents reported that they would contact the staff. Forty-seven per cent of the residents in Area 2, 30% of those in Area 1 and 24% of those in Area 4 said they would do so. The comparable figures for Areas 3 and 5 were only 14% and 11% and these were the areas where the parents reported the greatest difficulty in getting to the homes. If the residents in Area 2 were basing their expectations on what they had seen, this suggests a role for homes which other areas have not exploited.

To return to the central theme of this section, where did the young people wish to go? Table 4.4 sets out the distribution of their first and second choices. As can be seen there were three popular options, a flat, the parental home and—to a far lesser extent—fostering. These choices seem to fly in the face of professional opinion—flats are difficult to manage and lonely, and the guidance to the Children Act emphasises the importance in most cases of returning a child to her/his home and, failing this, of using foster care as a homely alternative. We were therefore particularly interested in which young people chose which options.

Two variables stood out as very strongly related to choice. Those who entered care for reasons connected with relationship breakdown were much less likely to want to go home—only one in five of them did so. Age was an even stronger predictor. Two-thirds of those aged 10 or 11, around half of those aged 12 or 13, around a third of the 14 year-olds but only one in six of those aged 16 or over wanted to go home. 'Care', a preferred

Table 4.4 Where residents would ideally like to go when leaving present home

Preference	First choice		Second choice	
	(n)	(%)	(n)	(%)
Birth parents	65	29.7	16	8.1
Other relatives	9	4.1	33	16.8
Foster parents	18	8.2	23	11.7
Adoptive parents	3	1.4	2	1.0
This home	12	5.5	15	7.6
Another home	5	2.3	12	6.1
Hostel	1	0.5	5	2.5
Flat	83	37.9	37	18.8
Lodgings	4	1.8	28	14.2
Other	19	8.7	26	13.2
Totals	219	100.0	197	100.0

Source: Interview with residents.

option for around a quarter of those aged under 14, appealed to only one in eight of 15 year-olds and to even fewer (8%) of those aged over 16.

It should not be thought that this preference for independent living was synonymous with a total rejection of parents. We asked those who did not want to go home, how often they would then like to see their parents. One in 10 had no parents or were so out of touch with them that the question was judged inapplicable. A further one in 12 said that the answer was 'never'. The most common answer (given by 42%) was more than once a week, and a further 22% said at least once a week. Only one in eight wanted contact as infrequently as once in every two weeks or once a month.

These figures for desired contact with parents correspond with what actually happens—to judge from Biehal and her colleagues' (1992) research—in the case of care leavers. So it seems that young people take a less extreme view of parental contact than that promulgated by some of the more extreme advocates of 'permanency' or in some of the more ideological interpretations of the Children Act. Residents recognise, perhaps, that they have a bond with their families that cannot, or at least should not, be broken. They also recognise that families and children are not necessarily good for each other and can certainly get on each others' nerves. So after the age of 11 they increasingly opt for a compromise, 'care' with contact for those aged 14 and 15, independent living with contact for those who are older. Contact in these cases is seen as good in itself and not, as it is by some professionals, as a means for ensuring return home.

Finally, then, in this section, how satisfied were the young people with the plans actually made for them? 'Very' to judge from what they told us. Only one in seven reported themselves as unhappy or very unhappy and a further third as having mixed feelings or not able to comment. Around a half said they were happy, or very happy (13%). As we should by now expect, these percentages varied significantly by area but in all areas only a minority were unhappy with what (quite often incorrectly) they believed their plans to be.

CONCLUSION

The young people's views of the reasons for placement were similar to those of the social workers and parents. Two-thirds saw the reason for placement in 'care' as having to do with a breakdown in relationships between themselves and their families. The remainder were more or less evenly divided between those who saw the placement as having to do with their behaviour and those who saw it as arising because they were in some way in danger.

There were very large differences between authorities in the proportion of young people who felt that 'care' had been a 'good idea'. It was least popular in the authority which was possibly under the greatest pressure, possibly because in this area 'care' had to be rationed to those who were perceived as being in the greatest need, rather than offered to those who might want it.

In general the young people would not have gone into a residential home if the choice had been theirs. Nevertheless, around a third would have done so and this choice was much more popular than fostering among those who had, as well as among those who had not, experienced the latter. Interestingly, around a quarter of those who would have chosen residential care would not have chosen the home into which they had in fact gone. Younger residents were more likely than others to wish that they had gone to some other residential home.

In terms of the future, it was startling to find how many residents did not know when they were expected to leave their current placement or where the social worker thought they were going. Where on our evidence the social worker had plans, disagreement over the basic details occurred in over half the cases and most commonly when the social worker's plans did not match the young person's wishes. Again, there were wide differences between areas in the amount of disagreement which occurred.

Asked whether they would have anyone to whom they could turn after leaving the home, a quarter of the residents mentioned a member of staff. In this respect, too, there were interesting differences between areas, with the proportion rising to nearly 50% in one of them. Generally, the young people envisaged staying in contact with their parents on a frequent basis but not living with them. These preferences, however, varied with age. Two-thirds of those aged 10 or 11 but only one in six of those aged 16 or over said they wanted to go home on leaving their current placement.

These findings give pause for thought. It would seem that the young people have what may be interpreted as a more ambivalent or more sophisticated view of the role of care than popular views of the Children Act would lead one to expect. Their view varied with age. Younger residents were more likely to regard 'care' as a bad idea, to want to be in a home other than their present one and to wish to return to their families as leaving it. However, the majority of residents did not regard being looked after as definitely a bad idea—a finding in keeping with the work of Fisher and his colleagues (1986). Neither did most of them want to return to their families. Instead, most of them seemed to see residential care as a halfway house—a bridge to an independence that would nevertheless include a relationship and frequent contact with their parents. In this independence they foresaw the need for support from a variety of sources and, in a significant minority of cases, from the staff.

5

THE ROLES OF RESIDENTIAL CARE: THE VIEW IN RETROSPECT

INTRODUCTION

One way of describing this book is that it tries to discover what makes for successful residential care. So we need to answer two questions. First, what are the criteria of success? Second, what kind of homes tend to produce it? This chapter explores the first of these questions. It examines the way in which young people and social workers evaluate the placements in a home and what makes them say that the placements were good or otherwise. Implicit in these criteria are the respondents' views on the role of residential care—as the judgement that a good knife is sharp depends on the view that its role is to cut.

The chapter is based on data collected comparatively late in the study, when nearly half the young people were no longer in the homes. The advantage of starting at this point is that residential care is an episode in a career. It takes its meaning partly from the experience in the home but also from what went before and what follows (cf. Whitaker *et al.* 1985). By studying our sample at this point we can gain two perspectives on residential care—one current and one retrospective. And this may be helpful, for an incident which may later be seen as a turning point or a new start may be seen at the time in quite a different light.

Our data came from our follow-up studies. Six months after the residents had been interviewed in their children's home we approached their social workers again, asking them to complete a brief follow-up questionnaire. At the same time we sent a brief follow-up questionnaire to the young person through the home if they were still there or through the social worker if they were not. Almost two-thirds (63%) of each sample responded and, putting these two sources of information together, we had some information on eight out of 10. At the time of the follow-up, just under six out of 10 of the young people were still in residential care and just over one in six with their parents. The remainder lived independently or, in a few cases, in prisons or hostels. We give more detail on these outcomes later in the report. This chapter is about what the young people and their social workers felt about what had happened.

VIEWS OF OUTCOME

The approach we adopted was to ask the social workers and young people how successful residential care had been and why. Table 5.1 gives the social workers' views of the success of the placement. In roughly two-thirds of the cases they considered the placement in residential care on balance successful and in one in 10 they considered it very successful. In very few instances did they consider that it had been a marked failure.

This distribution of answers was very similar to that we obtained when we had asked, at the time of the first interview, how happy they were with the placement. At that stage, too, roughly a third were unhappy or very unhappy about it, while the majority were reasonably content.

The young people who returned our questionnaire were, on balance, even more positive (Table 5.2). Asked to reply to the question, 'Do you think it was a good thing you went to that home?', nearly half said 'Yes, on the whole', a quarter said 'Very much so' and only a sixth said 'Not at all'.

Table 5.1 Social workers' views on success of placement

	(*n*)	(%)
Markedly successful	14	10.1
Successful	76	54.7
Unsuccessful	44	31.7
Markedly unsuccessful	5	3.6
Totals	139	100.0

Source: Follow-up questionnaire to social workers.

Table 5.2 Residents' views on whether a good thing to go to home

	(*n*)	(%)
Yes, very much so	39	27.9
Yes, on the whole	63	45.0
No, on the whole	15	10.7
No, not at all	22	16.4
Totals	139	100.0

Source: Follow-up questionnaire to residents.

When asked to explain the reasons for their ratings, the social workers and young people showed a wide measure of agreement on the criteria they seemed to apply. In general, they judged the experience on five dimensions:

1. Whether it was a good idea in the first place.
2. Whether the home was a reasonable place to live.
3. Whether it had, in some sense, helped them.
4. Whether they had been able to move on when they were 'ready' and at their own pace.
5. Whether they had had acceptable help after leaving.

In making these statements we are not implying that all the young people or social workers covered all these areas in each of their replies. Rather, it was that we noticed that their explanations for why the placement was a good or bad idea generally seemed to cover one or more of these issues. It was as if there was a model in their heads of what the care experience should be, but they referred to elements of the model selectively, depending on the stage in the young people's care careers (e.g. whether they had yet left) and its salience in their experience (e.g. whether they had been in a particularly 'good' or particularly 'bad' home).

These requirements related to a set of stages: deciding on the placement, settling in, a period of change or development, moving on, and getting appropriate support on leaving. What seemed, unsurprisingly, to be wanted was that there should be a genuine need for 'care', an appropriate type of placement, a home which was a good place to live and which contained behaviour, and better still improved it, a system which allowed a move at the right time, and resources to support the young person in the new environment. We use this broad framework to explore the social workers' and young persons' views.

STAGE 1—DECIDING ON THE NEED FOR 'CARE'

Stage 1 involves the answers to two questions. First, is any form of 'care' needed? Second, if so, what is the appropriate placement?

In the first postal questionnaire to social workers, we asked them whether there were any other arrangements which they would like to have made or to make for the young person but could not. In 70% of the cases they said that there were. Generally, the social workers accepted that the young person needed to move away from home. However, in around one in eight cases the social workers would have liked the young person to remain with his/her family or go to relatives. Quite often this was an ideal rather than a realistic possibility, since it was known that the young person or family would not agree to it. Sometimes it took the form of wishing that there had been more time for preventive work in the past. One social worker said that things were much better handled now. Others complained about the lack of resources to handle even a minimal amount of preventive work:

This family were crying out for help but referrals were not picked up as a whole, only investigated as incidents. Emergency placement could have been avoided, I think.

I would like to resume contact with the family for this young person, but at the moment this is unlikely as his parents do not want to see him (Social worker goes on to suggest a need for better post-adoption support).

In some cases the social worker appreciated that the young person wanted to be at home but felt, with regret, that this was not possible:

I have been her social worker for five years. She has always been unhappy in care and only wished to return home but we could not let her because of our concerns. . . . To conclude then, care has not helped Sharon but there was no alternative, so what's the answer?

For some young people things were not so complicated. One wrote in capitals on her form 'I WANT TO GO HOME'. In general, they evaluated their placements comparatively. So, if the young people had not been getting on at home or had been ill-treated there, in a sense the placement got off to a good start. Not 'getting on' could relate to abuse, to a breakdown in relationships or to the young person's worries about his/her own behaviour or mental state. So it could be a good idea to go into a home to:

Get my head together.

Or because:

I had some trouble where I was before. It is A GREAT home to live in.

Or because:

I had a very bad time with my mother and the home back you when you need it . . . you don't get hit here.

Conversely, 'care' got off to a bad start when it was seen as engineered against the young person's will. This could occur because the young person was remanded, because of *force majeure* in the care system ('my home closed down'), because the young person and the social worker viewed the situation differently ('I was living independently at my Mum's, looking after my sister'), or because of what was experienced as an arbitrary or duplicitous use of power ('I was set up and tricked'):

When I first came here I was lied to. They said I would only be here for one overnight. I have now been here for two years.

A man called . . . he said that I would be going in a children's home and I wouldn't. I just went in to my room and locked myself in.

Some young people seemed able to take in their stride the fact that they had not wanted to be in 'care':

I shouldn't really have been in care. But yes, when I was there I enjoyed it, and was looked after very well by all of the staff.

Others, however, were less forgiving:

I would like to go home with my parents to live with them. It is better than staying in a home. That means any home.

I never wanted to live here and would like to go home.

STAGE 2—GETTING THE RIGHT TYPE OF PLACEMENT

The young people knew the kind of placement they wanted—that it should, for example, be homely and, for some, close to their families (one exception to the last point wished to be farther from home, where he had heard that there were youths out to get him). They were, however, less ready to distinguish between placements by their designation (e.g. as a children's home or a foster placement). Asked directly whether they wanted foster care, a children's home or something else, they were prepared, as we will see later, to make a choice. However, they rarely explained their view of their current placement on the grounds that fostering would have been better or worse.

To this general rule there were some exceptions. Some young people explained their liking for their placement on grounds which would be less likely to be duplicated in foster care, referring, for example, to the presence of young people of their own age or to the existence of organised activities:

The people are very helpful to me when I have a problem and the other young residents are great friends to me.

Because they took me out to a different place like camping.

Other young people valued residential care specifically because it was not foster care and not trying to duplicate family life:

I like it here as I didn't seem to be able to get on with families after trouble at home—I prefer it better than a foster home.

Due to my recent life, I cannot cope in a family. So the kids' home is the perfect place for me.

Social workers, when invited to discuss possible alternative arrangements, were rather more forthcoming. The most common specific request (made by one in six and most commonly for those aged between 13 and 15 at interview) was for more foster care suitable for adolescents. It was sometimes acknowledged that this was impractical because the young person would not agree to it. More commonly, however, the difficulty was seen to be that such placements were simply unavailable or that those which were available would not be able to manage a difficult teenager. The solutions advocated by those who gave them were basically for a more professional, specialised fostering service with better pay, better training and more back-up support.

Around one in 10 of the social workers would have liked a different form of residential care—most commonly, very small local units, with generous staffing ratios and trained staff. Some wanted more therapeutic units—and there was criticism of the reluctance of managers to pay for placement in therapeutic communities and/or of the health service to provide them. Some wanted the same kind of residential service as at present, but with units specialised by length of stay (short and long), age and delinquent record, and perhaps with facilities for teenage mothers and their babies.

Small groups wanted better support for independent living (5%), educational provision (2%) or a mix of measures (4%). 'Supported' independent living was almost entirely wanted for those aged 16 or over at interview, where it had been or was wanted by nearly one in seven.

The largest group apart from those who mentioned no ideal consisted of a miscellaneous 'other' category. This included those who wanted some form of treatment for the young person (or who complained that the NHS was not set up to provide it, or ceased to be willing to provide it when the young person passed 16). It also included advocates of diversion who wanted an expansion of bail support and remand fostering.

Lack of resources was not the only problem leading to inappropriate placement. Social workers also complained of pressure to find places quickly—for example, being given a list of telephone numbers and told to find a secure placement within three or four hours and, conversely, of the adverse effects of failure to find a place quickly when one was needed. In some cases a placement originally found as an emergency and expected to last for only a week or so had dragged on for months.

Despite this litany of wants and complaints, nearly one in three social workers appeared to feel that residential care was the best place (or at least did not respond to the invitation to say that it was not):

In hindsight it would have been better for [young person] to have gone immediately to the community home because he could not cope with living in a family. The community home has certainly improved him in many ways. It gave him confidence, security and a voice.

There will always be children who cannot accept a permanent alternative family (emphasis in original).

So overall, what the social workers seemed to be seeking was choice.

The young people were less concerned with designing a kaleidoscope of services, but their views, if implemented, would nevertheless probably have required one. What they wanted was for someone to listen to their views and find a placement that fitted.

STAGE 3—GETTING A HOME YOU CAN SETTLE IN

The attributes associated with good homes by social workers included 'homeliness', 'security' (in a psychological sense), 'structure' (in the sense of having a predictable routine) and a committed and caring staff:

This young person has clearly illustrated to the workers involved that she has been very damaged by the rejection experienced in two foster placements, and feels 'safe' in a residential unit.

This young person has received a high commitment and a high level of individual input from residential staff.

Provided structure and advice to the young person while respecting their individuality and working in an open manner.

The deviations from this model were seen as arising from various factors. Some blamed reorganisation:

Too much uncertainty for the young person. Placement is so-called 'short-term' and the residential unit is due to be reorganised. However, the plan for this young person is long-term accommodation—therefore the concern is around where this young person will be moved to (if at all).

Recent change in role and function of placement has meant that it is no longer a stable environment in which to live.

Staffing issues were again seen as important:

I am very unhappy about the regime . . . There is a very obvious split between the attitude and behaviour of the management and a small number of staff and the rest of the staff . . . His keyworker and other staff like him and have a good relationship with him but certain workers and managers do not. This comes across very clearly to me and is clearly harmful to him.

Some homes were seen as chaotic and unsatisfactory in a wide variety of ways:

The placement the child is currently in has a number of short-comings, such as: (1) poor state of repair/decor; (2) lack of containment of the young people; (3) high change-over of workers making environment unsettled and no consistency of care; (4) poor record in getting children to school.

Others mentioned bullying:

Young person placed in residential establishment following a violent assault against her. Then under attack from other residents who did not want her in their space. Smuggled out at night to prevent more harm.

The young people's description of what they liked and did not like about homes was less lengthy than the social workers' and less analytical about the reasons for success or failure. Some were not very specific about the reasons for their evaluation:

I just want you to know that this home is great for me and for all the others to live here.

Because a children's home like Acacia View is not suitable for any young person.

Others, however, were more specific. In essence, the positive qualities they picked out were the same as those identified by the social workers, although they sometimes referred to 'fun' and 'freedom', aspects of life which did not feature in the professionals' accounts and to the closeness of the home to their families, something whose advantage the professionals perhaps took for granted. So, they valued safety and security:

Because I felt cared for and secure.

Because it is an all girls home so you don't have to worry about boys abusing you. Also the staff are very kind here.

They valued good relationships with the staff:

I get on with the staff and the kids here.

Because of the freedom I am able to have and also the help members of staff give to me.

And they preferred homes which were not chaotic:

Because things don't get smashed and things don't get nicked much and staff are nice most of the time.

They did not want to be bullied or abused:

I get bullied quite often. Does my head in living here. I just can't do with it at all.

Because it was very good, except when I got sexually abused by Matthew.

Disordered homes were criticised:

I needed a family environment and Tamarisk Road just made me upset. I see a lot of violent acts and breaking the law in the children's home. Also, most of the kids took solvents, drugs or alcohol.

Because it wasn't very settled and because the staff knew it would shortly be closing down, they didn't seem to bother as much. Also, when things broke they didn't bother to get it fixed because there was no point if it was closing.

Some excitement was, however, wanted:

Coz it done nothing for me and was boring. Never owt for to do.

Pear Tree Road is a settled home with a friendly environment. It offers stability for the young persons living there but doesn't have much excitement.

Some of the young people's comments conveyed some understanding of the difficulties under which the staff were working. This, however, was exceptional and the social workers were rather more understanding in this respect. Their negative comments were accompanied by a recognition that the residential staff had a thankless task in terms of both the difficulty of the residents and the frequently incompatible nature of the resident group:

The [young person] was fortunate that the mix of young people in the unit was favourable. Placing a youngster without an offending record in a unit which deals with remands is not, in my opinion, a good idea.

Due to emergency placement, no choice of community home. John is inappropriately placed—he attends school regularly and has no behavioural problems. The other residents have continued to bully him and try to mock his attendance at school and his other interests.

Such comments need to be balanced by others, which reflected the dedication of the residential staff and the potential of residential care:

I have been impressed by the standard of care and support offered in the home. . . . The staff do their best to provide a caring and stable environment.

After a difficult start and a degree of reluctance, now well settled, established and liked by staff and residents and calls it home. Excellent support from keyworker and staff members. Result = young person feeling wanted and cared for.

A young person put the point graphically:

Thorn Avenue staff are not just residential social workers, they are my family and they should be thanked by a medal of some sort. They are very kind and helpful. Again I would like to say thanks.

So if this is the quality of care that can be offered, what can it achieve for good or ill?

CHANGES IN RESIDENTIAL CARE

The young people quite often acknowledged that they had changed in residential care but were not specific about the nature of the change or what had led to it. They liked it because 'It was helpful' or because it 'Helped me to be good'.

As might be expected, the social workers were more explicit both about the nature of the changes produced by care and the way in which they were brought about. Their most frequent comments on change referred to changes in behaviour. Improvements were either unexplained or attributed to the effects of a 'good atmosphere':

Behaviour improved and enabled fostering.

Home able to help young person with some problems—improved behaviour, started visiting mother and returned to education.

Some of the young people referred to similar changes:

Because I think I have settled down a lot and there are a lot more people that understand and listen.

As I am now living in a settled home, I have become settled and a lot less aggressive.

These changes enable changes in the pattern of the residents' lives which might outlast their time in care:

Things have worked out well for me since I've come into care. I started to go back to school, did my exams, went to college. If I was at home I wouldn't have done any of that. Now I'm waiting for a flat.

Other changes in behaviour could also have potentially long-term but less desirable effects. A number of our questionnaires were returned from prison establishments or secure units and those returning them were not pleased with the way their lives were going:

*I'm pretty pissed off, actually. I'm in Oak Tree Secure Unit for doing nothing bad. Some people in here are in here for something they have done bad. They seem to have taken three months away from my life for no **REASON*** (emphasis in original).

Changes in behaviour for the worse were sometimes explained by the social workers on general grounds (e.g. 'failure to meet needs'):

Needs were not met by home. The young person began to reoffend and increased truancy.

Sometimes the explanation was given as the influence of bad companions:

The young person became open to even more bizarre behaviour as she took up the habits of the other young people in the group.

or a lack of structure:

The lack of any ability to establish clear boundaries and order within her residential placement meant that her needs were not properly addressed and her problems compounded.

or a negative spiral with bad behaviour leading to rejection and this in turn to further bad behaviour:

Saw staff as nagging and was abusive to female staff. His offending behaviour increased and the home was not able to contain it. He abused solvents and began to influence younger residents to the alarm of staff. There were problems with staff and the placement came to an abrupt end.

Reflecting on their experience, the young people referred to similar pressures and changes. Commonly they referred to the influence of their peers:

Well, the reason being is simply because when I went into care I had no police record whatsoever, but you get in with the wrong crowd in care and end up coming out with a record as long as your arm.

I felt that while I was in care the rest of the world just passed by and me'n the lads just stood still. Then when I left I had nothing like qualifications, etc.

Poor behaviour was sometimes seen as leading to rejection:

Because I've got myself into more trouble with staff and police and in the end they didn't want to know me, so they just kicked me out.

Because it encouraged me to stay out all night and take drugs and things like that.

Responsibility for poor behaviour, however, was sometimes attributed to the home rather than the young person:

Well if I never came into Apple Avenue I wouldn't have tried to kill myself, take drugs or get into trouble with the police. At the moment I'm in a new children's home . . . so I've got the chance to start again. So I'm petty happy at the moment.

In introducing the above quotations we referred to pressure, but in some ways it is not so much pressure as the lack of it that is the trouble. One young person commented that he always fell on his feet. Nevertheless:

I feel sorry for other kids in care, because after a while social services just give up and the kids are prepared to just sit around all day. While you're in care its like that's where you belong and nothing else is important apart from what's happening in the home. You forget about school and stuff and when you leave that matters. Social services try but they need co-operation from the residents and without that it's like they are banging their heads against a brick wall.

A second advantage of the placement as seen by the social workers was that it gave time for reflection—a period in which the young person was freed from immediate family pressures and could consider what they really wanted to do. These advantages particularly applied when the young person was at odds with her/his family or when there had been a breakdown in foster care. There was time then for absence to make the heart grow fonder, for bridges to be built, and for the young person to 'work through issues' and come to terms with the past.

Helped to determine young person's plans and wishes.

Enabled [young person] to come to terms with foster breakdown and move towards accepting a further placement.

James had time and space to think through what he really wanted; eventually he concluded that he would like to return home and did so with few difficulties.

Some of the young people referred to similar benefits:

Because it gave me a break from home and a chance to see what a children's home is like.

It gave me a chance to think about the different things I can do with my life, plus a chance to change.

A chance to sort things out was sometimes enhanced by the willingness of the staff to listen. The young woman quoted above who felt that she had been given the chance to change noted that when she was upset she could get on the telephone to her social worker, who would help her to sort out why. The importance of sensitive and responsive listening was mentioned by a number of current and former residents, but not everyone felt that they had been heard:

It gave us the chance to tell an independent person what it's like and what needs to change.

I don't feel that I have been listened to. . . . I used to have counselling from Hettie Atherton, she was a student and had to leave so I don't feel I have anyone to talk to now.

Difficulties over listening were not always seen as the fault of the staff:

Thorn Avenue has gone downhill due to kids coming in and not being willing to obey rules. That has made the staff very busy and we haven't had much one-to-one with staff, but they're not to blame.

A specific benefit to which a number of social workers and young people referred was that the homes enabled the young people to acquire the skills of independent living. Not all social workers felt that the training was realistic. Training for independent living does not seem to involve preparation for loneliness, neither is a regime which requires the young person to, for example, eat at the same time as everyone else, or which subsidises them if they run out of money, a full preparation for the stresses of living on income support in a tower block flat. Nevertheless, there were a number of appreciative references to the training from the young people.

They also taught me a lot of skills and helped me mature and [become] more responsible.

Social services has helped me get more independent (i.e. visiting my dad twice a week using public transport and going to college). They have spent a lot of time on me trying to get me to improve my hygiene.

Social workers generally, but not always, concurred:

It achieved the ultimate aim of independence and prepared young persons for it.

Recently we looked at a placement in teencare. It was surprising to hear that she receives approx £30 p.w. to spend on herself. This is completely unrealistic if any serious attempt is to be made on moving her on from this establishment.

Either because of improved behaviour and a chance to reflect or for other reasons, the young people and their social workers felt that a number of more general changes occurred. Some young people became more mature or more confident and they related to others better and gained in self-esteem. In this allegedly post-modern world, it might seem that the bases of self-esteem may be different for different groups. If this was so for the young people, they did not reveal it to us. Their comments reflected values that would not have been out of place in the 1950s:

Social services have helped me to be respectful to members of the public. Also they have helped me to rehabilitate my character and become a man of authority and a respectful member of the community.

I think I am doing well. I am now working and living happily with my Mum and Dad.

I seem to be doing quite well. I have started college and I am doing very well.

As usual, social workers picked up similar themes but in less colourful language.

Built relationships with adults—helped develop self-esteem.

One tends to progress downwards in the care system. It's impossible to help someone who doesn't feel they're worth helping.

So work, good behaviour and a family base all seemed to be valued and important props to a good view of oneself. The young people were not looking for sources of self-esteem at odds with those valued by the rest of us. Unfortunately, the sources they sought were frequently unavailable to them.

STAGE 4—MOVING ON

These general changes might signal the readiness of the young person to move on. Two contradictory dangers were apparent—that the young person would move too soon or that he/she would be ready for a change and 'go off the boil' while he/she waited to make it. Some chafed at the lack of change:

*Things have not really changed for me at all. I have meeting after meeting and nothing ever seems to come out of it. . . . I have been left in a short-term unit (4–6 weeks) for **10** months with no education and nothing to do. At times I have felt really depressed about it.*

It was OK at first as I thought all my being with foster parents just doesn't seem to work. So I thought being in a children's home was the best thing for me, but as I came to be 16 I had grown out of it and wanted to be with a family again. So I was unhappy at this stage and misbehaved a lot.

Others complained of pressure to leave before they were ready:

I don't think they realise how big a step you are taking when [you move] into your own place, but I think that they never seem to take what you say seriously. I don't think I should have been pressurised the way I was into my flat.

Another, by contrast, was grateful for the fact that she had (most unusually) been allowed to stay until she was 18.

I am very grateful to the children's home for accommodating me until the age of 18, but unfortunately leaving care with little support does not make me feel so happy.

Social workers were similarly aware of the importance of timing but were more likely than the young people to feel that *children should be moved out as soon as possible.* So they commented, for example, that:

Lack of resources has caused this young person to remain in a children's home longer than intended.

The main lesson is having the appropriate placement available when the young person is ready to move on.

Social workers seemed less likely to comment on the dangers of too quick a move. Indeed, there was emphasis on the danger that the young person would become too happy, would become dependent on the level of material goods in the home, and would stay in the home in order to get a leaving care grant and so would resist the social worker's plan to get them out. A rather different source of difficulty for the social workers arose in the rare cases where the young person had committed a grave crime and the social worker's plans for change were frustrated by the involvement of the Home Office and the Department of Health.

STAGE 5—HELP ON LEAVING

The problems facing the young people on leaving varied considerably, depending on where they went. In what follows we will deal separately with four groups—those returning home, those entering foster care, those going to some form of residential care (a miscellaneous group), and those living independently in flats, lodgings or hostels. The question in each case is what connection there might be between what happened in the home and subsequent events.

Returning Home

In the case of those returning home, all concerned seemed to agree that the home could have an impact on how things turned out. In some cases the influence was not exactly of the form that had been intended. Jessica Taylor, for example, thought that care had been a good idea on the whole because it gave her a break from her family and made her realise how much they really meant to her. It also gave her her 'independence'. She was, however, far from feeling gratitude:

In around the past year I have been in two children's homes. Neither of them has done anything for me. Now and again staff talked to me, but not as much as what I would have liked them to. Social Services have done next to nothing for me and now I have left a Children's home and am living with my elder sister, my social worker hardly comes and I get no help from anyone from Social Services.

Social Services have made me realise that I don't want to be moved into a children's home again. It was unhappy and I didn't like it one bit. It turned out alright because I am away from that place at last.

The lack of connection between the quality of care in the homes and the quality of the subsequent experience in a family was also apparent in the case of Miles Williams. His comment on his first children's home was that he had been very unhappy at first as he was getting picked on, was not doing well at school and not eating well. He had also been picked on at his second home (where we interviewed him), but felt that he had settled down there a lot better, so that it had been a good thing on the whole that he had gone there. Despite this somewhat unhappy history, Miles was pleased with social services:

Social services have done a lot for me in the past 6 months. They've got me back living with my real mum. They helped me settle in and talked to me about any problems I'm having. They got me out of the way if things got too upsetting. Social Services even gave my mother a grant to do up my room and get me some decent clothes. Rick Weaver from Magnolia House staff, my ex-keyworker, came out and did some extra outreach work with me. If it wasn't for him I'd be back in a children's home. He helped me to talk about my problems to my mum. I've still had a few arguments but nothing serious.

So for Miles what mattered now was his current situation and the help that his former keyworker was able to give him with that.

As far as could be judged from the young people's questionnaires, this pattern of separation between the quality of previous and subsequent experience was something that applied to almost all those who were back with their families. However, a small number had returned home and appeared to feel that their current lives had benefited from their previous experience in a children's home. The link was generally that the home had helped them desist from delinquent activity:

I am very happy I went there because I went to prison first and I wouldn't have got any help, only learn to become a better criminal. I have learnt from my mistakes by the help of Thorn Avenue. . . . Social Services are there any time I want to talk to them since I have been home.

Things have turned out well for me. I've got a job and I'm living with my father. Social Services helped me in a lot of ways, i.e. helped me off drugs and also helped me to stop committing crimes, i.e. burgling, nicking cars.

Other Residential Care

A small number of respondents had moved from one residential establishment to another. Where this other was a prison, they were unhappy with their situation and, as discussed above, not uncommonly blamed it on the adverse influence of their former home.

Others, by contrast, had moved homes and here the quality of the new home seemed to be the determining factor in their experience. Fortunately it was possible for the environment to change even though the home did not. Tommy Parnel had had a difficult history which had hardly been improved by his initial experiences in the home:

Because my mum could not cope with me, I was fat and not looked after properly. But matters have changed. I weigh nine stone, I am nearly 5 foot 4 and instead of growing outwards I am growing upwards! A couple of residents abused me. They made me stand in the nude. But they have left. I am living a happier life than before.

Foster Care

We had four questionnaires returned from young people in foster care. All said they were happy or very happy with their current situation. All but one also thought that it had been a good idea for them to go into residential care. Flora Turner was the most enthusiastic:

I think this is because when I went there just for two days—these two days were the 2nd and 3rd September 1992. I was made welcome and I felt as if I was in a home, not as in a children's home but in a family home. After those two days, when I went to live there all the time, I was loved and cared for and this is why I think it was good for me to go to the Rowans.

Happily, her experience of her foster home was equally positive:

I feel that I am in the right place with the foster carers that I am with. They have made me a part of the family. They love me and care about what happens to me in the future. I love the foster carers as much as they love me . . . I have thought that [social services] have not done anything for me. But now I look back and think I would not be with such a loving family and lovely home without them.

It might seem that the experience at the Rowans contributed to this happy outcome. However, it should be noted that her positive response to the Rowans was immediate and apparently waiting to be produced by any sign of concern. It was also noteworthy that one member of this group was not happy with her placement in a children's home (because of a 'personal problem with a member of staff'). She, however, was also very happy in her new placement:

Things have turned out well for me. Pat Spooner has helped me to get away from Ash Court into my new placement. I am happy in my new home and like my new school.

Independent Living

The problematic relationship between what happens in the home and what happens after it was further illustrated by our final major group—those who left for independent living. The issue is illustrated by one of the most apparent successes in the sample. This young woman considered that it had been a very good idea that she had gone into her children's home. Her comments on her experience in residential care were balanced but also very positive:

Before moving to [town] I lived in [city]. When I was living there I got into a lot of trouble with the police and drank heavily. I'd moved five or six times in a matter of months, didn't have anyone who really cared. So when I went to Hazel Street, because people cared for me, I stopped getting into trouble and, more importantly, felt settled and secure there.

This interesting and heartening story might have been expected to have an unambiguously happy ending. In fact, however, she said that she was unhappy ('This is because I dislike it living in this bed-sit'). Her responses to our standard 'happiness scale' suggested that she thought well of herself but the responses were otherwise unambiguously gloomy. She explained her feelings in more detail at the end of the questionnaire:

I received some outreach, but it wasn't for as long as I'd have liked it to be. Leaving care is so scary, being independent after years of being dependent on others is really hard and is very lonely. I had some very good times at Hazel Street but also I have some horrible memories which I'll live with forever. A lot of changes need to be made with living in care, to me it's a false look at life and world of material goods. It's only now after leaving care reality has come home to me.

The themes of this account include the importance of realistic preparation, the value in these situations of adult support from social workers or others, and the influence of the quality of the accommodation offered. Time in the home was valued, for the usual reasons, but also if it was perceived as having provided realistic preparation for independent living. Social workers were valued if they were there for you, got you flats, and generally helped you over the rough bits. They were not valued if they never came to see you, 'fobbed you off' with bed and breakfast or a hostel for the homeless, or failed to acknowledge your new adult status. And even with these supports, life could still go wrong if you were burgled or got in with the wrong crowd.

Organisationally it seemed that social services still had some way to go in realising the importance of known and trusted back-up in these situations. So perhaps have some social workers, about whom mixed feelings were expressed:

Jim Stewart my social worker has been brilliant and helped a lot.

My social worker is sod all use.

Some complaints were more specific:

Everything is alright for me at the moment. There is just one thing. My social worker is to leave me because she is too busy. I have to have a new one, but I don't want one . . . I really like my social worker and don't want to lose her. I think social workers that start with you should finish right to the end with you.

I am really cheesed off with everything that's happened since I moved into my own flat. Because I'm 16 with a baby I'm put into a category and stereotyped. They don't listen to my needs or even try to listen.

Some social workers, who have not been given a voice for some time in this chapter, were clearly well aware of these issues. They commented at various points on the deleterious effect of changes of worker, recognised the difficulty raised by the young people's belief that they were ready for living in a flat when the social worker felt they were not, and argued for the importance of sticking with the young person until the latter's life began to get into some kind of shape:

S has continued to need support, both practical and emotional, after leaving 'care'. This has been reduced as appropriate and he is now living independently fairly successfully—this has increased his self-esteem. **Lesson:** *children do not automatically become able to cope when they reach 18 years of age. Intensive support with gradual reduction can work.*

For some, however, as for the young woman first quoted in this section, the reduction in support was too rapid. We close this section with the account of a young woman who had very warm feeling towards her former home and who had been supported for a time by staff from it:

It is a very good home. It was like a normal home environment and staff showed you that they cared and I knew they were there 24 hours a day if I needed them for some reason, no matter how small . . . When I left [there], Social Services said they would give me all the help and support I needed but they did not. They just forget about you when you leave. The staff at the home were alright until a few weeks ago. As I don't have family and friends live to far away I am always on my own and Social Services don't seem to understand why I always have a go at them. They don't believe it is that bad.

CONCLUSION

Followed-up six months after we first contacted them, the young people and the social workers generally seemed moderately pleased with the way that things had turned out. We asked them to reflect on what had been good and bad about their experiences, and their comments clustered around five main areas.

First, both were keen that entry to the home should reflect a positive choice. For the young people, this meant that their previous life had not been happy and sometimes that they did not want any more experiences of foster care or family life. For the social workers, what was important was that there should be a variety of provision and adequate resources devoted to prevention, so that residential care was chosen rather than forced. The resources required included additional professional foster care placements (particularly for the 13–15 year-olds), greater support for independent living arrangements, and resources for prevention, diversion (through bail support and remand fostering) and treatment (including specialist psychological services and therapeutic communities). It would also include residential care, albeit not necessarily quite in the form that it currently exists. The hoped-for result would be that more placements would be made in a considered way, fewer would be inappropriate and there would be less pressure to keep young people in those that were.

Second, both social workers and young people were keen that the home should provide a secure, caring and comfortable environment. Conversely, it should not be a place where there was bullying or young people became part of a delinquent culture.

Third, it was important for some that the home had encouraged or enabled change. The mechanisms through which this had occurred were various. For example, the young person had got into college, which had both helped her self-esteem and given her a start for her future life, or there had been a reconciliation between a resident and his family, or somehow the resident had just calmed down.

Fourth, it was important that the move from residential care was well-timed. For the young people, this usually meant that it was not forced before the young person was ready for it. For the social workers, it usually meant that the move was not too long delayed by lack of resources or the young person's reluctance to leave what was sometimes seen as the 'lotus land' of a residential home.

Fifth, it was important that the young people were adequately supported after they had left the home. In this respect experiences seem to have been very varied. Some were very grateful to their social workers; some had received important follow-up support from their keyworkers; but others complained that their social workers were always 'otherwise engaged' and that social services were unaware of the loneliness and fear in their lives.

So the chapter makes the obvious point that the effectiveness of residential care depends on the provisions that precede, follow or, in the case of education, accompany it. In two respects, however, residential care can be expected to make an impact on its own. First it can, if the young people and social workers are to be believed, provide either a stable, caring environment or a frightening den of thieves. Second, it seems to have within it some capacity to enable or promote change, which again may be for good or ill. Our task in the remainder of the book is to determine what enables a residential home to deliver stable and effective care. Before turning to this, it may be useful to summarise some issues raised by our data on the role of the homes and described in the last four chapters.

Issues in the Role of Residential Care

Two-thirds or more of the residents, their parents and their social workers thought that the young person should not have remained at home. However, only about a third of each group thought that residential care was the best option. Their preferred alternatives were strongly related to age and included the options that the young person remained at home, was placed with relatives, foster carers or adoptive parents, or went into a flat or supported lodgings. Given that the young person was in residential care, the general expectation was that he/she would not return home (although here, too, preferences were age-related, with the parents of younger residents tending to want them back and the younger residents themselves wanting to return).

Against this background, the social workers saw the homes as having four main functions. They contained crises in the community, enabling situations to be assessed and the young person returned as soon as possible. They responded in a similar way to crises in 'care', but here the aim was more likely to be that the young person was enabled to change so that the next placement could be better-managed. They took adolescents for whom further fostering was seen as undesirable, so that they could remain for the foreseeable future. And they prepared young people to live independently in the community. Irrespective of the role the homes were playing, it seemed to be common ground among residents, social workers and parents that the home should be a good place to live, that it should not corrupt (a point particularly stressed by parents) and that it should, if possible, enable change.

A major difficulty was that most residents, parents and social workers were not getting the placements they wanted. Residential care was more likely to be chosen than foster care by both parents and residents, but both groups were more likely to choose something else. Parents and, to some extent, residents and social workers commonly thought that the regime was inappropriate for the particular young person and this was particularly so for younger residents. The timing of moves in residential care was often contentious, with residents feeling that they had been left in homes too long or, more commonly, that they had been pushed out too early. Information which might enable choice was lacking. So parents were often hazy about care plans, while residents and social workers often differed over what they were.

The problems of providing more choice were severe. The residents were difficult. In eight out of 10 cases some other arrangement had been tried in between their exit from their family and their entry into their current home. Foster care placements which would cope with them were commonly not available or, if available, might not be accepted. The views of residents and parents often conflicted, so that neither could have what they wanted. Most placements were emergencies, so that there was little time to look around for placements which would satisfy everyone's wishes. And the resources were not available, either, to provide a range of placements or to enable a smooth transition from the home to a new placement at a time which everyone chose.

In theory, solutions to these problems are possible. They are likely to involve:

- *The use of resources* to enable more intensive preventive work and a wider range of properly resourced alternatives to residential care.
- *Buffer facilities*, enabling crises to be held while properly considered choices are made.
- *Skilled social work*, enabling a rapid and intensive response to problems in the community, and clearer and agreed contracts with the family and the young person when plans are contingent on changes in each.
- *Integration*, for, as the social workers see it, the success of residential care depends partly on its links with the resources outside it.
- *Defence in depth*—a recognition that the more adults a young person has to whom he/she may turn, the less likely he/she is to be without support. So many young people want neither to return to their families nor to sever contact with them, and many want a continuing relationship with the staff.
- *A variety of residential care*—some of which might approximate to the alternatives which the young people say they want (e.g. flats).

We will return to these issues in the conclusion to the book. Their resolution depends on the availability of good quality choices—and hence in part on the ability to provide good quality residential care. It also depends on the provision of extra resources or the ability to make better use of the resources already available. The rest of this book is relevant to these questions.

6

THE HOMES—THE BASIC DETAILS

INTRODUCTION

The central focus of this study is on the homes themselves. This chapter is the first of four which concentrate on *the homes as units*. Over the course of the book we will have much to say about how the homes are run and the way the residents react to them. Immediately, however, our concern is with the more fixed and static variables—buildings, size, staff ratios and so on—which provide the setting for the life within.

Such 'structural' factors interest those who have to make policy. Potentially they provide the levers through which administrators may be able to improve standards, if not in individual homes, then over the system of homes as a whole. Sir William Utting, for example, places considerable importance on keeping the size of home low, the staff ratio high and the proportion of qualified and trained staff as high as possible (Utting 1991, 1997). So it is important to see whether there are large differences between homes in terms of these structural variables and if so whether they have an effect on measures of process and outcome.

A second aim of the chapter is to see whether we can produce a simple classification of homes in terms of their purpose and characteristics (e.g. whether certain homes are typically larger, tend to take certain kinds of residents and to have particular kinds of function). Our previous chapters have shown that residential care serves different purposes and these may need to be reflected in differences between homes. We will see whether these differences exist.

As already described, our study is based on 48 homes. Four of 'our' homes were based on sites which contained more than one unit, so that we could have treated them as comprising two large homes rather than four separate ones. By contrast we chose to treat other homes containing sub-units as single establishments. The basic criterion we adopted in making these judgements was whether the homes were listed separately in the *1993 Social Services Year Book*.

In the course of this chapter we present a relatively large number of descriptive tables. We find them fascinating, and hope some readers will do so as well. Others who are less enamoured with statistics are invited to skip these. Anything that is essential to the argument is said in English.

BUILDINGS

The interviewers claimed that with experience they could identify the most unobtrusive home. Nevertheless, some homes were clearly more unobtrusive than others:

'Ash View'. A large detached house in a long road of similar properties, all in red brick. Easily missed when driving past—completely inconspicuous. A small garden to the front side and rear. Inside, well-decorated with lots of pictures and ornaments. There is a large modern kitchen and a large-ish dining room. An adjacent living room is divided from this by glass doors—it has a comfy suite, TV, video, satellite dish (I think—there is certainly a dish outside) plus smart sideboard, etc.—a homely feel. Nearby is the office and a smoking room with table and chairs.

So, overall an unobtrusive, comfortable children's home, an establishment which the public might pass without a second glance, and which the interviewer felt could be 'easily missed'. The impression created by the description of 'Ash View' is very different from that formed of many other homes, for example, 'Beech View':

'Beech View'. A sad and gloomy place—all long, gloomy corridors and locked doors. It is difficult to convey the sense of unhappiness that Beech View exudes. It is a large, very obviously institutional building. Built in the 60s on two levels with a flat roof around four sides of a paved area not unlike the exercise yard of a prison. Impersonal dining room. A left turn takes you into a huge kitchen . . . with stainless steel surfaces and catering style eight-ring gas cooker and mega-grill etc . . . [upstairs] three landings of bedrooms, divided by sex, plus a flat (formerly used for independence training) but trashed by residents and now full of smashed furniture and graffitti. Quite nice grounds . . . even a tennis court . . .

So 'Beech View' is clearly an institution whose gloomy aspect conveys the impression of a juvenile prison. The home is redeemed, if redeemed at all, by the presence of sporting facilities in keeping with the tradition of boarding establishments. Its contrast with 'Cedar View' could not be more apparent:

'Cedar View'. A truly astonishing exterior for a children's home. Set on a regular row of council 'semis', the house is festooned with colourful hanging baskets, has a well-pruned hedge, florid borders and short grass. Step up to the shiny new front door and enter a recently decorated hall with posh wallpaper and borders. To the left is a nicely decorated and furnished lounge, ahead is a dining room (by now with a brand new French window) and the corridor to the right has a small office, toilet, laundry room and kitchen (soon to be refurbished and made into two kitchens within the present space) . . . So, a pristine and improving environment.

These pen portraits illustrate the very different immediate impressions which the appearance of children's homes can make on those who visit them. They vary in the type of neighbourhood, the physical appearance of the building itself, the standard of internal decoration and the degree to which the homes fit in with the neighbourhood or stand out as an institution. In order to capture these variations we asked the interviewers to make a small number of ratings for each home.

Table 6.1 gives the overall breakdown of the interviewers' impressions. As can be seen, the vast majority of homes were perceived by the interviewers as located in at least respectable areas and only four were located in areas described as 'run down'. External and internal décor was rather more harshly judged, although here again most homes were perceived as reasonable. In contrast to the examples given earlier, nearly half the homes were judged to be 'clearly institutional', while only five were

Table 6.1 Interviewers' impressions of the homes

Feature	(n)	(%)
Immediate area		
Run-down	4	8.7
Respectable	35	76.1
Up-market, leafy	7	15.2
External appearance of home		
Run-down	16	34.8
Average upkeep	23	50.0
Smart/well maintained	7	15.2
Internal appearance of home		
Run-down	13	28.3
Average upkeep	26	56.5
Smart/well maintained	7	15.2
Fit with neighbourhood		
Clearly institutional	22	47.8
Some institutional features	19	41.3
Ordinary/homely	5	10.9

Source: Interviewer ratings.

considered homely. The institutional features, however, were generally less dramatic than those at 'Beech View'. For example:

'Elm View' is a standard size home identical in design to 'Fir Tree View' and several other units. It stands on its own in a large area of open space and clearly is an institution. The interior is clean and well maintained. Some of the building is quite neatly decorated. Other parts have not been decorated for a while. It is quite comfortable in a 'lived-in' way (rated 'clearly institutional').

Such differences immediately strike an outsider and raise questions about how they affected the residents. That the residents notice them is undeniable and former residents have advised the Social Services Inspectorate (SSI) on the importance of avoiding institutional features. Similarly, residents in this study commented on the depressing effect of failures to attend to breakages. Nevertheless, there is a question of how far the effect, if any, of the environment depends on the way in which it comes to reflect or symbolise the atmosphere in the home and how far it has a direct effect in its own right. We return to these questions later in this report. As one of the interviewers wrote, 'It does not necessarily do to judge a book by its wrapper'.

SIZE AND OCCUPANCY RATES

An obvious difference between homes relates to their size. The importance of this has partly to do with cost. Previous evidence suggests that at least up to the size of 14 beds, there are economies of scale, with larger homes being less expensive than small ones (Knapp and Smith 1985). By contrast, professional opinion (e.g. Utting 1991) generally inclines to the view that 'the smaller the better'. Table 6.2 sets out the 'official size' of the 44 homes for whom the heads returned the information.

Officially the homes catered for numbers of residents varying between four and 20 with an average of 7.9. Nearly three out of four had fewer than nine 'official' beds and the most popular number, nearly a third of the sample, was six. The four large homes each catered for between 16 and 20 residents but each was divided into sub-units or projects so that their residents were still in many respects living in small groups.

These figures varied comparatively little between areas. Area 3 was an exception in this respect with three large homes, each catering for 16 residents. The median size in the other four areas varied only from 5.5 (Area 2) to 8 (Area 5). Area 2 was also something of an exception, with one very large home (20 residents) but a comparatively large number of small homes of five or less.

Table 6.2   Registered number of beds per home

Size (number of beds)	Number of homes	(%)
4	3	6.8
5	4	9.1
6	14	31.8
7	5	11.1
8	6	13.6
9	4	9.1
10	1	2.3
12	3	6.8
16	3	6.8
20	1	2.3

Source: Details of Home Questionnaire.

A striking feature of the homes was the degree to which their actual numbers matched the numbers for which they were intended. Inevitably there were a few homes with low occupancy rates—the lowest in the study was 38%—but the average occupancy across all homes was 90%. Nearly six out of 10 homes were full or even more than full—and only eight out of the 44 returning figures had an occupancy rate of less than 80%. Table 6.3 provides a summary of the occupancy rates for the five authorities, based on the 44 homes which returned the relevant information.

The small size and high occupancy rate of the homes are both encouraging and disquieting. On the positive side, the information on size shows how far the residential system has come from the large institutions of the 1960s and 70s, when an Approved School or even Probation Hostel designed for only 15 residents would have been regarded as small. Even the Department of Health statistics, which distinguish between establishments of over and under 12, seem designed for an earlier age. The small

Table 6.3   Occupancy rates in the five areas

	Registered places	Young persons in residence (*n*)	Occupancy (%)
Area 1	108	95	88.0
Area 2	75	65	86.7
Area 3	48	42	89.6
Area 4	83	82	98.8
Area 5	46	38	82.6
Total	360	323	89.7

Source: Details of Home Questionnaire.

size of homes should allow a more geographically based distribution of establishments and the high occupancy rate shows that they are used and presumably valued.

On the potentially negative side, the size of homes raises questions of justification. The traditional institution may not have been homely but it could point to facilities, such as classrooms or sports pitches, which made it clear that its justification lay in its education or training rather than its role as a substitute home. A tennis court was one of the redeeming features of the otherwise depressingly institutional 'Beech View'. However, a home catering for four residents is starting to resemble a large foster home. Costs and staffing may be higher, but the aim of both is presumably to provide a homely environment, and if that is the aim why not go the whole way and use foster care instead?

A further problem relates to the question of how the home is to confront the dilemmas inherent in its high costs, high occupancy rates and aspirations towards geographical catchment areas. Considerations of cost more or less require the homes to keep their occupancy rate high, while considerations of geography suggest that they should be prepared to take all those from a given area. The resulting clientele may make it difficult to keep a homely atmosphere or to adhere to a specialised role.

STAFFING: STAFF RATIOS

The costs of a home are mainly determined by its staffing—primarily by the ratio of staff to residents but also by the relative proportions of staff who are on higher or lower grades. For this reason, and because staffing is a feature of the home which managers can change, it was important to examine how far homes varied in their staffing and what seemed to determine any variations.

In general, there were more staff in a home than residents. One exceptional home had 64 members of staff, but the size of the staff group among the remainder varied from six to 29 with an average of 10. A quarter of the homes had a staff group numbering between six and eight, and a further quarter one of 16 or more. Staff groups of this size clearly allow for more differentiation of roles than would be possible with smaller numbers. Whereas one 'housemother' may have helped with the cooking, dealt with the children and managed the staff group on her own, her successor has the option of specialising in paper work and organisation and delegating the cooking to a specialist and the day-to-day dealings with young people to care staff. The use made of this opportunity varied by area. Table 6.4 gives information on the staffing structure in the different authorities.

Table 6.4 Staffing structure by area

	Area 1 n = 166 (%)	Area 2 n = 179 (%)	Area 3 n = 79 (%)	Area 4 n = 129 (%)	Area 5 n = 53 (%)	Total n = 606 (%)
Post						
Unit Manager	8	6	4	9	13	7
Deputy	5	12	4	7	11	7
Group Leader	0	6	17	9	2	6
Care Officer	73	38	60	52	49	54
Domestic Assistant	6	7	9	16	4	8
Cook	2	4	4	5	0	3
Night Care Officer	0	0	0	3	0	1
Other	8	28	4	1	21	13

Percentages rounded.
Source: Staff Log.

Overall roughly two-thirds of the staff were described as care staff or 'other' (a designation which in two areas covered staff who seem to do care work), one in five were group leaders or above and the remainder were cooks, domestics or night care officers. These broad figures conceal considerable variation. Compared with Area 1, Area 2 was distinguished by its relatively low number of care assistants and the proportionately high numbers of deputy managers and 'other' staff (many of whom will have done the jobs carried out in other authorities by care staff). The staffing structure in Area 3 reflected the existence of only three large homes, leading to a low proportion of heads but a relatively high proportion of group leaders attached to the units into which the homes were divided. Area 4 was notable for its high proportion of domestic assistants and its four night care officers, and Area 5 for the absence of cooks and the presence of the second highest proportion of 'other' staff.

An even more important variation relates to the ratio of staff time to residents. This figure varies by home and by authority. Table 6.5 gives data on the ratio of weekly staff hours to resident in each authority.

Table 6.5 Ratio of staff hours to residents in homes by area

	Area 1 n = 14	Area 2 n = 10	Area 3 n = 3	Area 4 n = 10	Area 5 n = 6	All n = 43
Maximum	99.4	141.5	75.0	68.1	80.3	141.5
Minimum	31.0	32.5	55.5	35.4	23.1	23.5
Median	54.0	87.4	67.6	48.6	39.7	55.5
Average	58.2	82.8	66.1	51.0	48.4	61.4
Overall ratio	57.2	82.2	68.9	51.2	43.2	60.5

Source: Staff Log and Resident Log.

On average there was a ratio of just over 60 staff hours for each resident. The extent of the variation revealed was, however, striking. As can be seen from Table 6.5, all but one of the authorities had some homes with relatively low ratios and some with relatively high ones. Thus, with the exception of Area 3, all authorities differentiated sharply between homes in the hours they allocated to residents. The authorities also differed in their overall ratios, with the most 'generous' (Area 2) allocating nearly twice the number of hours per resident allocated by the least 'generous' (Area 5). Overall, 25% of homes had less than 41 hours per resident and a further 25% had 75 hours or more.

In considering the explanation for these variations it would be wise to ignore the home with the largest number of hours, since it had a particular role to play with young people who had committed grave offences. If this home is omitted, the ratio of hours to residents is unsurprisingly related to the proportion of young people on remand taken by the unit ($r = .34$, $p < .05$). 'Generous' staff ratios were also associated with a high proportion of care staff who had some relevant qualification, suggesting that homes which were well resourced in terms of hours were also well resourced in terms of training ($r = .42$, $p < .01$). As Knapp and Smith (1985) found, below 14 beds there were economies of scale, with larger homes having less generous staffing. Above this figure, however, this relationship breaks down as authorities subdivided their homes into smaller subunits, each of which required staff.

Finally, nine heads of homes said that more than 14% of their resources were devoted to activities outside the home (e.g. after-care, supporting foster carers, preventive work with young people in the community) and hours in these homes were significantly higher than in the remaining homes.

In the light of these findings we examined whether the differences in hours between authorities were explained by the characteristics of their homes. To do this we omitted the one exceptional home and took into account the occupancy rate and proportion of remands. We repeated the analysis with and without the nine homes that, according to their heads, devoted at least 15% to their resources to work outside the home. We also did the analysis with and without Area 3, whose small number of homes with similar ratios of hours to residents made our technique of analysis somewhat dubious. None of this analysis shook our conclusion that authorities differed quite sharply in the number of hours they allocated per resident.

QUALIFICATIONS

Historically, much hope has been placed in staff qualifications as a means of improving the quality of homes. Barr (1987) listed around 50 major reports which saw an increase in trained and qualified staff as a key ingredient in the improvement of residential care. Subsequent reports by Norman Warner (1992) and Sir William Utting (1991, 1997) suggest that the strength of this belief has not waned.

In this research we distinguished between the qualifications traditionally thought appropriate for staff (CQSW, CSS, Dip.SW) and other relevant training such as the Certificate for the Care of Children, Nursery Nurse (NNEB) or Teaching Certificate. As can be seen from Table 6.6, the likelihood of a member of staff possessing these qualification varied by post.

Most heads of homes were qualified—58% had a CQSW, CSS or Dip.SW, and a further 16% had some other relevant qualification. About a fifth had none. Just over 50% of the deputies also had some qualification, in most cases a 'relevant one' (i.e. social work or 'other professional') but it was very rare for any other member of staff to have any qualification at all.

Table 6.7 sets out the variation between authorities in the proportions of their staff who were qualified. Area 2 had a policy of promoting parity of esteem between field and residential staff and 19% of their staff had a relevant social work qualification—a low figure perhaps, but still nearly four times as great as the comparable one in Area 4. Nevertheless, even if domestic and night staff are omitted, no area has even a quarter of their staff with a social work qualification or some other form of relevant professional qualification.

The situation in relation to individual homes was more varied. Over a third of the homes making a return had no staff with 'appropriate' qualifications, a quarter had more than one in eight, and in two

Table 6.6 Staff qualifications—by post

	(n)	No quals (%)	Social worker quals* (%)	Other professional quals** (%)	Unspecified quals (%)
Head	43	20.9	58.1	16.3	4.7
Deputy	43	46.5	37.2	7.0	9.3
Group Leader	34	76.5	8.8	—	14.7
Care Officer	309	83.8	2.3	5.2	8.7
Domestic Assistant	45	100.0	—	—	—
Cook	17	82.4	—	—	17.6
Night Care Officer	4	100.0	—	—	—
Other	74	77.0	6.8	2.7	13.5
Totals	569	76.3	9.8	4.9	9.0

* Includes Dip.S.W.; CQSW; CSS.
** Includes NNEB; Certificate In Child Care; Teacher Training Certificate.
Source: Staff Log.

Table 6.7   Staff qualifications—by area

	(*n*)	No quals (%)	Social worker quals* (%)	Other professional quals** (%)	Unspecified quals (%)
Area 1	153	73.9	9.2	7.2	9.8
Area 2	150	66.0	19.3	4.7	10.0
Area 3	69	88.4	8.7	—	2.9
Area 4	80	72.5	3.8	12.5	11.3
Area 5	51	78.4	7.8	—	13.7
Totals	503	73.8	11.1	5.6	9.5

* Includes Dip.S.W.; CQSW; CSS.
** Includes NNEB; Certificate In Child Care; Teacher Training Certificate.
N.B.   Domestic Assistant, Cook and Night Care Officer are omitted from this table.
Source: Staff Log.

exceptional homes the figure rose to around half. The picture in relation to 'relevant' qualifications was slightly more encouraging. Only six homes returned no qualified staff and nearly a quarter had a fifth of their staff qualified. From the Williams Committee onwards, official reports have bewailed the absence of trained staff. If this is a genuine cause for concern, it must remain one, and at the same time provide a strong argument for the use of 'on the job' NVQ style training. At present the question arises of whether at these low levels the presence of a few staff with qualifications makes any difference, and in particular whether, as the authorities appear to assume, the presence of a qualified head is important. We return to these issues later in the book.

STAFF CHARACTERISTICS: SEX, AGE, ETHNICITY AND TIME IN POST

Table 6.8 indicates the proportions of women among heads and the staff in the five areas and the length of time they had been in post at the time of the study. The proportion of heads who were women was less than the proportion of staff (see below), although the difference was not as marked as in many other professions.

One feature of Table 6.9 is the large number of women staff in the homes, bearing in mind that 60% of the residents were boys and young men (see next section). These figures again need to be related to the situation in individual homes, where the proportion of staff who were women ranged from a third to a 100% (three homes) with an average of around two-thirds.

Table 6.8 Proportion of women heads of home; length of time in post of all heads

	Number of homes	Women heads (%)	Time in post (all heads)		
			< 1 year (%)	1–2 years (%)	3+ years (%)
Area 1	14	64.3	14.2	21.4	64.3
Area 2	11	45.5	9.1	54.5	36.4
Area 3	2	50.0	50.0	—	50.0
Area 4	8	62.5	50.0	—	50.0
Area 5	6	33.3	16.7	—	82.3
Total	41	53.7	22.0	31.7	46.3

Source: Staff Log.

Table 6.9 Proportion of women staff: length of time in post of all staff in homes

	All staff (n)	Women (%)	Time in post (all staff)		
			< 1 year (%)	1–2 years (%)	3+ years (%)
Area 1	149	66.4	18.8	16.8	64.4
Area 2	152	66.7	7.9	18.4	73.7
Area 3	76	52.6	18.5	19.7	61.8
Area 4	85	60.7	36.5	14.1	49.4
Area 5	40	60.0	7.5	5.0	87.5
Total	502	62.9	17.6	16.3	66.1

Source: Staff Log.

A further feature of the table is that two-thirds of all staff had been in their current post for at least three years. Indeed, 40% had been in post for at least five years. There was some variation between areas, with Area 4 having, for example, a lower proportion of long-stay staff than Area 5. The overall impression of a low turnover may have been a reflection of staff satisfaction or, conversely, a lack of job mobility and opportunities among the large proportion of unqualified staff. Either way it suggests that the experience of staff is an important factor to be set against any lack of qualifications.

This impression of stability and experience is reinforced by examination of the individual homes. The proportion of staff in the home who had been in post for five years or more varied from 0% to 92%, but in two-thirds of the homes it was over 30% and the average was around 40%. Conversely, the average proportion of staff who had arrived within the last six months was less than 10%.

In keeping with these figures, most staff (77%) were in their 30s or above. The average age was 38 (varying from 32 to 48 in individual homes). Younger members of staff were significantly more likely than older ones to be black or Asian, but only 7% of the sample fell into this category and they were almost entirely found in Areas 2 to 4. Twenty-two of the 44 homes making a return had no black or ethnic minority staff, but in one home 42% of the staff fell into this category and in another 64%, suggesting a conscious policy of concentrating black and ethnic minority staff in a specialist home. One of these homes had indeed had 17% of residents who were other than white-British, but the comparable figure for the other was only 6%. In assessing all these figures it should be remembered that in none of our areas did ethnic minorities constitute more than 6% of the population (see Appendix C for further information).

RESIDENTS

Part of the collection of information about the 'structure' of homes was the census of current and past residents completed by 44 of the 48 homes in the study. One of these homes specialised in remands, whose high turnover could have given a misleading impression of the overall picture. We have omitted this home from the calculations which follow. Two authorities had also excluded high turnover 'remand' homes from the study. The remainder of the exercise yielded information on 1090 young people—344 current residents and 746 past residents, the latter defined as young people, other than current residents, who had been resident in the home during the last 12 months.

These figures reflect the highly significant fact that most residents only stay for a brief period. Table 6.10 compares the length of stay of those who were in the home with those who had left it in the past year. As can

Table 6.10 Length of stay of current and past residents

Stay in months	Current residents		Past residents	
	(n)	(%)	(n)	(%)
Less than 1	31	9	304	41
1, less than 2	31	9	133	18
2, less than 3	47	14	65	9
3, less than 4	22	6	50	7
4 or 5	41	12	69	9
6 or more	172	50	125	17
Totals	344	100	746	100

Source: Resident Log.

be seen, half of those in the homes had been there for six months or more, whereas this group only make up around a sixth of those who had left.

These figures cast new light on the costs of homes, which look altogether less frightening if one is considering cost per resident served as against cost per yearly place. At the same time, they highlight the fact that a small group of residents, probably around a sixth of those admitted, are taking up around half the places.

Not surprisingly, length of stay varied by the purpose for which the placement was made. The average length of stay for those said to have been placed 'long-term' was 13 months. The comparable figures for other categories were to the nearest half-month, respite (2 months), emergency (3 months), assessment (3.5 months) and other (3 months). The comparable figure for young people on remand (13% of the discharges) was also low, at around two months. Table 6.11 gives the overall figures for the nature of the admissions, their legal status and the length of stay.

From the point of view of homes, these figures raise the question of whether they should try to specialise in long- or short-stay residents or should stick to their role of community resource and take all-comers. As a measure of the degree to which they adopted one or the other policy, we computed the proportion of short- (less than two months) and long-stay (over six months) residents each home had had in the course of the past year. There was considerable variability. If calculations were based on all

Table 6.11 Nature of admission, legal status and months in home of residents

	Current residents n = 344 (%)	Past residents n = 746 (%)
Nature of admission		
Emergency	57.0	84.9
Respite	12.9	6.5
Assessment	6.1	3.2
Long-term	21.5	3.9
Other	2.5	1.5
Legal status		
Accommodated	66.3	61.7
Order	26.5	12.7
Remanded	7.2	25.6
Months in home		
Under 1 month	10.8	50.5
1–2 months	21.1	22.2
3–5 months	17.3	13.2
6–12 months	28.0	8.7
Over 1 year	22.8	5.4

Source: Resident Log.

the residents in the home over the past year, nine homes were clearly 'short-stay', with more than half the residents staying for less than two months and less than one in six for six months or more. Eleven homes were long-stay, with more than 50% of their residents having stayed for six months or more and less than 25% for less than two months. Twenty-four were mixed.

Table 6.12 sets out the total and average numbers of residents who had been in these different types of home over the past year. It might have been expected that short-stay homes which catered for a disproportionate number of residents might have had higher staffing ratios, but this proved not to be the case.

AGE, SEX AND ETHNICITY

Table 6.13 provides a summary of the age, sex and ethnic background of current and past residents. As Berridge (1985) has pointed out, the phrase 'children's home' is a misnomer. The great majority of residents are teenagers. Very few, however, are older teenagers. Only 6% of the sample were over 17 and only 0.2% 18 or over. Older teenagers are perhaps less suited to a regime geared to a younger age group but more likely both to be seen as able to cope on their own and to want to do so. At the other end of the spectrum, the youngest child was seven (we did not count babies with their mothers) and less than 5% were 10 or under. Around a quarter, however, were less than 14. So two problems arise—the need among homes to discharge residents at a much younger age than that at which teenagers commonly leave home, and the difficulty of coping with an age range which, although restricted, still gives scope for older young people to bully or corrupt younger ones.

At the level of individual homes, the average age of residents who had been in the home over the previous year varied from 10 to just over 15½.

Table 6.12   Residents over last year by length of stay

Type of home	Number of homes	Total number of residents in last year	Average number of residents	Percentage of total
Short stay	9	416	46.2	38
Mixed	24	511	21.3	47
Long stay	11	163	14.8	15
Total	44	1090	24.8	100

Source: Resident Log.

Table 6.13 Age, sex and ethnic background of current and past residents

	Current residents $n = 344$ (%)	Past residents $n = 746$ (%)
Age		
12 and under	12.9	11.3
13–14	32.3	30.8
15	28.0	29.3
16 and over	26.8	28.5
Sex		
Females	41.2	38.4
Males	58.8	61.6
Ethnic origin		
White-British/White-other	91.1	94.7
African-Caribbean	1.8	1.1
Asian	0.4	0.1
Mixed	6.4	2.4
Other	0.4	0.1

Source: Resident Log.

The great majority of homes, however, had had residents with an average age of between 13 and 15.

Three homes were exceptional in that they clearly catered for a younger age group (average age less than 12). These homes provided a service for 'pre-adolescents' who were 'unfosterable', either because of their behaviour or because abuse had made them too disturbed to tolerate a family. The aim was to work with them so that they could be fostered or returned to their families.

Demarcation at the other end of the age scale was less clear cut, although one home defined itself in terms of preparing older adolescents for independent living and a number of other homes specified age ranges (e.g. '10–13 year-old boys and 10–16 year-old girls). Sixteen per cent of the homes had had residents with an average age of 15 or more. As discussed elsewhere, the natural desire on the part of homes to cater for a manageable age range must conflict with other equally natural aims, notably the wish to serve a local catchment area, to respond to emergencies, and to move young people on in accordance with their needs rather than at a predetermined age. So other homes were less demanding in their official age requirements, catering, according to the heads of homes, for all ages from 10 to 17.

The population of homes was also divided according to sex. Overall, 42% of those who had been in the homes over the past year were girls, although this proportion varied sharply with age, rising from 11% at the age of 10 to 50% at 13 and 14 and then falling off slightly. However, of the 43 homes on which we had the necessary data, five took only females, five took only males and the remainder were mixed.

Homes which specialised by sex were varied in other ways. Among those catering for girls, one was intended for young girls who had been sexually abused; another catered particularly for girls with delinquent histories (e.g. on remand) or who had been 'inappropriately' placed in other homes; while another sought to offer a 'secure, caring environment' on a relatively long-term basis. Homes for young men seemed to be designed for a somewhat delinquent group (the proportion of residents with previous convictions was much higher than for the homes as a whole) and to be similarly divided between those intended to provide a short-term response and those intended to keep the young people on a longer-term basis.

A large majority of current and past residents were described as white. In this respect there were variations between homes, with a third having had no residents from ethnic minorities over the previous year, a further third having had less than 11% from such backgrounds, and the remainder between 11% and 27%. In keeping with other research (Bebbington and Miles 1989; Rowe, Hundleby and Garnett 1989) and with our own survey (see Chapter 2), dual-heritage young people seemed particularly likely to be looked after. Contrary to our expectation, the correlation between the proportion of residents and the proportion of staff from ethnic minority backgrounds was low and not significant ($r = .22$). (See Appendix C for further information on black and ethnic minority residents.)

PURPOSE AND TYPE OF HOME

The variations between homes raise the question of whether these have to do with the purpose or remit of the establishment, and if so whether the differences cluster in some way so that, for example, we can detect 'typical' short- or long-stay homes. 'Purpose', of course, may mean different things to different people, so that social workers or young people may not define the purpose of a home in the same way as a unit manager. From the point of view of the latter, three dimensions seemed to be involved—the kinds of young people the home was to take, the length of time for which they were to stay and the objectives the home was to pursue while they were there.

Even heads who felt they had been given no clear remit nevertheless indicated there were dimensions along which their home could have been defined:

What are we? We take so many different young people of all ages and problems, and there is no agreed definition of how long they are here for and what we should be doing for them.

Other heads who felt that they were clear about what they were doing picked up one or more of these major dimensions. One, for example, did not specify a clientele for the home but did define a length of stay and three purposes (rehabilitation home, preparation for a further placement, and support). The home was seen as offering:

Four beds, an emergency response for up to six weeks, support for after-care, foster parents, respite and day care.

Other heads described their homes as differing along all three dimensions—type of resident, length of stay, purpose of stay—simultaneously:

We are a treatment unit, not secure, we provide a family-type atmosphere for boys, diagnose the problem and maintain contact with families.

We provide short- to medium-term care for five young people, together with outreach for 25 young people in the community . . . We aim to return kids home as soon as possible.

As can be seen from these quotations, the heads defined the kinds of young person in various ways. Most were prepared to take both females and males but, as we have seen, some specialised in one or the other. Some saw their role as dealing with delinquents, young people on remand and those displaying 'challenging' behaviour (categories which were sometimes distinguished), while others tried to take non-delinquent young people, and others were prepared to take any young person irrespective of delinquent history. Others defined their roles in terms of dealing with particular kinds of problems ('emotional problems' or 'sexual abuse') or negatively in terms of the kinds of young people they would not take (e.g. those who were on an 'order' or those who 'had been previously accommodated').

Other heads of homes implied that the criteria for admission varied, in that they needed to take young people who were compatible with the group who were in the home at the time or who would not exacerbate a potentially explosive situation. One, for example, commented that the home took 'long-term young people, non-offenders who are compatible with each other'. Such selectivity, however, conflicted with the demands that homes serve geographical areas, the high occupancy rate of homes and the high rate of emergency admissions. One home had in the past dealt only with black and ethnic minority young people but it now took 'anything that they throw at us'. Other heads of homes commented that they took 'any young person' or 'all types'.

Descriptions of the role of the home and of the length of time for which its residents were expected to stay were often combined. Some homes, for example, saw themselves as providing a short-term response to emergencies, which were to be responded to in a purposeful way involving the use of community resources and close contact with the young person's family. Some of these homes described themselves as 'general-purpose' but the most thorough-going community philosophy seemed to be adopted by one or two of those, which described themselves as 'family centres'.

This vision of a residential home as a focus for and back-up to work in the community is an attractive one but it was qualified by the head of home, who noted that residential work still took up the bulk of resources. As we have seen, few heads of home said that they devoted more than 15% of their resources to it.

Other homes saw themselves as offering 'therapy' or as preparing the young people for a further destination, such as fostering, independent living or rehabilitation home. The assumption seemed to be that the young people would only be able to make use of these destinations if they changed in some way and that these changes required time. The ways in which this was to be done are discussed later in the report, but broadly they fell into four categories: the provision of a secure environment or a 'homely atmosphere', 'therapy', the maintenance and hopefully improvement of family relationships, and social training designed to prepare the young people for independence (e.g. the use of 'trainer flats').

In general, these more ambitious aims were seen as requiring a longer period of time. Whereas those who saw their role as offering short-term provision seemed to be resigned to emergency admissions as a way of life, heads who saw their homes as offering longer-term care were less happy about this practice:

We want planned admissions because it is a settled, structured environment.

In contrast to these apparently focused establishments, however, a number of homes described themselves as general-purpose or said that they had no remit at all, or that a remit which had been clear had been eroded by emergency admissions, difficulty in moving young people on, reorganisation or the unsuitability of their staffing or environment.

The picture was further complicated by the existence of four homes in the study which were larger than the others (16–20 beds) and which provided a variety of relatively specialised services through different units on the same campus. These larger homes inevitably took residents from a wide catchment area, and in one authority their sub-units basically served the different purposes of reception/assessment, preparation for fostering or return home, and preparation for independence. In the other authority, the home offered some secure accommodation, some accommodation seen as 'alternative to secure', a 'bungalow project' and an independent living project.

The general impression, therefore, is of a small number of distinctive homes, generally defined in terms of their clientele, purpose, or length of stay or some combination of these variables, and a number of other homes which, by accident or design, fulfilled a variety of purposes for a wide variety of young people staying for varying lengths of time.

As a check on this impression, we examined the designation which the heads of homes used to describe the roles of their home when presented with a small number of categories originally developed by the Social Services Inspectorate (1985). Obviously this classification will be more useful if sizeable numbers of homes fall into each category and if the categories distinguish between the homes on a range of variables. Table 6.14 sets out the results of some analyses designed to find out if this was so.

As can be seen, most homes described themselves as general-purpose. On average, around a third of their residents had had a previous conviction, around two-thirds of them were considered to enter as emergencies and nearly four out of 10 stayed for less than two months (short-stay in the table). The only other sizeable categories of home were family centres and homes which described themselves as specialist. These differed little from the general-purpose ones on the variables we have been considering, with

Table 6.14 Category of home and features of resident admissions

		Features of resident admission		
Category of home	(*n*)	Previous convictions (%)	Emergency (%)	Short-stay (%)
General/multi-purpose	21	31	69	40
Home with education	1	70	24	42
Family centre	8	32	65	62
Specialist	5	27	51	41
Home for remands	1	75	100	77
Other	3	35	71	42
No response	9	—	—	—

Source: Resident Log and Details of Home Questionnaire.

the exception that family centres catered on average for an even high proportion of short-term residents.

A rather different approach was to see whether the variables which heads of homes described as important in defining their homes clustered together in any way. Following this line of thought, we found that homes which had an above-average number of emergency admissions also tended to have an above-average number of short-term residents ($r = .33$, $p < .05$) and a correspondingly low number of long-term ones ($r = -.44$, $p < .01$). These homes differed from others in that they were less likely to take residents for assessment or relief breaks and, by definition, for planned long stay. For reasons no doubt connected with their high turnover, they tended to have had more residents in the past year than other homes ($r = .57$, $p < .01$) and, for reasons which were less obvious, they tended to have a lower proportion of staff with relevant training ($r = -.31$, $p < .05$).

Homes with relatively high proportions of residents taken for other reasons than as an emergency tended to have a less distinctive profile. Homes that took a relatively high proportion of young people for relief breaks tended to have a relatively high proportion of trained staff, particularly staff with a social work qualification ($r = .41$, $p < .01$). Almost none of the variables we have been considering distinguished the homes that took a high proportion of residents for a long stay, with the obvious exception that they tended to have longer-staying residents and fewer emergency admissions. Homes taking a higher proportion of residents for assessment seemed to have no other distinguishing characteristic. A rather different grouping was provided by homes which took a relatively high proportion of young people on remand and not surprisingly tended to have higher numbers over the course of a year and higher proportions of residents with previous convictions.

These associations suggest that there may be some general differences between short-stay homes catering for emergencies and the others. Emergencies, perhaps, are seen as antithetical to the more settled atmosphere required for relief breaks, assessment and treatment. The difference, however, is one of degree and is not particularly marked. Many homes serve all-comers and try as best they may to be all things to all young people. In what follows we will need to bear in mind that the homes we are studying are highly varied—the home that tries to deal with four pre-adolescent girls who have been sexually abused is clearly a very different place from the large campus home performing a variety of functions or the home that seeks to prepare older adolescents for independent living. At the same time, many homes are 'general-purpose' and those which do not define themselves in this way may nevertheless find themselves constrained to act as if this was their function.

CONCLUSION

The simple description we have so far provided casts further light on the crisis in residential care discussed in the introduction. By the standards of earlier years, the homes in this study were small, non-institutional and generously staffed. These factors are related (for smaller homes had more staff hours per resident and were less institutional), so the rising costs which menace residential care are in part a response to changes which professional opinion has seen as desirable. At the same time, these developments were far from evenly spread across all homes. There were major variations, both within and between authorities, in buildings, size of home, staffing ratios and the proportion of staff with professional qualifications—all factors likely to have an impact on cost, and probably performance.

The findings also suggest some possible reasons for the difficulties the homes have found in running a smooth regime. Some homes specialised in idiosyncratic ways but a majority carried out or enabled a wide variety of functions, including assessment, provision for remands, the provision of relief for families and long-term care. Occupancy rates were high and the residents were almost all teenagers, most of whom spent less than two months in the home, and most of whom were admitted as emergencies. So it would not be surprising if some heads of homes found it difficult to create a clarity of purpose and a supportive culture in what might be seen as transit camps serving adolescents with (temporarily at least) nowhere else to go.

These findings raise the important questions to which we will return later in the book. Is it desirable to have further specialisation? What are the implications of having a high or low staff ratio? What difference does it make, whether there is a relatively high proportion of qualified staff? Does it matter that only some of the heads are qualified? The lack of association among these variables is particularly striking. On the face of it, one would have expected longer-stay homes to be less fully staffed (to keep down costs and reduce the pressure on residents to move before they were ready [see Chapter 5]). Medium-stay homes might be expected to exclude short-stay residents (to make it easier to develop a culture which supports treatment). Are the lack of these associations evidence of deliberate policy or of 'making do' under pressure?

These questions are given particular urgency by the heavy use of resources by a small number of residents. Residential care takes up a proportion of resources from substitute care which is much greater than its number of beds would suggest. Within residential care itself, a small group, probably about a sixth of those admitted, takes up about a half of the beds.

7

THE HOMES—
MANAGEMENT AND
REGIME

INTRODUCTION

The last chapter considered some structural aspects of our sample of homes: the relatively fixed features, such as size and staffing ratios, and the characteristics of their clientele. In this chapter we turn to process: the interactions and negotiations that take place within the home and between the home and significant actors in its environment. For the moment we have dealt, as it were, with the bricks and mortar and need to turn to the life that goes on within.

In practice the distinctions between structure, process and outcome are more convenient than precise. Should one count the aims of the home as a structural variable, something fixed, laid down as it were in tablets of stone by an unwavering management? Or should one consider it a process variable—something endlessly redefined and renegotiated as life goes on, so that each decision to admit answers a new existential question about the purpose for which the home exists? Similarly, should one count the friendliness of the contacts between staff and residents as a process variable concerned with interaction or as an outcome because of its intimate connection with the residents' quality of life?

The existence of such unanswerable questions does not, we believe, negate the value of the basic distinctions which give rise to them. We need, however, to realise that some variables (like quality of interaction) can be treated both as process and as outcome, and also that the impact of structural variables will often depend on the meaning they are given in the cut and thrust of home life. The effects, for example, of a given staffing ratio will depend partly on whether the staff feel that it is fair and adequate and also on the way in which staff are deployed on a day-to-day basis. For this reason, variables will reappear in this chapter which have already been discussed in Chapter 6. In this chapter, however, our focus will be on the way these variables are perceived. For example, in Chapter 6 we discussed the staffing ratios of homes and in this chapter we examine whether the heads of home consider these to be adequate.

In organising the chapter we will concentrate on four major arenas within which important transactions take place:

- *The home and the organisation*—the degree to which the home has freedom to organise its own affairs, and the degree to which the head of home feels that she/he has a clear task, adequately supported in terms of procedures, resources, training and the like.
- *The home's regime*—the framework within which residents live in terms of times expected in, freedom to enter different parts of the home, invite in guests and so on, and also the rules that exist and the punishments that are invoked to enforce them.
- *The home and its social environment*—the nature of the support which the home receives, as the head experiences it, from other individuals who have a key influence on the home's well-being (police, neighbours, social workers, teachers, DSS officials, careers officers, employers and so on).
- *The transactions within the home*—the degree to which the home is in a stable state and the staff and residents are supportive of the home's overall approach.

The purposes of this part of the investigation are partly descriptive—for these are important issues on which there is currently little information. However, we also want where possible to develop summary measures which can later be related to measures of outcome.

The chapter is based on three sources of data—the views of the heads of homes as given in an interview with one of the researchers, staff responses to some questions in the staff questionnaire, and interviewer ratings of the home. The main source of data from the head's interview was provided by a checklist which invited the head of home to state whether a certain aspect of the home's life was a support to them or a problem. As in the last chapter, we give an unusually large number of tables in the expectation that readers will skip those which do not interest them.

THE ORGANISATION AND THE HOME

Two key issues in the relationship between the Social Services departments and the individual homes concern the degree to which the home is controlled by the department, and the way in which any control is exercised. Recently there has been increasing emphasis on the need for external controls. Berridge and Brodie (1996, 1998) summarise the concerns of recent reports on scandals as including, among other things; inadequate line management; minimal direct contact between children and staff on the one hand and external managers on the other; unsatisfactory placement policies and processes. They themselves were critical of the lack of management involvement in the homes, which they felt represented a deterioration in the situation since 1985. This approach represents a contrast from the literature in the 1970s, which emphasised the importance of adequate autonomy for staff. So, it is important to describe the extent of external controls and then evaluate their effect.

We deal first with the issue of the home's autonomy and then with the nature of the support and influence it received from the surrounding department.

Autonomy

Research in the early 1970s suggested that the amount of autonomy possessed by the staff and the head of home had a major impact on the effectiveness of small residential units. The effects were believed to lie partly in the way autonomous staff behaved—their interpersonal style. Thus, Tizard (1975) found that quality of communication between staff and young children in residential nurseries was improved if the former were not immediately under the eye of their superior. However, it was also felt that staff in autonomous units had more freedom to respond to needs if they did not have to refer requests to their superiors and were not constrained by the demands of a centrally organised regime (Heal and Cawson, 1975). Sinclair and Heal (1976) produced data which suggested that autonomy was not without a cost, in that it tended to lead to a greater variability in performance. On average, however, greater autonomy still produced more supportive units. More recently, professional opinion has identified obstacles to good practice in order books and other methods of constraining the freedom of staff to negotiate with residents over what they buy or over menus.

Given this research tradition it seemed important to assess how far the various homes could be regarded as autonomous residential units with a view to later establishing whether variations in autonomy were related to variations in performance. For this reason we asked the heads of homes about the amount of autonomy they felt they had in certain key areas and to say whether they considered this 'a lot', 'some' or 'none'. Questions about appraisal were not answered by a number of respondents, presumably because they were unaware of any appraisal system. With this exception, all but three of the heads answered all the questions. Table 7.1 sets out their replies.

The majority of heads reported that, on balance, they had at least some autonomy in most areas, and in the areas of buying food, paying for entertainments and buying clothes and presents the great majority felt that their autonomy was considerable. The only areas for which more than a third felt that they had no autonomy was over payments connected with aftercare, paying for repairs, and accepting or rejecting admissions. Potentially, such a lack of autonomy could cause problems, with homes waiting for urgent repairs, unable to respond to the needs of former residents who turned up at their door, and forced to take in difficult admissions at points when they would upset the balance of the home. Indeed, 40% of heads said that they had no choice whatsoever about accepting or rejecting residents.

As might be expected, heads who felt they had autonomy in one area of their operation were more likely to feel that this was so in others, and a scale constructed on the basis of the items listed in Table 7.1 had a reasonable reliability (alpha = 0.72). To our surprise, however, this scale did not distinguish significantly between areas, so that there is no evidence that homes in one area were generally more autonomous than those in another.

The Home and the 'Management': What Heads Wanted

Inevitably, the attention of heads of home was heavily focused on the triangle formed by themselves, the staff and the residents. Thus, in

Table 7.1   Head of homes' views on degree of autonomy

	Degree of autonomy		
	A lot (%)	Some (%)	None (%)
Paying for clothes	82.3	11.1	6.6
Paying for repairs	29.0	35.5	35.5
Paying for food	71.4	28.6	0.0
Paying for entertainments	75.1	19.9	5.0
Paying for presents	68.7	24.3	5.0
Paying for after-care	23.2	37.3	39.5
Accepting/rejecting admissions	12.8	44.6	42.6
Appointing staff	34.2	58.6	7.2
Recruiting relief staff	49.7	43.1	7.2
Training staff	27.2	66.6	7.2
Supervising staff	81.8	18.2	0.0
Appraising staff	47.1	37.3	15.6
Moving money between budgets	20.8	61.4	17.8

Source: Head of home interview.

contrast to a number of reports which place great importance on the role of strong management in ensuring high standards in homes, some heads seemed doubtful if management had much of a role to play at all. For such heads, the key lay in the staff and the hard work, honesty and humour they brought to their task:

A home is only as good as the staff in it.

The honesty and strength of the staff is what works here: not the department's policies.

So much acknowledged, the heads would have been less than human if they had not taken up the opportunity to comment on the role— sometimes but not necessarily helpful—which they felt management played in their working lives. A number of the issues were raised by a somewhat critical head:

There's no clear remit, emergency admissions occur and aren't supposed to. In effect we are working with 15 to 16 year-olds with no place to go . . . We want more staff please, and [we want to be] a five-bedded unit so everyone has their own room. We want more training and time to do it—a peripatetic team to cover small group homes where they need it—more support and a better knowledge of how homes actually are by management.

Other staff were much less critical than the one just quoted but the issues covered were often much the same. Staff wanted a clear remit, and they did not want to be required to play roles which they considered incompatible. They wanted these roles to be feasible and negotiated with them, and they did not want them to change too often. Given such a remit they wanted it supported by adequate resources, training and management backing. These points are worth brief elaboration before we consider how many felt sufficiently strongly about them to identify them as a problem in their home.

Clarity of remit was clearly appreciated where it occurred:

The remit is very clear—[we're a] rehab unit for under 12s to return home to parents or to go to foster care within three months.

Quite often, however, the clarity of the remit was said to be undermined by emergency or unsuitable admissions with, according to one head, a *tendency to undermine me as a manager and make inappropriate admissions in an underhand way*, a reference perhaps to the lack of adequate information about admission of which others complained. Even if the admissions were in accordance with the home's official purpose, they were not always thought to be compatible with existing residents. In one home an official 'emergency bed' was seen as a continuing source of trouble. Other heads complained about mixing sexes (seen as inappropriate for some abused girls and some immature youths), bail returns (with their own problems and unlikely to fit the home's routine), and a wide spread of ages, so that it was difficult to give all ages the response they required.

A concern of a number of heads was that these roles were not properly negotiated and that too often they themselves were neither adequately consulted nor informed. The advent of the Children Act, and the heightened profiles of inspection and children's rights had given rise in some to a feeling that they were subject to unrealistic expectations and had too little influence in shaping a response. Policies on restraint might be seen as unrealistic and as giving no positive guidance on what should happen if, for example, one young person was assaulting another and could not be verbally restrained. Decisions about the future of the home were also thought to require consultation. One home was aware that it might be about to close but no clear decision has apparently been taken; another knew it was to close but not when—a fact which posed some difficulties for the head, who was trying to maintain the staff's morale. Reorganisations involving major changes of function were common—36% reported one in the previous 12 months—and were rarely welcome.

Given a feasible, clear, negotiated role the heads wanted the resources to back it up. This was partly a matter of buildings—homes should be well located and well designed—so that, for example, they were not placed in highly delinquent estates or attempting to accommodate 'eight giants' in rooms designed for children under 12. For many it was a matter of staff—either more staff *per se* or staff of particular kinds, such as deputies who could take over from the head when necessary. Others again wanted ancillary resources—better foster parents, so that inappropriate children should not be placed or kept long in the home for want of a suitable placement; psychologists or other therapists, so that treatment could be provided for those in residence; backup resources, so that help could be available at times of stress, to provide special care for a particularly difficult young person or to allow the whole staff team to go away for a day's workshop; or facilities for young people who had been excluded from school.

Finally, there was a desire for support for themselves and for staff. Training was seen as one way of providing this and there were requests that there should be more training or training of different kinds. Support for the head was also seen as important and one head in particular was eloquent in praise of a manager who was seen as having had practical experience in the field and as being a doughty fighter in departmental battles concerned with the home's interests.

The Home and the Management: Heads' Perceptions of Problems of Support

These wishes and comments have been taken from individual staff and, of themselves, give no sense of the degree to which a high proportion of heads were satisfied or otherwise with particular areas of management. In order to get some quantitative measure of this, heads were asked to say whether a particular area was a problem for them or a source of support. Table 7.2 summarises the results.

To judge from Table 7.2 certain aspects of management are better appreciated than others. First, it seems to be a truth fairly universally acknowledged that, from the point of view of the heads at least, social work managers are nice people. Nearly half the sample gave the most supportive rating possible with management, and more than two-thirds found this relationship more supportive than not. Other areas of success were training and the amount of autonomy possessed by the home. In both these areas, nearly half the sample found management practice at least more helpful than not, whereas only around a quarter identified problems.

Two areas which elicited rather more mixed opinions were clarity of roles and the expectations of the Children Act. The latter had its strong defenders but some heads were concerned about the implications for control and the degree to which the Act provided a suitable framework for dealing with delinquency. More than four out of 10 heads sat on the fence, ticking a 'mixed' response and presumably feeling either that the Act was a curate's egg or that it was, like the air, a context for their endeavours which it was inappropriate either to praise or blame.

Three issues seemed, from the responses given in Table 7.2, to be particularly problematic. These were reorganisation (where nearly half felt

Table 7.2 Heads' reported experience of aspects of management

	Problem (%)	Some problems (%)	Mixed (%)	Some support (%)	Support (%)
Expectations of 1989 Act	18	4	42	13	22
Reorganisation	23	23	37	9	7
Autonomy	7	18	29	22	24
Relations with management	9	11	11	25	43
Mix of roles	16	24	40	11	9
Clarity of roles	22	11	24	13	29
Training	13	16	22	22	27
Staffing ratio	27	22	18	11	22

Percentages rounded.
Source: Head of home interview.

there were problems and only one in seven felt that there were, on balance, advantages), mix of roles (similar figures) and staffing ratios. In contrast to the Children Act, staffing ratios were matters on which heads had definite opinions. Nearly half felt that their staffing ratios were at least something of a problem to them, although by contrast nearly a third felt that the ratios were at least something of a support to their endeavours.

We were concerned to see how far these attitudes to various aspects of management were inter-related. The advantage to us of a high degree of inter-relationship would be that we would be able to develop a single score (called, for example, supportive management) and relate this to measures of outcome. In this way we could avoid a much greater number of tests between particular aspects of management and outcome, and the possibility that in so large a number of tests some at least would prove significant by chance.

We thought in advance that some degree of inter-relationship was likely. This was partly because of the subjective nature of our measure—heads who had low morale or were disaffected would, we thought, be likely to see problems in many aspects of management. In so far as the heads' perceptions of problems reflected genuine differences in management arrangements, we also expected some degree of correlation—homes that were well-managed in one respect would be expected to be well-managed in others. At the same time we did not expect a very high degree of association between different aspects of management. It would clearly be possible for a department to have, for example, good training arrangements but at the same time to be almost ceaselessly involved in reorganisation.

We explored these issues initially by looking at the inter-correlations between certain elements of management (expectations of the Children Act were seen as relevant to management, since we judged that it was the business of management to work through the Act with their staff). Table 7.3 sets out the relevant figures. As can be seen, 11 of the 28 pairs of correlations were significant, most of them highly so. By contrast, there were also a number of negative or zero correlations.

All this suggests that Table 7.3 might be explained by variation between heads on a small number of underlying dimensions (e.g. the degree to which they felt 'empowered'). A method of exploring such dimensions is provided by principal components analysis, which explores how far a set of variables can be seen as the product of a smaller number of underlying uncorrelated dimensions. The analysis identifies the loading that each variable has on a component. The nearer this loading approximates to one, the more plausible it is to interpret the component as representing that variable. It is also possible to calculate a score for each individual in a given component.

We carried out such a components analysis on the data summarised in Table 7.3. The first component identified seems to represent clarity and

Table 7.3   Correlations between heads' assessments of aspects of management

	Expect-ations of 1989 Act	Reor-ganisa-tion	Auto-nomy	Man-age-ment relations	Mix of roles	Clarity of roles	Train-ing	Staff-ing ratio
Expectations of 1989 Act	1.00							
Reorganisation	.24	1.00						
Autonomy	.49**	.42**	1.00					
Management relations	.31*	.27	.25	1.00				
Mix of roles	.02	.40**	.40**	−.11	1.00			
Clarity of roles	.35*	.26*	.54**	.26	.26	1.00		
Training	.27	.12	.24	.01	−.19	.18	1.00	
Staffing ratio	.35*	.10	.35*	−.01	−.04	.35*	.39**	1.00

* Significant at .05 level.
** Significant at .01 level.
Source: Head of home interview.

stability of purpose. It loaded highly on a positive attitude towards the home's mix of roles, the clarity of these roles and the home's experience of (or, more probably, lack of experience of) reorganisations. It also loaded highly on autonomy. High scorers on this component typically felt that they had been given a clear, internally consistent remit, that they were not going to be plagued by reorganisations, and so were 'empowered' to get on with the job. Low scorers did not feel so sanguine about their role and its stability and may have been correspondingly disempowered. As one of the heads put it, the first requirement is a clear aim.

The next two components accounted for less of the variance, and were, for this reason, and because of the small number of variables, less interesting. They remained, however, reasonably easy to interpret. The second component loaded heavily on training and staff ratios. It will be remembered that homes with a high level of qualified staff also tended to have better staff ratios, and the second component may represent the perceived willingness of the organisation to invest in the home. The component also loaded quite heavily on a positive attitude towards the Children Act 1989—a fact which may have reflected the training devoted to it. The last component was very heavily loaded on relationships with managers, something which was perhaps dependent on personal chemistry and which seemed to be relatively independent of attitudes to the more formal aspects of management.

THE COMPONENTS OF REGIME

Research in the traditions we are talking about has been concerned with issues of 'liberality' or 'permissiveness' in regimes. This partially reflects the salience given to these variables in professional debates, and partially the all-pervading influence of Goffman (1961). Goffman emphasised the similarity of residential regimes. However, it was natural that researchers looking for differences should be concerned with dimensions that Goffman identified (most of which had to do with restrictiveness in one form or another). King, Raynes and Tizard (1971) followed this approach as, later, did Colton in 1988. In describing the regimes in our sample, we therefore had at the back of our minds the hypothesis that these would differ along some dimension of 'permissiveness' or 'institutionalism'. If we could measure this dimension, this would again simplify our analytic task, and in order to attempt this we developed seven separate scores which, on the face of it, should distinguish between permissiveness and strict regimes. These measures were:

- *Open to parents*—a measure based on the relative willingness of homes to receive parents at any hour without prior appointment.
- *Open to friends*—a similar measure but this time concerned with the home's willingness for friends to visit.
- *Bedtimes*—a measure based on the hour at which residents were expected to be in bed on weekdays and at weekends.
- *Movement*—a measure based on the ability of residents to visit certain rooms (e.g. office) or facilities (e.g. fridge) without restriction.
- *Rules*—a measure based on the replies of staff in the home on the rules in place.
- *Punishments*—a measure based on the replies of staff in the home on the punishments usually used in the home.

In developing the first three measures, we roughly divided the answers to each relevant question into three equal groups (e.g. late in bed on weekends was defined as 'no definite time or after 12' and gave a score of three for the most permissive answer, two for the next most permissive and one for the least). All the variables were scored in such a way that a high score suggested permissiveness and a low score strictness. We were interested in whether variations on these measures were reflected in similar differences in the rules and punishments employed. Information on these came from the staff questionnaire.

The information presented in Table 7.4 was used to create a score for each member of staff. For technical reasons, the variable 'open correspondence' was omitted as it reduced the reliability of the score we wished to create. We added the remaining variables, counting 'never' as 3, 'sometimes' as 2, and 'often' as 1.

Table 7.5 was also constructed from the staff questionnaire and was treated in the same way. As can be seen, the methods of control which

Table 7.4 Frequency of certain rules and restrictions

Rules and restrictions	(n)	Often (%)	Sometimes (%)	Never (%)
Open correspondence	299	0.7	17.1	82.3
No unsupervised telephone calls	303	8.9	44.6	46.5
Look after pocket money	299	17.1	59.5	23.4
Restrict way bedrooms can be decorated	301	5.3	54.2	40.5
Forbid certain items of clothing	301	1.7	32.9	65.4
Forbid certain styles of haircut	302	0.7	16.2	83.1

Source: Questionnaire to staff.

were most likely to be described as 'routinely' used seem relatively benign. These common methods depend on relationships (as do counselling and telling off by 'closest' adult) or on the withdrawal of treats and outings. Those punishments which other research (Whitaker *et al.* 1985) and common sense suggest are most likely to be resented (e.g. sending early to bed) were rarely used in this sample. Punishments which are officially discouraged and perhaps of dubious legality were hardly ever used routinely, although the great majority of staff said that physical restraint had to be used on at least some occasions.

As with the data on rules, we developed a score on the basis of this table, omitting the variables concerned with counselling and medication. We found that there were highly significant differences between homes on our scores for both rules and punishments. It seemed logical, therefore, to use a home's average score as a measure of the use of punishments and the existence of rules within it.

Table 7.5 Frequency of certain controls and punishments

Controls and punishments	Routinely (%)	Rarely (%)	Never (%)
Transfer or threat of removal	9.3	70.1	20.6
Gating/keeping in	27.6	45.8	26.6
Exclude from treats/outings	49.0	47.0	4.0
Extra chores	23.8	40.3	35.9
Send early to bed	25.0	28.7	46.3
Drugs/medication	1.0	2.7	96.2
Stop pocket money	22.1	30.9	47.6
Telling off by closest adult	48.1	34.7	17.2
Public reprimand	8.4	32.4	59.1
Group punishment	8.2	49.7	42.2
Physical restraint	14.0	69.2	16.7
Counselling	75.7	17.7	6.7

Source: Questionnaire to staff.

The next step was to examine the correlations between these variables to see if a home that scored high on one of these variables was likely to score high on the others. Table 7.6 sets out the results. As predicted, these measures correlated quite highly together. Of the 15 correlations in Table 7.6, five were significant at .01, four at .05 and two more at .06. Only the home's willingness to receive friends before lunch and late into the evening failed to show strong correlations with the other variables—indeed, it was responsible for four of the six correlations which failed to reach significance.

In keeping with the strategy we had adopted earlier with management variables, we used a components analysis to try and describe the variables in Table 7.6 in terms of a small number of dimensions—one of which, we hoped, could be described as reflecting a dimension of 'permissiveness'. The analysis identified two major components, of which the first seemed to reflect the permissiveness or flexibility of the home, with high loadings on the relative absence of rules and punishments and the relative freedom of young people to use the home's facilities without restriction. The second component loads most heavily on the readiness of the home to receive visitors, whether parents or friends, at different times of the day, although it, like the first component, loads quite heavily on the readiness of the home to let its residents stay up late. We examined whether authorities differed in the average scores obtained by their homes on the first component and found that they did so significantly.

EXTERNAL SUPPORTS

Traditionally, research into residential care has considered the home environment, as it were in isolation. Some justification for this approach comes from the dramatic variations in the quality of care in residential

Table 7.6 Inter-correlations between measures of regime

	Open to parents	Open to friends	Bedtimes	Move-ment	Punish-ments	Rules
Open to parents	1.00					
Open to friends	.64**	1.00				
Bedtimes	.50**	.30	1.00			
Movement	.31*	.20	.56**	1.00		
Punishments	.39**	.12	.35**	.30*	1.00	
Rules	.20	.04	.30*	.36*	.43**	1.00

* Significant at .05 level.
** Significant at .01 level.
Source: Head of home interview.

establishments over time, even given that the surrounding environment
has remained the same (see Sinclair 1971, 1975) and their proven ability to
produce scandals under the eye of managers and inspectors. Nevertheless, no home is an island, entire and of itself; the continent of which each
is part includes not only the Social Services department but also its neighbourhood and the national and local services to which it must relate. The
influence of these environmental factors affects the day-to-day running of
the home and also the efficiency with which it is able to achieve its overall
objectives in enabling young people to move on and settle.

Our coverage of these environmental factors was less complete than
was the case with some others. Nevertheless, the heads of home left us in
no doubt about their importance. If the young people were not able to go
to school, they might stay up late when others wanted to be in bed, and
then hang around the home, bored and ready for mischief when staff
wished to be getting on with other things. Relationships with schools
were therefore of considerable importance, as were any suspicions that
schools under local management and spurred by competition over league
tables were too willing to impose indefinite suspensions on difficult
pupils in general and those in the care system in particular.

Relations with neighbours, the police, local employers and the careers
service were also important. Most people want to be welcome in their
neighbourhood, protest meetings about one's very existence lower morale, and lighted material shoved through one's letterbox tests morale to its
limits. At such times, and also when trouble brews within the home,
relations with the local police can help or hinder. The knowledge that
police will call and restore order is reassuring: the knowledge that they
regard the home as a source of delinquency and its staff as insufficiently
willing to impose control is not. As for the local employers and the careers
service, their potential value to homes with older young people needs no
saying.

Of particular importance for homes are their relationships with social
workers and the arrangements for ensuring future housing. As we have
seen, many young people are birds of passage who stay only briefly in the
home and all young people move on eventually. The efficiency of the care
planning system, the ability of social workers to tackle problems which
may impede movement (e.g. relationships with family) and the possibility of providing suitable housing for those who do not return home,
are clearly vital.

As with different areas of management, we wished to get some quantitative measure on the degree to which the heads of home regarded these
different kinds of external relationships as sources of support or problems. Table 7.7 sets out the results. The first impression given by Table 7.7
is that, whatever the anecdotal evidence, most heads found most of the

professionals with whom they dealt reasonably helpful. The police seemed to be outstanding in this respect, a finding repeated by Berridge and Brodie (1998). Four out of 10 of the heads gave them the most supportive rating, and none considered that they were a major problem. High praise, however, also seems to have been earned by the Careers Service (perhaps for trying, for other evidence does not suggest many residents were placed in work), the education service and, to a somewhat lesser extent, field social workers and the care planning system.

Neighbours and the DSS received somewhat more mixed ratings but for very different reasons. Forty-seven per cent of the heads found the neighbours a problem or somewhat of a problem. By contrast, 40% found them at least a moderate support. Very few heads sat on the fence and gave a neutral rating. A neutral rating was, however, the most common one given to the DSS, and this seemed to reflect a low level of contact. Seventeen of the 45 heads who responded to this part of the interview did not answer this question, and few of those who did expressed strong opinions.

The most serious problems, according to the heads, fell into two main areas—the employment market and housing for young people. More than half the respondents felt that there was at least something of a problem in these areas and very few felt that the situation in either respect was good. The problem in relation to housing seemed to be the quality of what was available, rather than its absence—the heads were not keen, for example, that their residents should end up on 'sink estates'. In relation to employment, the problem seemed to be that very little was available.

In contrast to the situation in relation to regime and management, we could see no particular reason for trying to group these external supports into a smaller number of dimensions. There was, for example, no reason to think that relations with the police should in any way reflect that with

Table 7.7   External relationships as perceived sources of problems or support

	Problem (%)	Some problems (%)	Mixed (%)	Some support (%)	Support (%)
Contact with fieldworkers	7	18	36	16	24
Care planning system	11	13	31	18	27
Relations with neighbours	27	20	13	20	20
Relations with police	—	13	20	27	40
Relations with careers	3	5	30	32	30
Relations with education	14	11	23	27	25
Relations with DSS	7	21	54	7	11
Local employment market	30	28	23	8	13
Housing for young people	39	13	31	15	3

Percentages rounded.
Source: Head of home interview.

the Careers Service. Even if—conceivably—both were affected by the importance given by homes to external relations or by the local reputation of the home, their effects would most probably be felt in particular areas—the likelihood that older young people would get jobs or that residents would be cautioned rather than charged. For these reasons we have generally analysed these variables on their own, rather than as part of some composite measure.

RELATIONSHIPS

So much for relationships outside the home, what about relationships within them?

In our interview we asked the heads of homes to say whether they saw their home as currently in a stable state. We rated their replies on a four-point scale, assessing just over a quarter as very stable, just over a quarter as very unstable and the rest as more or less evenly divided in between. This question effectively repeated one which had been asked in the questionnaire to the head of home and in both their verbal and written replies the heads of homes attributed their difficulties (if any) to the same causes—the arrival of particularly difficult residents who upset the others, turnover, unrest or lack of experience among the staff, and management uncertainties (e.g. impending closure).

This summary may give a rather bland picture of the nature of the difficulties when they occurred. Such was not our impression or that of our interviewers. We close this chapter with two vignettes provided by our interviewers of two contrasting homes:

'The Laurels'   *The staff group appeared to share common concerns for the residents, and demonstrated these constantly with warmth. They were also one of the most welcoming of staff groups, including long-serving staff members and newer staff members.*

Relationships between staff and residents appeared relaxed and comfortable on almost all occasions that I visited. 'The Laurels' had a pet dog, which seemed to reflect the homeliness of the establishment.

'The Hawthorns'   *I felt incredibly sorry for all of them—a large staff team at sixes and sevens with itself and a resident group, some of whom are in permanently manic/chaotic mood and the others trying to keep their heads down and survive.*

Brutal assaults on staff and residents by a few in the resident group are commonplace (e.g. just last week a female member of staff was so severely kicked in the crotch that she had internal bleeding and is off sick for the foreseeable future . . . she is pressing assault charges against the individual concerned as this is just the last in a grim catalogue of his attacks).

Verbal, physical and sexual abuse reign—I am not overplaying this— residents constantly swear at staff, bullying is endemic and one older male resident makes it his business to copulate with all younger females who are admitted—last week a 13 year-old.

So, an extremely frightening, threatening and abusive environment. A dumping ground for . . . uncontrollable kids. A shocking place.

These vignettes suggest major differences in staff unity and relationships between staff and residents which may reflect, or perhaps be influenced by, the resident 'culture'. The penultimate sentence of the second vignette suggests that the influence may have flowed from the residents to the staff and that the place was in a mess because the residents were 'uncontrollable'.

We return later in the report to the issue of the direction of cause and effect (from residents to home or vice versa). In doing this we will use, among other things, the ratings made by the interviewers of staff–resident relationships and of relationships between staff. They made their ratings on a four-point scale and Table 7.8 sets out the results.

CONCLUSION

In general, the homes gave the impression that they had reasonable autonomy in most areas of their affairs, and that their regimes were benign and relaxed. There were, however, exceptions to these generalisations and differences between homes over how far the rules applied.

In relation to management, staff expressed most concern over the mix of roles the homes were expected to fulfil, reorganisation and aspects of

Table 7.8   Relationships—staff with staff; staff with residents

	Relationships	
	Staff with staff (%)	Staff with residents (%)
Very warm/friendly	35.4	14.6
Mainly warm/friendly	39.6	56.3
Some tension/hostility	16.7	18.8
Considerable tension/hostility	8.3	10.4

Source: Interviewer ratings.

their staffing ratio. A number of differences clustered together, so that homes could be differentiated along some dimension of 'empowerment'. Heads who felt that they had a clear remit, compatible roles for the home, and who did not feel they were prevented from fulfilling them by reorganisation or lack of autonomy, would be at one end of this dimension. Heads who felt they lacked these advantages would be at the other.

Homes also differed in their flexibility or permissiveness. At one end of the continuum, homes let their residents stay up and come in late, welcomed parents at most hours, had a low level of institutional restrictions and made little use of punishment. The other end of the continuum represented a more restrictive regime in all these respects.

There were also differences between homes in the degree to which the heads reported problems in relation to a variety of outside 'actors' with a potential influence on the home. The greatest diversity occurred in respect of neighbours, who were seen as very helpful by some and the reverse by others. There were shared opinions about the police, who were almost universally seen as helpful (a finding also in Berridge and Brodie's study), and about the situation in relation to housing and employment, which was very generally seen as bad. The enthusiasm for social workers was on average less marked than that for the police, another finding on which our study agrees with that of Berridge and Brodie.

These differences again raise questions about their impact. Does it matter whether homes run a relatively liberal or restrictive regime? Does 'empowerment' (as defined above) make any difference to the quality of care?

The importance of these questions was highlighted by the number of heads of home who reported that their establishment was not in a stable state. They attributed their difficulties variously to problems relating to staff, to residents or to other factors, particularly reorganisation. The importance of determining the factors that influence such instability was highlighted by vignettes of the home, which, as our earlier material from residents and social workers would suggest, clearly varied from the benign to the malignant.

8

THE HOME—THE HEADS' PHILOSOPHIES

INTRODUCTION

Common sense suggests that the head of home will be a key figure in any small residential establishment. Researchers have been strangely reluctant to test or even entertain this hypothesis, but where they have done so they have given it strong support. Evidence on the central role of the heads in residential care has been provided for probation hostels (Sinclair 1971, 1975), children's homes (Berridge 1985), establishments for autistic children (Bartak and Rutter, 1975), and homes for elderly people (Allen 1983; Evans *et al.* 1981; Gibbs and Sinclair 1992; Townsend 1962). More recently Brown and her colleagues (1996) have emphasised the importance of coherence between the head's view of care and that of their staff and the outside management, while Berridge and Brodie (1998) found that the coherence of the head's philosophy of care was strongly associated with the quality of care in the home. Any attempt to explain the quality of care in children's homes must take the views of the heads into account.

To this general justification for considering the views of the heads of homes, two more specific points can be added. First, the heads of home are highly experienced men and women, whose views on what makes for good residential care have in the past been too little considered. Any developed theory of what counts for good practice in this field should at least start with the hard-earned wisdom of its practitioners. Our research provides, albeit in a rudimentary way, an account of how these professionals think about their aims and practice.

Second, and more specific to the aims of this research, the heads provide the link between the structural characteristics of the home and its remit on the one hand and day-to-day practice on the other. It seems, on the face of it, unlikely that structural characteristics such as size or staffing ratio would exercise an overwhelming impact on the process of care within a home. In understanding the latter, the views and beliefs of the head of home are a natural place to start. For these reasons, this chapter presents a simple account of the views and concerns of heads of homes, as expressed in a semi-structured interview which lasted between one and five hours.

METHOD

The interview focused in part on general concerns—how to maintain a reasonable degree of order or promote consistency in the approach adopted by the staff. Our main concern, however, was with the aims of the heads, the means they used to achieve these aims, the difficulties they experienced in doing so, and the results they thought they achieved. The areas on which we focused were mainly those suggested to us by the *Looking After Children* project (Parker *et al.* 1991). So we examined how far the heads expected to change behaviour, help with emotional difficulties, improve health and educational attainment, repair damaged relationships between home and young person, help the young people find work, and manage their move out into independence.

The method we used relied on an initial open-ended question in each of these areas. The interviewers then followed up these questions with more detailed probes, designed to elicit the expectations in more detail and then explore how the heads set about achieving them, what problems they faced in doing so and what outcomes they achieved. All interviews were tape-recorded and the recordings were used as a basis for ratings made by Carol Stimson at the University of York. Our fear is that the ratings will be used inappropriately—as reflecting an absolute judgement rather than judgements made against our own relative standards. For these reasons we give only one table reporting the ratings actually made as examples of the method we used.

Later in the book we will explore how far these ratings were statistically related to our measures of quality. Our aim in this chapter is more modest. In it we set out to give an impressionistic account of the heads' approaches and achievements. In doing so we will sometimes behave as if one head has spoken for all, and also as if to say something is to ensure that it happens. Thus, in describing approaches to health, for example, we note that these include routine practices (e.g. initial examinations), attention to diet, the provision of health education information, rules on smoking, insistence on the importance of staff example, tactful, well-timed interventions with individual residents over hygiene, and attention to the fears of individual residents in such matters as dentists. Obviously, not all heads mentioned all these points and of those who mentioned them, some may have given them only perfunctory attention. Nevertheless, we believe that there is a point in drawing together these points from different interviews, if only to give a sense of the range of practice wisdom which is potentially available. Moreover, it is generally apparent that some heads have much more thorough approaches to some areas than others. This will allow us, later in the report, to analyse the relationship between these differences and outcomes.

ORDER

We don't expect to be sworn at . . . we don't swear at kids. At the end of the day they can do what the hell they want—that's where respect comes in—mutual respect.

At this young age there needs to be a routine. It's probably the first time in their lives someone has said, 'This is what we now expect of you . . . this is the time you get up . . . this is what will happen to you if you're not in time for tea.

Tell an adolescent they're not going to swear. They'd probably tell you to 'fuck off'.

There's got to be consistency . . . You've got to have a good staff team. We have got a good staff team.

Issues of order and discipline are central in residential care. Historically, residential establishments have used their approach to discipline to define their purpose and approach. Many of the former approved schools defined their role as training young people within a secure disciplined framework: by contrast, therapeutic communities felt that a lack of formal controls was a necessary condition for an approach which sought to encourage young people to take responsibility for themselves. Even if this historical tradition is ignored, it is obvious that issues of control must arise when any group of people live together, particularly when this group consists largely of adolescents, the majority of whom are there because they find themselves unable to get on with their families. Such issues range from the apparently trivial—smoking in bed, banging doors or swearing at staff—to matters that anyone would regard as serious—sexual exploitation, arson, bullying and delinquency. In this study parents, residents and social workers have all emphasised the importance of such issues in children's homes.

In questioning the heads of homes about the issue of discipline, we concentrated on areas where there was room for legitimate disagreement rather than on issues such as abuse, where it is obvious that some forms of behaviour are quite unacceptable. We asked them:

Could you tell me about the standard of behaviour you expect over things like swearing or the way residents talk to staff, and where you draw the line and intervene?

The questioning then went on to probe their answers, establish the means by which they aimed to keep control, the difficulties they had in doing this and the results they felt they achieved. Table 8.1 sets out the ratings we gave in these various areas.

Expectations

As already pointed out, Table 8.1 could easily be misinterpreted as imply-ing, for example, that nearly a third of the heads of homes had low or very low expectations of the standards of order they expected to achieve. Such an assumption would be unfair without more detailed examples of the kinds of evidence we used to make the ratings and the kinds of expectations which we rated 'low'.

Generally, a rating of 'low expectations' reflected an acceptance on the part of the head of home that staff could not control behaviour and should only step in in a forceful way where there was a danger that someone would come to harm if they did not. Swearing was seen as part of the young people's culture and as something that they may have learned also from their parents. Life was easier if the staff did not make an issue of getting residents up to breakfast if they were not going to school. Those going to school could then get off in peace. Some damage to prop-erty was seen as inevitable, and would only call for action if the culprits repeatedly broke things or had caused a very serious amount of damage.

Some justification for these low expectations was provided by acknowl-edgements that individual residents would lose control and that to inter-vene forcefully might make matters worse. For the most part, however, the justification seemed to be a pragmatic one—bad behaviour was inevit-able and the thing was to learn to live with it.

Table 8.1 Distribution of ratings related to order

Dimension	Very low (%)	Low (%)	High (%)	Very high (%)
Expectations	17	17	34	32
Means	11	30	40	19
Difficulties	22	17	44	17
Outcomes achieved	17	17	39	26

Percentages rounded.
Source: Head of home interview.

At the other end of the spectrum were a group of heads who did not see bad behaviour as a necessary part of home life and who were quite prepared to be specific about what they wanted in a number of areas—school attendance, bedtimes, swearing, 'boundaries', and generally behaving in a 'reasonable', manner both inside and outside the home. Allowances were sometimes made—reactions to swearing in some homes were said to depend on the context within which the forbidden words occurred. In contrast to those with low expectations, these heads justified the standards they wished to enforce by appeal to concepts of 'respect' and what is required if a group is to live happily together. The young people had to realise that they should treat each other and each others' possessions 'decently', and this not necessarily because this was therapeutic but because it was right.

In between these extremes—and difficult to rate with any reliability—were those heads who would take some swearing or some boisterous behaviour but would step in if things were getting out of control, and those who saw slamming of doors, swearing and other forms of anti-social behaviour as expressions of unhappiness. They did not excuse all, but they were prepared to live with a certain amount of disruption and to accept that at some times, but not others, the home would be a difficult place in which to live.

Means

Some strategies were geared to controlling the behaviour of particular young people—'anger management' was popular and so was counselling, and not giving rewards to bad behaviour, and discussion of the incident after the event. It was important to make clear to the resident when behaviour was not acceptable and to make use of any relationship between the young person and the member of staff. Other strategies involved the actual or pretended use of power—staff were expected to bluff if necessary, but their bluff could also be backed by sanctions—for example, by removal of pocket money or 'grounding'.

As with the standards expected, heads of homes varied in the degree to which they had an extensive, thought-out repertoire of means for ensuring reasonable order in their homes. One admitted that she did not really have a policy on how to do this. Instead, efforts in this direction involved attempts to appeal to the young people's better nature—group meetings at which the extent of the problems were acknowledged and it was pointed out that the staff did not really deserve the treatment they were getting, or attempts to get individual young people on the side of the staff. By contrast, other heads reported a wide variety of means of the kind reported above and the rater was instructed to code a very high level of involvement where:

The standard of behaviour expected is definitely sought through a variety of means, both formal and informal, which taken together constitute a coherent policy on order.

Some means involved an effort to build up a culture of expectations which were then consistently reinforced. Thus, it might be seen as important that there was agreement between the staff on the standard of behaviour that was expected, that efforts were made to ensure that the young people themselves were involved in agreeing what was acceptable, and that the staff set a good example themselves (or, in the language usually adopted, 'modelled' acceptable behaviour).

These strategies could be reinforced by routine practice within the home—for example, efforts to ensure staff agreement on standards could require staff meetings; the exclusion of difficult young people at points when the home was not in a state to help them required attention to admission policies; and heads might try to ensure good relationships with individual residents by ensuring that more than nominal attention was paid to the keyworker system. It might also be seen as important to ensure that difficult young people did not enter the home at points when the resident group was not settled.

Difficulties

In keeping with the general pattern of this part of the interview, we also asked the heads of homes about difficulties they had in ensuring the standard of order they wanted. In general, these were seen as centring around the culture from which the young people came, the dynamics of the particular group and factors connected with the staff. Some residents were seen as particularly difficult but the difficulties they posed could be compounded by peer pressure to behave badly, the bad example given by other members of the group who might threaten or abuse staff, and the general need of the young people to gain acceptance from their peers, if necessary by difficult behaviour, or to compete for status, again if necessary through delinquent or anti-social actions. Trouble could also be seen as stemming from differences between members of staff, the arrival of new staff who were not able to adopt an approach consistent with that of their colleagues, and overload on staff, which meant that they were under stress and liable to make mistakes in dealing with the residents. Running through this section of the interview was a feeling that nothing succeeds like success. The threatening and abusive behaviour of young people was seen not only as evidence that there were difficulties but also as a direct cause of further difficulties. It was difficult to intervene without provoking yet further trouble and yet failure to intervene meant that undesirable behaviour was being accepted as the norm.

Success

As has been implicit in much that we have written so far, there were large differences between homes in the degree to which the heads felt that they had achieved the standard of behaviour that they wanted. Some reported 'no order' or a 'constant battle', 'fortnights of hell' or the fragile maintenance of control through physical confrontations. Others less graphically reported 'quite a good standard of order' or an acceptance that things were 'not too bad', that the young people accepted the constraints, had a moral code or conscience, and were even considerate, although these virtues might be latent and not initially apparent to the naked eye. Others, as we have pointed out before, stressed that these things went in cycles, that it depended on the mix of young people in the home at the time and also on what else was going on in young people's lives.

Thus, the interviews with the heads of home reinforced, if reinforcement was necessary, our perception of the salience of order in children's homes. More importantly, perhaps, it illustrated the practice wisdom which exists over how this order may be maintained, and suggested the beginnings of a theory over what might be important in maintaining it. This would emphasise above all the establishment of a culture of what was and was not acceptable. This culture would depend on a consistent and agreed approach by the staff, and the acceptance by the young people that what was wanted was what was necessary if the members of a community were to deal decently with each other. It would also require strategies for dealing with residents who were difficult on an individual basis, so that neither bad behaviour by residents nor bad examples by staff can be seen as anything other than exceptions. If such a culture becomes established, it would feed on itself, for nothing succeeds like success.

BEHAVIOUR

If you literally sat on him for half an hour he would laugh and you could have a conversation with him. He was not aware of how to seek attention.

I see it as very much the role of the staff to [foster] self-esteem and self-worth.

The larger the group, the more chance there is of losing them to the disruptive behaviour . . . The kids like being here and they get a great deal of respect for the place. It works.

After discussing issues of control, our interviewers turned to issues of behaviour. As we have seen, a high proportion of residents had a history of difficult behaviour of one kind or another and in a minority of cases social workers had hoped that placement of a child would achieve a change in this area of his/her life. It was natural, therefore, that we should ask about the degree to which homes set out to modify the behaviour of residents in the long-term. This was not necessarily synonymous with efforts to keep order—indeed, some might argue that too much attention to order could deprive residents of responsibility for their own acts and thus undermine efforts as long-term change.

Our ratings suggested something of a gap between expectations and outcomes. All but a fifth of the heads were rated as having high expectations in terms of what they wanted to achieve in this area but only around a half felt that their outcomes reached similar heights. As before, however, these figures mean little without some illustration of how we made the rating.

At one extreme were heads who felt that the nature of their enterprise precluded attempts at long-term change. The young people were with them for too short a time, it was not possible within these constraints to foster the kinds of relationships with them on which long-term change could be built, their problems in any case were too entrenched and the children themselves too damaged. These low expectations were sometimes reinforced by an appeal to philosophies developed in the fields of addiction and sex education. The aim, it was explained, was not to modify behaviour but to offer choice. A distinction was made between aggression and abuse, on the one hand, and problems connected with drink, drugs and under-age sex on the other hand. The former were wrong and should be contained, but the latter should be approached from the point of view of risk rather than of morality. The philosophy was that of 'harm reduction', which was explained as the offer of information designed to reduce risk.

At the other extreme, some heads accepted that their aim was indeed to modify behaviour. They felt that the young person's break from a previous environment offered a chance for change. Standards needed to be set, behaviour challenged, self-esteem encouraged and new opportunities offered. Hopefully, the resulting changes would be long-term, although there were variations in how far heads felt that this was likely.

Means

Heads also differed over the means by which any change was to be achieved. One felt that as expectations of change were unrealistic, discussions of means were unnecessary. Others, however, relied on varying mixtures of the climate of the home, contact between individuals and members of the staff and the use of outside agencies. Those who relied on the culture of the home emphasised similar means to those we have discussed in the section on control. Peer group pressure was seen as able to work for good as well as ill. Staff were able to set a norm by clear definitions of what was and what was not acceptable and why, and were able to act firmly when necessary. Individual influence was largely seen to depend on talking things through with the individual young person, an activity for which the key worker system could provide a framework. However, some also saw a place for just 'hanging on' and for some use of behavioural approaches in terms of rewarding good behaviour rather than bad, and modelling acceptable behaviour. A variety of outside agencies were mentioned—psychologists, units for those with problems connected with drugs, and projects which redirected the young people's energies. Outside agencies could also be sources of information and leaflets which would help the young people take control of their own lives.

Difficulties

Most heads saw quite considerable difficulties in the way of any attempt to modify behaviour. Most importantly, perhaps, many young people were seen as not wanting to change. The other difficulties have all been mentioned before—the destructive influence of the peer group, the instability introduced by the arrival of new staff and residents, and the difficulty of ensuring that new residents would suit the group.

Success

Generally, the heads were rather cautious about the degree to which permanent change was achieved—in part, perhaps, because they lacked the information on which to form an opinion. The most pessimistic felt that the young people did not even modify their behaviour within the establishment, citing particular incidents or the exhaustion of members of staff as evidence for their opinion. Others felt that if realistic aims were set, modest success was possible. Difficult behaviour gradually reduced over the period a young person was in the home; the heads could not promise that this improvement would be permanent, but they were pleased with the changes that occurred and hoped that they would last.

EMOTIONAL DISTURBANCE

Following our questions on difficult behaviour we asked the heads of homes about the possibility of dealing with emotional disturbance. The two sets of questions were closely linked—for many heads saw difficult behaviour as a form of 'acting out'. Their task, they felt, was to enable the young people to talk about their problems rather than 'act them out' through aggressive or self-destructive behaviour.

Most heads placed considerable emphasis on this aspect of their work. Nevertheless, there were differences in the degree to which they felt that they should try to deal with the emotional problems of their residents. At one extreme were heads who felt that staff were not trained to help with emotional problems and that in this area the path of wisdom was to leave well alone. Others felt that it was the task of their establishment to 'try and unlock some of the emotional pain—help them find ways of dealing with emotional outbursts'. The head of home just quoted had a strong ethical view of what the young people should become—that is, 'sharing, caring adults', and this aspiration was seen as requiring measures to build the young person's self-esteem.

In discussing the means for achieving these ends, the heads emphasised the same broad areas they had mentioned in relation to dealing with difficult behaviour, to wit the influence of the climate or atmosphere of the home or staff group, work within the home with the individual young person, and the involvement of outside agencies with the relevant expertise. The atmosphere of the home was seen as important in either taking the pressure off the young person, relaxing him/her and enabling one-to-one work to take place or, alternatively, as destroying any possibility of constructive work. One-to-one work was generally seen to be based on the willingness of the staff to listen and on the existence of a relationship between the young person and a member of staff, something which the keyworker system might encourage. Self-esteem, however, could also be encouraged by a 'regulated lifestyle' and the existence of 'achievable goals'. A variety of outside sources of help were mentioned—psychological services, social workers, family therapists, school counsellors—and these might use a variety of measures—groupwork, family work or some form of counselling. Ideally, the whole was based on an individual assessment of the young person's needs which bound together a multi-disciplinary approach.

The problems in the way of achieving such ends should also by now be familiar. There was too little time to achieve fundamental change; the young people lacked the motivation to change and were in any case too damaged to do so; staff lacked the necessary skill, turned over too quickly, had low morale or too many emotional problems of their own; outside help was unavailable or took too long to get; families, or even local people, exercised a destructive influence on the young people and undid any good that the home might achieve. Such, at its blackest, was the composite picture of difficulties painted by the heads of home.

Such a bleak picture was repeated by some but by no means all the heads when they were asked to describe the outcomes they achieved in this area of their work. Some felt that they could 'not achieve anything' because of the peer group or because 'with 14–15 year-old kids you can only scratch the surface'. Others felt that they were slowly 'getting there', developing relationships, seeing some progress. A minority (15%) were prepared to stick their necks out and claim that this area of their work was going well.

FAMILY RELATIONSHIPS

Family relationships were mentioned in the last section as something which hinder the work of the home. Such a possibility is, of course, very much out of keeping with the spirit of the Children Act. From an official point of view, relationships with and hence contact with families are to be encouraged wherever possible and for a variety of reasons. It is believed that in most cases this is what families and young people want, that contact encourages return home, that lack of contact leads to problems of identity, and that in any case the last thing that anyone wants is a young person cast loose on the world at 16 or 17 with no family on which to fall back. The latter point at least seems to be in keeping with the behaviour of those graduating out of 'care', most of whom seem to have contact with their families, even if they do not necessarily stay with them or do so only for brief periods (Biehal *et al.* 1995; Bullock, Little and Millham 1993). As we have seen, this view also fits the views of the young people in our interview sample.

In the light of this official endorsement of family contacts the reactions of heads of home were somewhat more mixed. For one, the official policy was 'a joke—the problems kids have experienced at home mean responsibilities laid down for parents in the Children Act is (sic) a mess'. Others encouraged contact where they felt that there was something to build on but reported that some parents were relieved to be rid of their children or that parental interest dwindled over time. Two-thirds of the heads did, according to our ratings, strongly endorse the policy, feeling that the legislation required this, that it was desirable in itself and that if, for some reason, contact with parents was undesirable, efforts could be made to develop or sustain links with grandparents or other family members. Nevertheless, most added caveats to the effect that contact was not always desirable, and most were quite articulate about its difficulties and restrained in making claims for its outcomes.

The means for encouraging such contacts were partly related to the home in general—there should be easy access to a telephone and a welcoming atmosphere for parents when they visited—and partly to work with individual young people and their families. In the latter respect, keyworkers and social workers clearly had important roles. The key was to keep parents informed, involve them in decisions about what should happen, and mediate between parents and young person. 'A good relationship with the kids gives confidence to the parents', and on the back of such confidence the staff could take a more direct role with the parents and encourage them to keep in contact. There was an art, too, in moving at the young person's pace, not pressing for a reconciliation when neither side was ready but reinforcing any steps towards better relationships.

Only two heads implied that there were no difficulties over family contact. The others were more or less eloquent over a variety of problems. These included practical difficulties (transport problems for the families, lack of staff time to take young people to families), difficulties within the families (reluctance on the part of the young people or parents, feuds over who should have access) and the natural unease of parents in dealing with staff who were taking over roles which they themselves might have been expected to exercise. There could also be occasions when relationships had clearly broken down almost irretrievably or where the disclosure of abuse meant that contact was discouraged.

As already mentioned, claims for success were cautious. Some saw none: 'No success whatsoever with current group—no movement due to entrenchment of family situations and attitudes'. Others set their sights low and reported results in keeping with their low expectations. Others reported some success amid an uphill struggle or felt that while they had not achieved reconciliations—lines of communication had been kept open and this was all that could be expected in the circumstances. A minority reported that the majority of their residents returned home (in one case 95% of them were said to do so) and that where this was not so a dialogue had been maintained.

HEALTH

Homes may or may not be expected to change those admitted to them but they are certainly expected to look after them. This requires attention to the ordinary aspects of young people's lives, including their health and education. Concerns about the young people's health arise partly because they are likely to come from disadvantaged homes and partly because some may be putting themselves at risk through smoking, their use of drugs or alcohol, or the number of their sexual partners. As a result, social workers have been urged to pay more attention to the health of young people who are looked after and health constitutes a separate dimension in the new records developed for the *Looking After Children* initiative.

We felt that most heads of homes endorsed this official concern with health issues. Their doubts if any were over whether there was much of a problem ('In my experience the health of young people in care is good') and if there was a problem, whether there was much they could do about it. One or two implied that they were going through the motions: 'Dental appointments—that's as far as it goes', or 'Medical on admission, dentist, optician—the kids opt out frequently'. Others, however, appeared to place much more emphasis on this aspect of care, 'fighting for the kids to get a good deal', arranging for full assessments, checking that the young people were happy with their GPs, ensuring that individual issues were followed up, dealing at both a general and an individual level with problems connected with smoking, obesity, personal hygiene and sexually transmitted diseases, and priding themselves on the quality of the diet in the home.

The means adopted for promoting health have already been sketched above. The heads appeared to rely on some routine practices (medicals on arrival) and also on tactful intervention as required (for example, over diet or personal hygiene). Some prided themselves on being very systematic in the way they recorded information relevant to health. There seemed to be variation in the degree to which the homes provided general advice on drugs, smoking and HIV and in the smoking policies adopted. Contraception seemed to be dealt with as a health issue, with heads attempting to make sure that contraception was made available without the implication that sexual intercourse was being encouraged.

The main difficulties facing this aspect of the homes' work appeared to be the attitudes of the young people themselves. These were said to be uninterested in the dangers of smoking or HIV, either because of the heedlessness of youth or (by one head) because they had such low self-esteem that they did not believe there was any point in avoiding risk to themselves. The young people were said to be similarly intransigent over drink (which many of them enjoyed) and junk food, to which many of them were accustomed. A number were said to be afraid to go to the doctor. Fear of the dentist seemed to be even more pronounced. Other problems which did not arise from the attitudes of the young people related to the provision of services (for example, lack of female GP, delays in getting services) and the lack of training for staff on such matters as AIDS, contraception and accessing medical resources.

In general, most heads seem to feel that they were having a reasonable measure of success in this area of their work. They were able to tackle problems arising from previous neglect, they acknowledged ruefully that the young people's drinking, smoking and sexual practices had not changed as much as they might have desired, but they thought that in most respects the young people enjoyed reasonable health and that the homes dealt reasonably with any health problems that might arise.

EDUCATION

The education of young people in care is commonly regarded as even more of a neglected area than their health. There are, however, encouraging signs that a number of the educational issues are now receiving attention in the literature, a development due in part to the effort of Sonia Jackson (1989) in raising the issue. For example, Aldgate, Colton and Heath, along with other of their colleagues, have written about the educational attainment of children looked after by local authorities (especially young people in foster care) (Aldgate et al. 1992; 1993; Heath et al. 1989, 1994). On a related subject, Stein (1994) has written about the education and career trajectories of young people leaving care.

There is also concern that a high proportion of those looked after are excluded or suspended from school (Audit Commission 1994), that social workers have been uninterested in education, failing even to include information on it in their records (Fletcher-Campbell and Hall 1990), that the process of care itself disrupts educational careers, moving young people around without regard to examinations and stigmatising them in relation to their peers. For their part, homes have been accused of being unconcerned about education, failing to encourage homework and allowing a culture to grow which is hostile to school. More recent evidence suggests that the experience of care (or at least of long-term foster care) does not of itself worsen educational performance but that it certainly does not improve it.

All evidence suggests that the educational performance of children who are looked after is extremely low relative to almost any comparison group, and the consequence is that the young people leave care seriously disadvantaged, not only in relation to their families of origin but also in relation to employment. Not surprisingly, official guidance and the materials produced for the Looking After Children project both emphasise this aspect of the young people's lives.

This official policy was generally reflected in our ratings, since nearly two-thirds of the heads of homes were seen as having extensive expectations in this aspect of their work. A few heads, it is true, felt that this was an area in which they could do little, or that it was one which necessarily took second place to more urgent priorities. Others, however, said that they gave education great emphasis, and saw its value in providing qualifications and building up the social skills of the young people.

As might be expected, the heads of home were able to talk about a variety of ways through which the young people could be encouraged to go to school. These included establishing the reason for non-attendance (for example, bullying), rewarding attendance (and conversely ensuring that those not attending were expected to do something challenging), and encouraging homework. It was important that staff took an active role in promoting school work and that they made their interest clear through attendance at school functions. It was important to liaise with the school over strategies for getting the young person back (e.g. by building up gradually) and to make use of the Behavioural Support Units and other facilities which the school provided. Perhaps most important of all was the need to establish a culture whereby going to school was simply the normal thing to do.

So much said, the heads acknowledged that achieving high standards of school performance was often difficult. Some of the problems had to do with the young people themselves, who might feel stigmatised for being in care or who had in some cases been out of school for such a long time that they had simply given up on the idea of going back. Moreover, it was suggested that in some cases the problems of the young people were such that getting them back to school had to be low in the Social Services' priorities. Other problems had to do with the school system. It was alleged that the consequence of the *Local Management of Schools* initiative was that schools were excluding more and more young people. According to some heads, schools believed that young people in children's homes did not have to go to school and the staff were, in any case, prejudiced against their residents. There could also be specific problems about mothers with babies going to school. We rated very nearly four in ten of the heads as finding extensive difficulties in such areas.

As for outcomes, just under a third were rated as feeling that they had extensive success in this area. Around one in seven, however, appeared to have almost no success at all: 'The kids don't go, it's very difficult, there seems to be nothing one can do'. But by contrast, some reported that all their young people of school age were going to school, that it was just accepted that in their home young people went to school, and that there had even been some examination success.

WORK

If young people have left school they face the issue of what to do about work. Official guidance is less forthcoming about work for those looked after than it is about education. Partly, no doubt, this is a matter of age. The majority of those who are looked after are not of an age when detailed plans for their employment would be appropriate. Partly, too, it may be a matter of resignation—for employment is now very difficult to get. Both factors may have influenced the replies of the heads of homes. In a number of instances we could not make the relevant rating because the age range of their homes meant that they did not have policies in these areas. The ratings we did make emphasised the relatively low expectations which the heads had of enabling their young people to get work and the severe difficulties which they had met in trying to do so. Some simply implied that they could not influence this outcome and set no targets for it. Others were rather more sanguine, relying on boredom and the need for money to motivate the young people to go out and get work, and emphasising the importance of doing something. Even some of these, however, were not sure if the emphasis they placed on work was realistic.

Despite their pessimism, the heads of homes described a reasonable range of strategies for getting their young people into work or an appropriate alternative. Some of these involved the use of official channels (social workers, leaving care workers, the Job Centre and the Careers Service). Others involved the use of contacts—those possessed by the head of home or teachers or those built up through work experience. Others involved work with individual young persons—encouraging them to read the paper for job advertisements, praising their efforts at job seeking, taking them to interviews and helping them to present themselves at an interview, and attempting to ensure that those who had a job were rewarded in the sense that the rent they had to pay did not remove all financial incentive to them to work or obtain a place on an appropriate scheme. Again, some heads emphasised the importance of a work culture—young people in their home were expected to do something, whether this was going to college, going to work or being on a scheme.

Despite such purposeful approaches, the difficulties in the way of success were formidable. Some were related to a culture of unemployment. The young people's parents had been unemployed, the young people themselves had performed badly at school, had attracted the stigma of being in care and saw no reason to think that they would do better for themselves than their parents. Claiming the dole was a way of life and they saw no reason to risk the humiliation of a job interview, indeed they would rather lie in bed. Other reasons related to incentives. It was very difficult for the young people to get a job that would leave them financially better off. The most powerful reasons, however, were structural. There were no jobs for young people with the kinds of abilities of those in the homes; careers offices were thus 'a waste of time' and opportunities to buck the system were few.

Not surprisingly, our ratings for outcome in this area were not very optimistic. Around a third said that outcomes were 'not good' or 'very limited'. One doubted if a single young person from the home had found work in recent years. Others, however, reported somewhat better success—some by having a wider vision of what was possible than simply jobs or YTS. One currently had three young people out of school and of these two were working and one had gone to college. Another reported that all who had left had found something, whether this involved college, courses or work. Such examples, however, were beacons of light in a much less encouraging world.

MOVING ON

If the young people are not to go home—and to judge from the heads of homes many of them are not—they will have to move out to some form of independent living. Recent research, most notably by Stein and his colleagues (see, for example, Stein 1997), has graphically illustrated the problems faced by young people discharged from residential or foster care. Their likely or possible problems include debt, loneliness, difficulties in getting appropriate accommodation, exploitation by unsuitable friends, fear of burglars, quarrels with neighbours, and the need to budget, cook, handle bureaucracies and generally cope with managing on their own. These problems are now well known and have been illustrated in our own study (see Chapter 5). We asked the heads of homes how far they tried to forestall or manage them.

As with work, questions in this area were not relevant to all the heads of homes, since some of them were dealing with quite a young age group and had little experience of it. Nevertheless, most had high or very high aims for this area of work and most had a considerable repertoire of means for achieving it. That said, our ratings suggested that the outcomes achieved were less than the aspirations.

In terms of expectations, some heads acknowledged with admirable frankness that their work in this area could only be tokenistic. One commented that it was not possible to prepare young people for the loneliness of the world and that time spent on practical skills was almost a way of diverting attention from this unpalatable fact. At the other end of the spectrum were heads who said they put a great deal of effort into this area of work.

Evidence of such efforts was provided by the range of means they employed. Some of these were outside the control of the home—after-care schemes were the most obvious example. Others involved careful planning with the young person over when he/she would leave and what needed to be done if the move was to be successful. What was needed could well include the acquisition of skills in cooking and budgeting, and sometimes this was to be achieved by trial periods in independence flats, where the young person was expected to live on a realistic budget. Other means included assistance with getting accommodation, filling in the relevant forms and so on, and a willingness either to reach out to the young person after they had left, or to be hospitable if they wanted to come back for a couple of nights or the odd meal.

The difficulties in moving on included many which have been highlighted in other research. A key issue was that the young people were seen as wanting to move out and live on their own when they were not really ready to do so. Those who left at 16 were seen as particularly vulnerable and it was pointed out that group living was in some ways a poor preparation for living on one's own. Additional problems could arise from the lack of suitable resources—foster parents, semi-independent living arrangements of various kind. Many of the young people were lonely, and they might change their plans, fall out with their neighbours and fail to keep their accommodation.

As for the overall outcomes, there were differences in how well the heads felt they did. At one extreme, heads felt that outcomes were generally poor when the young people left the home, although things might settle down eventually. Some, however, felt that success could be achieved, particularly perhaps with young people who had been at the home longest. One head of home argued that the establishment was 'unique' in the effort it put into outreach and aftercare and felt that the outcomes were indeed very good.

CONCLUSION AND COMMON THEMES

So far, we have examined each issue, as it were on its own. Nevertheless, certain common themes have emerged as the heads made similar points in relation to different lines of enquiry. Much of the similarity can, perhaps, be caught under the headings of 'motivation', 'culture', 'treatment' and 'external arrangements'. Let us explain what we mean.

In relation to motivation, it was striking how often the heads returned to what the young people wanted as a determinant of what was possible. Young people did not necessarily want contact with their parents—so this was an important limitation on the Children Act. Young people were not motivated to give up smoking or swearing or to go to work—so aspirations in all these areas had to be tempered with the reality of what the young people were prepared to do. The explanations for this lack of motivation were various, depending perhaps on the theoretical disposition of the head or the varied motivations that in fact existed. So the blame was attributed to culture, to the nature of adolescence, to the experience of failure or to feelings of worthlessness. Whatever the explanation, the importance of motivation was generally acknowledged and provided an oblique justification for philosophies of harm minimisation. Some young people, it was implicitly acknowledged, would go on drinking, taking drugs or having sex with numerous partners—the path of realism was not to dissuade them from these actions but ensure that if they were going to undertake them they did so with the least risk to themselves or others.

A second key feature of the heads accounts lay in the importance they laid on the home's culture. The important thing to establish was that in this home young people did not break up the furniture, act delinquently, and generally display a lack of respect for others. By contrast they did go to school, did try to take up work, did respect the property of others. Success in this respect fed on itself, meant that the home was a secure and reasonable base for the young people, and provided a stepping stone for individual work with the young people in terms of controlling their behaviour, growing up emotionally, and going to school.

In keeping with this analysis, the heads' ratings of the success achieved in maintaining control were highly significantly related to the success they reported in terms of achieving behavioural and emotional change and achieving improvements in the young people's education. By contrast, it was not significantly associated with outcomes more dependent on factors outside the home—getting work, establishing good relationships with parents, and moving on—neither was it significantly associated with success in relation to health.

Although the culture of the home might be an important element in achieving individual change, the heads did not generally regard it as sufficient on its own. For this to occur the heads generally mentioned individual approaches, some behavioural (e.g. 'anger management'), some relying on talking (particularly enabling young people to talk out their feelings rather than act them out) and some generally dependent on raising self-esteem. Thus, in a context where reasonable behaviour was the norm, difficult behaviour could be seen as a reaction to individual pain and responded to accordingly.

Finally, there were issues outside the home that needed to be handled if the achievements within the home were to be translated into future happiness. The heads gave quite detailed accounts of work designed to improve relationships with families, obtain work, collaborate with school and other professionals, and enable young people to move on.

So if the heads' accounts are to be taken seriously, we need to look at separately at least three different aspects of the homes' work—their success in establishing an acceptable culture, their ability to work sensitively with individual children in the light of their problems and aspirations, and their success in dealing with young people's lives outside the home. These accounts are highly compatible with the way young people and their social workers evaluated residential care (see Chapter 5). Data presented later will cast light on all these issues. For the moment, however, we would like to stress the degree to which, without much encouragement from the outside world, heads have developed an implicit practice theory which is related to all these issues. As noted in Chapter 1, a criticism of residential care has been that it lacks a coherent and agreed theory. Such a theory seems in outline to exist in the practice wisdom of heads. It needs, *prima facie*, to be further articulated.

9

THE HOMES—THE STAFF WORLD

INTRODUCTION

The philosophy of the home may be set by the head in conjunction with more senior management. However, it is the staff who have to implement it and whose day-to-day actions will convey to the residents what the true philosophy of the home is. Brown and her colleagues (1996) have argued that the coherence between the staff's, head's and managers' definitions of what the home is about is crucial to its success. Berridge and Brodie (1998) found that their measure of the quality of care provided by a home was almost perfectly correlated with their assessment of staff morale; Whitaker and her colleagues (1998) suggest that the ability of staff to be themselves within an agreed context, thus providing 'unity in diversity', is a central element in a successful home. Clearly the staff must be an important element in any evaluation of residential child care.

Given their importance, it is unfortunate that the job of a member of staff is not an easy one. There is evidence that they often feel powerless in relation to the demands of their management and the outside world (Baldwin 1990; Whitaker, Archer and Hicks 1998), that it is difficult to ensure that they feel part of the wider department (Kendrick and Fraser 1992); that their theoretical orientation, if any, is often either ill-developed or at odds with that of the managers (Kendrick and Fraser 1992), and that they lack the training which, irrespective of whether it increases effectiveness, might be expected to give confidence in the face of confusing demands (Hills *et al.* 1997). Against this background, staff have to face residents who are almost certainly more difficult than those of a decade ago (Berridge and Brodie 1998), negative publicity, and frequently an undercurrent of sexual tension (Kendrick and Fraser 1992) and occasional violence (Soothill 1995; Whitaker, Archer and Hicks 1998). A recent study in Northern Ireland suggested that, compared with other Social Services staff, they are more discontented with their jobs, experience a higher level of strain and are much more likely to be physically attacked (McConkey *et al.* 1997).

Among the researchers quoted above, Whitaker and her colleagues (1998) have given perhaps the most graphic account of the staff's experience. In their detailed study of the day-to-day life of staff they outlined the pressures and rewards for individual staff members. On the positive side they found that staff drew strength and encouragement from working in a cohesive staff team in a distinctive home, from the progress of residents and their relationship with them, from organising special events and treats, from the variety of the work and the sense that they themselves did it well, and from a sense that their management listened to them and gave them resources. Conversely, staff felt stressed by difficult relationships with young people, violence or abuse from them, fear of allegations and worries about the residents' safety and progress. These stresses could be compounded by a feeling that they lacked control over admissions, and by lack of resources, lack of support from senior staff, high turnover or lack of cohesiveness in their own staff team, and the intrusiveness of the work into their own lives and those of their colleagues.

Our own study can complement these detailed accounts by exploiting its statistical size. In this way it can check the hypotheses generated by more qualitative work. For example, a number of studies suggest that staff morale is likely to be low if staff have comparatively little control over admissions, and we will be able to see whether this association holds up. We can apply a similar statistical approach to document the variations between staff in the different homes in the way they see their jobs and in morale. We can then go on to see how far these are likely to be explained by 'objective' factors such as their sex, age or seniority and how far morale appears to be influenced by policy and practice—for example, by the frequency with which members of staff receive supervision. Later in the report we will relate these differences in morale to a more general measure of success in homes and see how far they, too, coincide.

The main source of data was the Staff Questionnaire, which was sent to 526 staff in the 48 homes. A total of 304 questionnaires were returned, representing a response rate of 58%. This conceals a considerable variation between homes, whose response rates varied from none to 100%. The biographical information in the Staff Questionnaire is included in Appendix A, which compares the characteristics of those who returned the questionnaire with the characteristics of the whole staff group as, detailed by the head of home in the Staff Log. In all important respects the two were very similar. In these respects at least those staff who returned the questionnaire were, as far as we could reasonably tell, representative of the whole staff group.

INITIAL RESULTS

In this section of the chapter we concentrate on those items in the questionnaire which asked staff about their experience of the home, problems and satisfaction, and the training and support received. As in Chapter 7, we used components analysis to simplify and reduce the large number of variables involved. We used the factor scores in further analysis where we related them to:

- Age: Under 30; 31–40; over 40.
- Sex: Women; men.
- Post: Managerial/supervisory; care staff.
- Qualifications: Social work, other relevant.
                    Other qualifications.
                    No qualifications.
- Local Authority: Area 1 to Area 5.

'My Job—As It Is and As It Ought to Be'

Key aspects of any person's job are their understanding of what the job involves and their satisfaction with this. One section of the questionnaire, therefore, asked respondents to consider the list of tasks set out in Table 9.1 and to indicate, first, their current involvement in each of them and second, the degree to which they thought they *ought* to be involved in them.

The tasks that staff were most heavily involved with were keeping order and general supervision, showing concern for young people, social training and acting as a keyworker. The tasks they were least involved with were staff supervision and leadership (not surprising as most of those replying were 'care staff'), therapeutic work, after-care and contact with families.

Staff were certainly not dissatisfied with the tasks that occupied much of their time. They still wanted to be involved with them and to much the same degree as at present. However, many staff wanted more involvement in after-care, therapeutic work and contact with families. Like the heads of homes and young people, some staff were critical of the current situation in relation to after-care:

Outside the homes, I do not believe that they stand a chance in the community. This is a deeply depressing view of the work but it presents exceptionally difficult problems with few solutions. It is not my intention to remain in the job.

Table 9.1   Elements of job—'as it is now'; 'as I would like it to be'

		Involved in this aspect of the job			
		No (%)	A little (%)	Quite a lot (%)	Very much (%)
Domestic	I am involved	12.8	26.3	27.9	33.0
	I ought to be	14.1	28.9	31.5	25.5
Administration	I am involved	8.7	21.5	30.2	39.6
	I ought to be	4.7	17.7	38.8	38.8
Education	I am involved	10.2	31.5	30.2	28.1
	I ought to be	8.8	10.8	35.7	44.8
Work training	I am involved	13.9	27.5	31.7	26.8
	I ought to be	9.3	13.4	36.4	40.9
Keeping order and	I am involved	—	4.7	11.7	83.6
general supervision	I ought to be	0.3	5.0	11.4	83.3
Care planning	I am involved	3.4	15.2	24.3	57.1
	I ought to be	1.3	4.0	20.3	74.3
Contact with families	I am involved	15.6	30.5	30.2	23.7
	I ought to be	5.0	12.1	31.4	51.5
Showing concern	I am involved	0.7	3.3	16.0	80.0
for young people	I ought to be	—	2.7	9.0	88.3
Social training	I am involved	2.7	5.0	19.7	72.6
	I ought to be	0.3	5.0	15.0	79.7
After-care	I am involved	26.0	36.6	19.2	18.2
	I ought to be	8.4	14.8	27.3	49.5
Therapeutic work	I am involved	18.4	40.3	26.3	15.0
	I ought to be	4.4	16.4	36.6	42.6
Staff supervision/	I am involved	36.3	25.8	16.7	21.2
leadership	I ought to be	22.0	15.3	29.6	33.1
Acting as keyworker	I am involved	11.9	8.9	13.9	65.6
	I ought to be	6.3	5.7	14.7	73.2

Source: Questionnaire to staff.

A lot more could be done in after-care. Once they leave the security of the home, it's a ticket to disaster. Re-offending is a foregone conclusion.

Although overall I feel very positively about my job, it would improve 100% if I had more of a real effect in my clients' future plans, i.e. more real power to access and plan for them if, or especially if, their Field Worker is slack.

In short, there was a desire to expand the 'treatment', as opposed to containment, aspects of the staff's work.

We carried out a components analysis on the 13 items in Table 9.1. This suggested that the differences between staff could be most conveniently explained as lying along three separate dimensions:

C1 Items that could be categorised as reflecting a concern with Care Planning and After-care.
C2 Items that dealt with Order and Social Training.
C3 Items that cover Administration and Supervision of staff.

As already explained, components analysis makes it possible to allocate separate scores to each case (i.e. in this situation a member of staff). We examined how staff scores varied by our standard list of variables. Women were more likely to have greater involvement than men in care planning and after-care. Care staff were more likely to be involved than managers and there were significant differences between local authorities on this component. There were some differences by local authorities on Order and Social Training and on the Administration and Supervision scores, on which managers, unsurprisingly, scored higher than others.

Training

Our next concern was with how far staff received training in different areas of work and how relevant this seemed to them (see Table 9.2). None of the items about which we asked had been totally neglected by trainers. The least well covered were first aid, young people leaving care, sexuality and health education for young people, were between a third and four in 10 staff had had no training at all. By contrast, items concerned with control, race/religion/culture, the Children Act and child protection were comparatively much better covered. As we will see later, young people were frequently worried about their health and relationships with their peers, and were commonly offered drugs. So training clearly reflected many of the concerns of Social Services departments but still had difficulty in covering important aspects of the young people's lives.

Job Descriptions

We were interested (see Table 9.3) in the degree to which the staff felt that they knew what was expected of them and felt that they would be supported provided that they followed the guidance given. Our questions elicited mixed, if generally positive, responses. Thus, whilst two-thirds of staff felt that they had been given a 'clear job description', and that the job was much as described, a similar proportion also felt that they were not given a 'thorough induction' training. Nearly four out of 10 or more felt that they had not been given clear guidance on touch, handling violence or discipline. Roughly half felt that the guidance given was not realistic,

Table 9.2 Amount of training received for different areas of work

	None (%)	Less than one week (%)	At least one week (%)
Controlling young people	18.9	53.5	27.6
Child protection	14.5	45.9	39.6
Issues of race, religion and culture	29.2	44.7	26.1
Dealing with sexuality	36.3	43.7	20.0
Health education for young people	36.1	47.3	16.7
Implications of HIV and AIDS	21.5	62.6	15.8
Communicating with young people	20.1	46.6	33.3
Health and safety at work	30.3	53.7	16.0
Fire precautions	23.9	63.0	13.1
First aid	43.6	37.8	18.6
Drugs	29.1	54.7	16.3
Young people leaving care	43.0	44.0	13.0
Children Act	11.7	48.0	40.3

Source: Questionnaire to staff.

although they generally trusted management to back them if they followed it. In their open-ended comments, staff at this point drew attention to the lack of both 'back-up' and resources:

Two staff on duty with four very vulnerable, damaged children who have enormous emotional needs, require 24 hour care, control and supervision makes meeting even basic needs very difficult. Commitment to things such as swimming clubs cannot be given, as one member of staff would be left with three volatile youngsters and responsibility for the establishment . . .

Staff teams should also be able to have more sanctions to enforce on young people, as the sanctions we are restricted to do not work.

Despite the above, 84% indicated that they 'knew how they were expected to do the job'. The main area of criticism was the large number of staff (75%) who disagreed with the statement that they 'had had the training they needed'. Written comments suggested that the perceived need for training reflected both the difficulty of the job and its low status:

Improved training structure for residential workers. Removal of CSS. The number of staff gaining a professional qualification is dropping all the time. There is going to be a vacuum in the very near future, as qualified staff leave the residential sector for fieldwork teams.

Residential work does not receive the recognition it deserves. We are at the hard end of social care, caring 24 hours a day, but little is put into training and

Table 9.3 Response to statements about job

Aspects of job	Strong disagreement (%)	Disagreement (%)	Agreement (%)	Strong agreement (%)
I received a clear job description	12.8	19.3	37.2	30.7
The job was pretty much as described to me	11.1	21.8	44.0	23.2
I was given thorough induction training	38.6	27.9	21.1	12.4
There is clear guidance on touching	13.8	25.9	27.3	33.0
There is clear guidance on restraining	18.7	17.0	26.7	37.7
There is clear guidance on handling violence	18.5	28.2	27.9	25.5
The expectations on disciplining residents are clear	11.2	33.6	30.5	24.7
The guidance to staff is realistic	17.9	32.1	35.9	14.1
I am kept abreast of changes to care plans	7.8	20.7	48.3	23.1
I know all I need to know about events when I am not on duty	6.1	19.7	50.8	23.4
If staff follow guidance management back them	7.5	19.0	44.5	29.0
I know how I am expected to do job	4.4	11.5	48.2	35.9
I have had all the training I need	24.7	50.3	2.10	4.0
I am satisfied with job	9.5	24.7	41.0	24.7

Source. Questionnaire to staff.

development of staff and many staff come in with little or no experience in residential work.

Component analysis suggested that the 14 items in Table 9.3 contained three underlying themes or components:

C1 Items that dealt with Training, Information and Support.
C2 The underlying theme to these items was a need for Clear Guidance and Procedures.
C3 Items that covered Clarity of Job Description and introduction to the job (Induction).

Female staff and those in managerial and supervisory posts tended to be more concerned than their counterparts about Training, Information and Support, and there were also differences by local authority in the amount of satisfaction expressed about it. Local authorities also differed significantly in their scores on Component 2 (Clear Guidance and Procedures). Differences on Component 3 (Job Description and Induction) were limited to the age breakdown, where those under 30 had higher scores on this component than those over 40. This would indicate that the younger members of staff, and presumably therefore those most recently in post, were more satisfied with their job description and introduction to the job than older ones. The differences between authorities and between long-serving and recent members of staff suggest that variations in policy were having an impact on the experience of staff.

Support and Consultation

Job descriptions and guidance are no doubt important but they are hardly substitutes for the day-to-day support and advice which staff give to each other. Tables 9.4 and 9.5 give the results of our questions in this area. About a third of the staff indicated that they talked about residents with social workers most days and a further 41% said they did this about once

Table 9.4 Sources of support and forms of consultation

Support and consultation	Most days (%)	About once a week (%)	About once a month (%)	Less often or never (%)
Formal staff meetings	3.7	50.7	33.3	12.3
Receive supervision from senior staff	0.7	4.0	58.9	36.4
Talk about residents with SW	30.3	41.0	18.0	10.7
Talk about residents with other professionals	11.3	23.0	32.7	33.0
Talk about residents with their relatives	13.8	35.2	28.5	22.5

Source: Questionnaire to staff.

Table 9.5 Sources of help in performing job

Help from	Very helpful (%)	Helpful (%)	Unhelpful (%)	Very unhelpful (%)	No contact (%)
Other care staff	63.1	34.2	2.0	—	0.7
Social workers	10.1	70.3	15.9	1.0	2.7
Other professionals	8.1	67.2	17.2	2.4	5.1
Parents	4.2	61.1	26.4	3.5	4.9
Staff meetings	45.5	43.8	5.7	1.0	4.0
Supervision sessions	49.7	32.3	7.0	1.7	9.4
Informal supervision	54.2	36.1	2.7	0.3	6.7
Formal consultations	27.0	51.1	6.7	—	15.2

Source: Questionnaire to staff.

a week. Staff meetings and contacts with parents were also quite frequent. A majority reported that such events were at least weekly. By contrast, supervision sessions with a senior member of staff generally took place on a monthly basis. For a third of the staff it was even less frequent.

The vast majority of staff felt they received most help and support from other care staff, and staff meetings, supervision sessions and informal supervision were all experienced as very helpful by around half the staff. Social workers, other professionals and parents were rarely experienced as providing equivalent support.

The vivid accounts of staff experience in Whitaker and her colleagues' work were echoed in the more neutral medium of the postal questionnaire. One member of staff was able to contrast his/her current and previous homes:

Having worked in an establishment that was undergoing major changes and had allegations floating around, I was very impressed when I started here by the way the team works as a team and are very consistent with their work.

The positive comment above was very different to the experience of another member of staff:

Senior staff have no regard for workers. Normality is a long way away in residential care . . . bullying, children being moved and not told, little control and no-one to approach . . .

Although the eight items factored neatly into two underlying themes (C1, Meetings and Supervision; C2, Individuals) further analyses based on the component scores failed to identify any significant differences by our independent variables.

Problems

We invited staff to tell us about areas of their work which concerned them
(Table 9.6). Our questions covered problems which the research outlined
at the beginning of this chapter had suggested might be important. Not
surprisingly most were seen as causing at least some concern to most of
those replying. The three items for which staff experienced the least problems were their 'relations with colleagues' (confirmation of what had
been found in the previous section); 'relations with senior staff'; and their
'relations with young people'. The areas that caused them the greatest
concern were the 'progress made by residents' and 'keeping order'.

*I enjoy my job very much but find the restrictions placed upon staff very frustrat-
ing, not for the staff's benefit but for the boy's. It is almost impossible to provide
any boundaries or to moderate anti-social behaviour, thus giving the boys a false
sense of how life will really be and not preparing them for the outside world.*

*People seem less aware of the extreme behaviour these youngsters exhibit. Work-
ing closely with such emotionally needy children is extremely intense.*

Further analyses indicate that four main components or themes appeared
to underlie the 13 individual items:

C1 Items that dealt with different aspects of the job such as money,
    security and career prospects—Job Security and Conditions.

Table 9.6 Response to possible problems with job

Problems	No concern (%)	Some concern (%)	Great concern (%)	Not applicable (%)
Impact on our family	21.6	52.8	21.3	4.3
Impact on social life	18.6	53.8	25.2	2.3
Relations with senior staff	53.5	35.5	9.0	2.0
Relations with colleagues	63.9	30.8	3.7	1.7
Keeping order	20.0	49.3	29.7	1.0
Residents' progress	7.7	54.4	36.9	1.0
Relations with young people	52.3	38.3	8.1	1.3
Money	37.3	44.7	16.7	1.3
Hours	28.6	45.2	25.2	1.0
Job security	29.6	43.9	24.9	1.7
Career prospects	22.7	46.7	26.0	4.7
Feelings of uselessness	27.4	47.5	24.1	1.0
Status	35.1	41.5	22.1	1.3

Source: Questionnaire to staff.

C2 Items that covered the feelings of staff about their Relations with Young People and their own sense of usefulness.
C3 Items that dealt with hours of work and the Effect of the Job on Family and Social Life.
C4 Items that reflected Relations with Colleagues.

Male staff and staff in the 31–40 ('mid-career') age group saw Job Security and Conditions as more of a problem than did others.

Staff Morale

We asked the staff how satisfied they were with their jobs and—a subtly different question—how satisfied they were with the job they were doing (for one can say that one has a good job but is not happy with the way it is working at the moment.) Both questions were answered on a four-point scale and not surprisingly the correlation between them was highly significant ($r = .71$, $p < .01$). So we created a measure of morale by adding the two together.

There were a number of 'objective' variables which distinguished staff with high and low morale. Staff tended to have low morale if they had worked for a relatively long time in residential work, and, disappointingly, in the homes in which they currently were, and if they were relatively highly qualified. In keeping with their aspirations they tended to have high morale if they rated their jobs as involving relatively high amounts of contact with families, social training, counselling and after-care. Interestingly, morale was also higher if they reported relatively frequent supervision sessions and relatively frequent formal staff meetings.

We found that a regression equation with four 'objective' variables explained just under 20% of the variation in morale. The variables were length of time in post, qualifications, frequent supervision, and a 'job factor' which roughly reflected the keyworker's role (i.e. it included relatively high involvement in care planning, contact with families, after-care, therapeutic work and acting as a key/primary worker). So on this analysis, the secret of having a contented staff group would be to ensure that they were relatively new to residential work, were not qualified, had frequent supervision, and took on keyworker roles.

We next examined how far staff scores on the components we have identified differed between homes, and how far these differences were reflected in and explained differences in morale. Briefly:

- There were very highly significant differences between the homes in the degree to which the respondents said that their jobs involved after-care and planning and in the degree to which they said they involved care and control.

- There were very highly significant differences between homes in the degree to which staff felt they had (a) adequate information and support, (b) clear guidance and procedures, (c) clear job descriptions and adequate induction.
- There were highly significant differences between homes in the degree to which staff found the various meetings helpful and to which they found the individuals they contacted helpful.
- There were significant to highly significant differences between homes on all the main components which dealt with problems connected with the job.

In short, the homes were, for some reason, far more highly associated with the components of care than any of the basic variables which we have so far discussed. It was not surprising, therefore, that the homes differed in average staff morale at a significance level beyond 1 in 10,000.

Not surprisingly, the various component scores relating to job problems and the clarity with which the job had been defined and supported were strongly related to morale. From a statistical point of view these scores 'explained' the variations in morale between homes. This, however, is hardly surprising since they reflect, for example, the degree to which staff felt they got on well with their colleagues.

A more interesting question was the degree to which morale in homes was influenced by aspects of the environment which could be influenced by policy or management. Table 9.7 lists a number of aspects of the home which were significantly associated with high morale. Some of these are probably best seen as embodying management practice. Others reflect interactions within the home (e.g. the degree to which staff relationships

Table 9.7   Correlates of high staff morale in homes

	r
Head 'empowered'	.37*
Head trained (CQSW/DipSW/CSS)	.37*
High proportion of qualified (CQSW/DipSW/CSS) staff	−.42**
High proportion of emergency admissions	−.31*
Average frequency of supervision	.43**
Staff relationships cohesive (interviewer rating)	.30*
Staff–resident relationships warm (interviewer rating)	.37*
High proportion of residents report attempted bullying	−.39**

* Significant at .05 level.
** Significant at .01 level.
Source: Head of home interview; Staff Log; Details of Home Questionnaire; interviewer ratings; and resident interview.

or the relationships with the young people were harmonious). It seems most likely that the relationship here is circular—high morale may tend to produce good relationships, but these in turn will tend to produce high morale.

Some of the associations in Table 9.7 are as might be expected. Common sense and the studies cited at the beginning of this chapter would all lead us to expect that staff morale would be higher in homes where staff got on with each other and the residents, and where there was little bullying. Berridge and Brodie (1998), Whitaker, Archer and Hicks (1998) and Baldwin (1990) all emphasise the negative impact of unwanted admissions and so the association of low morale and admissions is not surprising. Heads who feel that they have a clear, consistent and feasible remit (key elements in our measure of empowerment) should be able to provide leadership, so it was to be predicted that they were more likely to be in charge of high-morale homes. We have already noted that staff valued supervision and so homes where it occurred routinely (if rarely more frequently than once a month) were likely to have higher morale than others.

There are, however, some more surprising and disturbing aspects of Table 9.7 and about the variables which did not have a significant relationship with morale. Homes which had relatively high staff ratios did not have high morale—a fact which would seem to argue against overwork as a major cause of low morale. The finding that homes with qualified heads had on average lower morale is likely to be equally disturbing to authorities—most appoint a qualified head if at all possible—and to Sir William Utting, who has been a stalwart supporter of the need for qualifications in this field. Part of the explanation may be that training is a source of disagreements—homes with qualified heads were significantly less likely to be rated by our interviewers as having a cohesive staff. Moreover, qualified heads were associated with a relatively high proportion of qualified staff—a group who even if not in the majority may have stood for different ways of doing things. After allowing for this latter association, we found that the association between the qualification of the head and the low morale of the staff dropped below significance.

We used the information in Table 9.7 to try and explain variations in homes. We began with variables which reflected policy and practice and found that a regression equation which used empowerment, supervision and the training of the head produced a multiple correlation coefficient of .64. We then added information about the processes within the home (proportion bullied, staff agreement, and staff resident relationships). This changed the variables in the equation (which dropped to two—supervision and staff agreement) but left the size of the multiple regression unchanged.

CONCLUSION

Staff in this survey were pleased with many aspects of their jobs. This satisfaction was enhanced if they felt that they had a clear feasible role, good support from their colleagues and management, adequate money, security and job prospects, and that their work did not interfere too much with their family and social lives. It was also importantly connected with their feeling that the residents were making progress, and with difficulties or otherwise in maintaining order. This is in keeping with common sense and it supports—albeit less vividly and with less graphic detail—the conclusions of the studies quoted in the beginning.

The particular interest of this study lies in its identification of specific features of management and policy which appeared to enhance staff morale. In this respect, some of the findings reinforce conventional wisdom, whereas others run directly counter to it.

First, the study suggests that many staff want a more therapeutic role and one which involves contact with families and after care. Berridge and Brodie (1998) included in their measure of quality of care in homes, which they described as 'focus of staff concerns on narrower or wider issues'. By this they meant that staff in high quality homes kept sight of the objectives of their work with individuals and were not solely concerned with life in the establishment. Staff in this study agreed with this viewpoint. They expressed a desire for wider roles in the questionnaire. Those staff who had such roles had higher morale.

Secondly, the study suggests that heads who are empowered, as we defined the term, will find it easier to generate a cohesive staff group with high morale. This finding is in keeping with the favourable findings of early research on the effects of 'staff autonomy' in residential care (e.g. Heal and Cawson 1975; Tizard 1975). Moreover, it is easier for heads of home to provide leadership if they feel that they do not always have to seek agreement for their proposals from their management and that they are not likely to be undermined by a change in the home's function. On the other hand, enquiries into scandals in homes had typically criticised external management for its 'hands off' approach. This apparent conflict is an important issue. We will return to it later when we have to wrestle with similar findings over the apparent effect of empowerment on outcomes.

Third, the study suggests that staff morale will be higher if the head of home is either not qualified or, if qualified, does not recruit a relatively high proportion of qualified staff. This finding is disquieting. A possible explanation lies in the difficulty of ensuring a coherent approach when a qualified head and a proportion of qualified staff have been brought into a home where most staff are untrained. (The explanations that qualified staff were more likely where the intake was more difficult were not supported by our analyses.) A further explanation is that qualified staff were themselves more likely to have low morale than others—a finding which may stem from the incongruence between their training and the job they found themselves doing.

Despite the above, the staff in our study wanted more training but the implication may be that this should be provided in other ways than at present. More specifically, social work education should, perhaps, acquire a far heavier emphasis on group processes if it is to be used to qualify heads of homes. The paramount need for coherence suggests that staff doubts over the realism of much of the guidance and their lack of training in a wide variety of fields such as drugs and sexuality might be countered by training delivered on an in-home basis. Such training could provide a mechanism for the development of a joint approach.

Fourth, the study suggests that regular formal supervision is important to morale. This finding is in keeping with generally accepted views. There is little to say about it, except to urge that it take place.

In short this evidence suggests that social services who wish to produce high staff morale in their children's homes should:

- Enhance the status, job security and career prospects of the staff.
- Develop staff roles, including where possible after-care and work with families.
- Empower the heads (in the sense in which we have defined 'empower').
- Develop training which enhances rather than disrupts a common approach.
- Encourage regular formal supervision.

Issues for the Homes as Units

We have now finished our description of the homes or units. Most commonly these homes are multi-purpose, either by design or because of difficulties in refusing admissions or discharging residents. Compared with the establishments of earlier years, they are small, highly staffed and permissive and they have a rapid turnover. Such changes call, perhaps, for a new theory of residential care, and the heads of home have been developing one. Other staff are rarely qualified but broadly satisfied with their jobs, although they would like these to be expanded to include elements of after-care, and they expressed a variety of other concerns.

This broad-brush picture needs to be complemented by an emphasis on the diversity which exists. Homes vary sharply in the clarity of their aims, the resources devoted to them, the proportion of qualified staff, their formal and informal relationships with management, their permissiveness, the philosophies of their heads, and the morale of their staff. As described by our interviewers, and by social workers, staff and residents, they can also be very different places.

So does the way in which the homes are resourced and run have an impact on the resident world? If so, does the nature of this relationship reflect the ideas of official reports and the views of heads and staff? Before answering these questions, we need to go further into the residents' experience.

10

THE RESIDENTS' WORLD—OUTSIDE CONTACTS

INTRODUCTION

So far we have considered the purposes of our 48 homes and the way they were resourced, managed and run. The next three chapters consider the experience of the residents. We look first at their life outside the home, and in particular at their accounts of their work, school and leisure time and their relationships with family, social workers and friends. The chapter is partly descriptive—examining how far the common aspirations for school involvement and family contact were being met—and partly analytical—seeking clues on the ways in which purposes which everyone agrees are valuable might be accomplished.

WORK AND SCHOOL

After a few preliminaries we began the interview with the residents by asking whether they had left school and if not whether they were in school, suspended or excluded, or waiting to go to a new one. Overall, nearly half (49%) said that they were at school. Nearly a third (29%) had left school and the remaining fifth were—according to them—suspended or excluded (12%), or waiting for a new school (9%). So on their own account nearly a third (30% of those of school age were not at the time of the interview getting full-time education.

Absence from school is no doubt undesirable from the point of view of the young people but it also has a number of consequences for the homes. Young people who are not at school when they might be expected to be are a management problem. They get in the way of the staff who want to be getting on with other things, set an undesirable precedent, and frequently go to bed late, thus causing difficulties at the other end of the day as well. In addition, they pose an awkward dilemma. Should they be rewarded for not going to school by being given an interesting programme, or should they be left to their own devices, which may involve mischief?

Current research by Isabelle Brodie (Brodie and Berridge 1996) has emphasised the imprecision with which terms such as 'suspension' or 'exclusion' are used in real life. A young person who is not going to school may be variously seem as excluded, suspended, absent without leave or waiting for some definite plan to be made. Different professionals (teachers, head teachers, residential staff, social workers and so on) may well have very different ideas on the formal status of what is going on. The reality, however, is simply that the young person is not going to school, and our own research suggested that it is this difference between those who are going to school and those who are not that is important. Briefly, variables such as the social workers' judgements or 'adjustment' or of 'involvement in school' did not distinguish between those waiting to go to school and those suspended or excluded from one. There were, however, very significant differences between those who were not at school and those who were.

Table 10.1 sets out the proportions of young people in the different authorities who were of school age and either at school or not. As can be seen, the differences were very large and very highly significant, varying from 14% in Area 4 to 54% in Area 2. These variations suggest that it is possible for education and social services to 'get their act together' and reduce the numbers of those in care who are not in school, but some do this to a greater extent than others. Given the importance of this subject, we looked at other variables likely to be associated with not being in school to see if they might explain the variations between authorities.

Briefly, male residents were much more likely than female ones not to be in school (39% and 18%); and those who were admitted for reasons

Table 10.1 Whether resident of school age at school or not—by area

	(n)	At school (%)	Excluded/ suspended (%)	Waiting for new school (%)
Area 1	37	78.4	10.8	10.8
Area 2	28	46.4	39.3	14.3
Area 3	26	65.4	23.1	11.5
Area 4	41	85.4	9.8	4.9
Area 5	24	62.5	8.3	29.2
Totals	156	69.9	17.3	12.8

Differences significant at .003 level.
Source: Resident interview.

connected with family breakdown or 'trouble outside the home' were more likely to be in this category (36% and 42%) than those we have described as 'victims' or 'other reasons' (21% and 0%). The proportions of females did not differ significantly by area but the proportions entering for different reasons did. A test which took this variable into account still showed a significant effect of authority on proportions in school even though the significance was lower ($p < .03$).

Another possibility was that the low proportion of young people in school in Area 2 might reflect the difficulty the interviewer had in obtaining a sample. The county is large and it was not uncommon for her to make a round trip of 100 miles but fail to find a resident in. She might therefore have picked up an unusually high number of young people who were not at school simply because they were more likely to be around during the day. Examination of the data on residents in the home in the past year suggested that this might be the explanation. According to the heads of homes, Area 2 did not contain an unusually high proportion of residents who were not in school.

However, the data provided by heads of homes still supported the idea that Area 4 might be doing unusually well in terms of school attendance. Among the residents who had left (and who on average spent only a brief time in the homes) Area 4 had a higher proportion of exclusion or suspensions than any other area. Among those who were still there (and who had on average spent much longer in the homes), Area 4 had the lowest proportion of suspensions or exclusions. This suggested that the longer a resident in Area 4 stayed, the better her/she did in comparison with other areas in terms of being at school. This effect (an interaction between length of stay, area and being at school) was very highly significant ($p < .0001$). Strictly speaking, this could be the result of selection rather than of good practice: Area 4 could have just decided to discharge anyone not at school earlier. We feel, however, that good practice is the more likely explanation. Area 4 did in fact have a specialised team of teachers attached to the department and responsible, among other things, for trying to reintegrate young people in mainstream education. So we have evidence of their success.

Similar but less conclusive evidence was available at the level of the home. The proportions of residents of school age who had been in the home over the past year and who were said by the heads to have been excluded or suspended from school varied from one (in four homes) to 92%. This proportion correlated significantly ($r = .41$, $p < .01$) with our measure of the degree to which the head of home had thought through the means for getting the young people back to school.

This analysis made no allowance for the fact that the homes were likely to have varied in the proportions of young people who came in when they were already suspended or excluded. Moreover, some homes kept their residents longer, increasing both their chance of getting them back to school and the chance that some residents would become excluded or suspended while in the home. We did, however, analyse our interview data after omitting those who said that they were excluded or suspended before arrival. This showed that the proportions not at school varied from 15% in homes where we had given the heads one of the two highest ratings to 33% in homes where we had given one of the two lowest ratings. Young people in the first category of homes were more likely (although not significantly so) to say that they had been helped over difficulties at school and significantly more likely to say that they had been helped with planning for education or work. So it seems likely that some heads were having an effect.

We asked those who were still at school whether this was the same as the one to which they had gone before coming to the home. The reason for this question was the evidence (Berridge and Cleaver 1987; Bullock *et al.* 1993b) that entry to 'care' is easier and return home less stressful if it is not accompanied by a change of school. In our sample, just over half (56%) of those in school had remained in the same one. On the whole they were pleased about this; only a quarter said that they would have preferred to have changed. But then, those who changed were equally satisfied: only a quarter said that they would rather have stayed where they were. If other things are equal, it is no doubt important that young people remain in the same school. However, they may not be getting on there, and if so they may be better off in a new one.

We next asked those at school whether they were proud of something they did there. This was one of a number of similar questions asked because they appeared relevant to the development of self-esteem. Nearly three-quarters of those at school said 'yes' to this question, and those doing so were on average judged by their social worker as significantly better-adjusted. They were also much more likely to say they were enjoying their time at school. Predictably, perhaps, only a quarter of those who had something of which to be proud mentioned an academic subject on its own. Others instanced sport, art and music, practical activities such as carpentry or a combination of different activities.

To judge from their answers to us, most of the young people (62%) who were actually there enjoyed school and a further one in seven enjoyed it very much. Only a quarter said they disliked it or disliked it a lot. These figures, however, varied sharply by age. Six per cent of those under 12, a quarter of those aged 13 or 14, and just over a third of those aged 15 or over said they were not enjoying school. Overall disaffection with school was widespread. Just over half those of school age said that they were either not at school or were not enjoying it if they were.

Of those who said they were excluded or suspended, about half said that this had occurred before their arrival at the home, and half that it was five months or more since they were last at school (the average was around eight). Less than four in 10 of this group said that they were receiving any form of education (e.g. a visiting tutor) and for those that were the input did not seem heavy. A quarter of this small number said they were getting 20 hours' teaching per week, but four out of 10 said they were getting five hours per week or less. They were less likely than their peers at school to think of anything they were doing in the home of which they were proud and they were less likely to say that they were enjoying the time which might have been spent at school.

Those at Work, on Youth Training or Unemployed

Thirty per cent of the sample were of working age. Their introduction to work, however, had not generally been very encouraging. Only one in seven said that they were actually in a paid job. Just over a third (35%) were on some form of Youth Training (YT). The remainder said that they were unemployed. The likelihood of unemployment varied by authority—from 75% in one authority to just 23% in another but, in contrast to the situation with education, there was no evidence that it related to the degree to which the head had thought out the means for getting the young people into work (most heads were, it will be remembered, pessimistic about the success they achieved in this respect).

Work and to a lesser extent YT seemed a very important element in their self-respect and quality of life. All the small group who were working said they enjoyed their time there, as did eight out of 10 of those who were on YT. By contrast, almost half the remainder said they were not enjoying themselves during the time when they might have been out at work. The question of whether they did anything they were proud of during this period produced similar answers (see Table 10.2).

Table 10.2   Liking of current employment status

	Working		Youth training		Unemployed	
	(*n*)	(%)	(*n*)	(%)	(*n*)	(%)
Dislike it a lot	—	—	2	11.8	4	12.9
Dislike it	—	—	1	5.9	11	35.5
Like it	6	85.7	8	47.0	15	48.4
Like it a lot	1	14.3	6	35.3	1	3.2
Totals	7	100.0	17	100.0	31	100.0

Source: Resident interview.

LEISURE

If school and work were somewhat dubious sources of self-respect (if only because so many did not take part in them) were the young people able to define themselves around their leisure activities?

We asked them what kinds of things they enjoyed doing, and then how they enjoyed their leisure time. A majority (58%) said that they did so most of the time and all but four that they did so at least some of the time. Young people who said that they mostly enjoyed their leisure time were more likely to say that they were proud of some leisure-time activity. Such pride was significantly more common among young male residents, residents under the age of 12 and those who entered the care system as 'victims'. The most common source of pride was sport (including swimming), but other leisure activities and hobbies were also mentioned. The numbers were small but it was interesting that young people in work or on YT were significantly more likely to say that they were proud of some leisure activity than those who were unemployed (58% of them did so, as against 27% of the others). This association could reflect the gloom with which those out of work regarded other aspects of their lives, the greater leisure opportunities brought by some limited finance, or the greater employability of those who take pride in something.

Whatever the explanation, the evidence supports the need to look at all aspects of a resident's life, including school, leisure and work in order to encourage and support those things in which he/she can take a legitimate pride.

FRIENDS

We asked the young people about their friends. These have been somewhat neglected in studies of 'care'. Such evidence as exists suggests that friends between peers within the home are likely to be somewhat superficial (Whitaker et al. 1985). Yet friendships or sexual relationships with young people of their own age (although not necessarily in the home) are likely to be of great significance to many residents. Understanding of this topic would benefit from sensitive interviews with a small sample. Our own approach has been necessarily more broad-brush but does allow us to examine the association between answers to questions about friends and other aspects of the data (e.g. our measures of subjective well-being).

Four out of 10 of the residents said that by entering the home they had lost touch with at least one 'important' friend. By way of compensation, just over half said that they had a particular friend or group of friends with whom they went around at the home and only a third were prepared to say unequivocally that they did not. Rather similarly, six out of 10 said they had enough friends, only one in 10 said they were definitely lonely and one in 10 said they were a 'bit of both'. As we will see later, homes differed very markedly in the degree to which they were perceived as friendly and this had to do with the characteristics of the home itself.

Loneliness (in the sense of clearly not having enough friends) was associated both with having lost touch with someone important and with not going around with particular friends. Loss of a friend and lack of current friends were not, however, associated. Perhaps loneliness in the young is like loneliness in the old—the same word is used to cover two different things—the desolation of losing someone particular and a lack of sociable contact.

FAMILY

Relationships with family have long been the centrepiece of policy, practice and research relating to 'care'. Fashions, however, have changed. Prior to the war, families were generally held to be bad for children in care, and contact was discouraged or forbidden. In any case, contact was usually difficult for the children and young people, who were often placed with foster parents a long way from their home or in large, inaccessible institutions. Things have changed. Mass evacuation during the war, the work and films of Bowlby and the Robertsons, the advent of the new Children's Departments, and the work of more recent researchers, such as Aldgate and Millham and his colleagues, have all emphasised the importance of maintaining contact between children and their parents (see Bowlby 1953; Aldgate 1980; Millham et al. 1986). The costs of 'care' (even foster care) are a sharp encouragement to treasurers to note the virtues of rehabilitation, and hence of the contact between parents and children on which rehabilitation can be built. Prevention, family contact in 'care' and rehabilitation are among the centrepieces of the Children Act 1989 and its accompanying guidance.

In this long march to rehabilitation there has, however, been the occasional detour or even retreat. Evidence from large-scale longitudinal studies has emphasised the benefits brought by early or even later adoption (e.g. Kadushin 1970; Maughan and Pickles 1990; Rathburn, Di Virgilio and Waldfogel 1958; Tizard 1977). Studies of high risk groups of young children (e.g. those believed to have been physically abused or those in residential nurseries) have likewise raised the possibility that these do better on a number of measures if they do not go back to their families (Hensey, Williams and Rosenbloom 1983; King and Taitz 1985; Tizard 1977). Adolescent girls in 'care' from 'discordant' homes appear to do best if they do not return to them (Quinton and Rutter 1984); there is evidence that adolescent boys from 'bad' families may be less delinquent if they are away from home (Minty 1987; Sinclair 1971, 1975); so the benefits of family visits to those in 'care' may reflect the mutual desire of parents and children to see each other, rather than the effects of visiting *per se*. More influential than these academic and largely ignored rumblings has been the impact of child abuse scandals, the discovery of 'drift' in 'care' and its corresponding financial and emotional costs, the emotions raised by 'tug-of-love' scandals, and the rhetoric of the permanence movement. The impact of these factors probably reached its high point in the mid-1970s, but the careful crafting of the Children Act allows social workers to reflect these concerns where appropriate.

Our own contribution to this political minefield lies partly in the fact that we have asked the young people what they wanted. That we have done so may appear naïve. These are painful issues. It is hard for young people to know what they feel about them themselves, and certainly hard for them to get across the complexity of their feelings in response to a standard question from a stranger. Nevertheless, we feel that the answers we reported in an earlier chapter—to wit that most residents want contact with their families on leaving care but not a return home—represent an interesting and certainly more sophisticated response to the issue of 'rehabilitation vs. permanence' than many given in professional debates. What then do the young people want by way of contact with their families while they are in 'care'?

We approached this question by asking the residents who was in their family. Subjectively, 'families' may correspond relatively little to the way they are defined for the purposes of censuses, income tax returns, birth certificates and contacts with social security. Grandparents, cousins, foster parents, unrelated 'uncles' and others may all feature in the family as a young person defines it, while natural fathers or even natural mothers may not feature at all. Moreover, within the family the young person may want contact with some individuals but not with others.

We grouped the residents' replies according to whether they referred to 'one family' (17%), 'one family with significant others' (10%), 'split (two-site) family' (38%), and 'split family with significant others' (32%). Only 4% could not be categorised in this way.

Only 5% of lone parent families were classified as 'single families', a further 7% were seen as 'single families with significant others' and the great majority (86%) of them were classified as 'split families' with or without significant others. Overall, 'significant others' were least likely to be involved when there were two birth parents living (as we believed) together.

Once the interviewers had established who was in the residents' families, they went on to ask how often the residents had contact with one or more of their parents. In a third of cases this turned out to be frequently (more than once a week). In a further quarter it was once a week. Around a fifth had contact on a two-weekly to monthly basis and a further fifth either had no contact (17%) or no 'family' (3%).

The frequency of contact was very strongly associated with sex and family composition. Over two-thirds of male residents but only just over a third of female ones had weekly or more frequent contact ($p < .001$); over 70% of those living with lone parents, as against 57% of those living with two parents, 50% of those with step-parents, and 41% of those with 'other' arrangements, had such frequent contact ($p < .01$). It seems likely that this situation reflected the young persons' wishes or interests. Situations which carried the risk or flavour of sexual abuse may have been avoided by female residents; those which raised issues of divided loyalty by all.

Contact with siblings was also frequent for those who had them. Just over a third said they saw them more than weekly and a further quarter (23% or so) at least weekly. Just under a fifth never saw their siblings and the remainder did so at intervals varying between once every two weeks and once a month. Frequency varied by household composition. Weekly contact was still most likely in the case of lone parent families, but it was next highest in step-families, rather than when two birth parents were living together. Parental separation may perhaps bring siblings together, as well as making for difficulties between them and their step-parent. Contact with siblings was also less likely when the young person had entered as a 'victim', perhaps because he/she was sometimes a victim of a sibling, or because other siblings blamed the young person for his/her role in the family misfortunes.

Interestingly, contact was *not* related to care career as we measured it. So there was no evidence that those who had been in care longer or who were in the home for a long-term placement had less frequent contact than others. This is encouraging, and contrary to what we had expected on the basis of other research (Millham *et al.* 1986).

We asked the residents whether they saw their families as much as they wanted, too much or not enough. In response to this rather crude question, only four said 'too much' and for the purposes of analysis we have grouped them with those who saw as much as they wanted. Sixty-two per cent of the sample fell into this last category, while just over a third (36%) said they did not see their families enough.

The frequency with which residents reported seeing their parents or siblings was only weakly related to whether they felt that they saw enough of their families. Indeed, in the case of contact with parents, the relationship was not even significant. There were, however, significant relationships with authority, reason for entering 'care', and age. Satisfaction with contact rose steadily with age (from 46% satisfied among the under-12s to 77% among the 16-or-overs). Older residents may wish to see their parents less and be better able to arrange contact when they want it. 'Victims' were particularly likely to want more contact than they received.

There was also some variation by authority, and perhaps by home. Whereas in two authorities around three-quarters of the residents were satisfied, the proportion in two others fell to around a half. Residents in homes where the heads received one of the two lowest ratings for having thought through the means for fostering family ties were twice as likely not to be satisfied with contact as those in other homes, but the numbers were too small to reach significance.

We wanted to go rather more deeply into this question and find out whom it was that the residents wanted to see more of (see Table 10.3). The replies supported some familiar messages. Contacts with siblings were particularly missed—half the sample would have liked to see more of at least one brother or sister. Mothers, fathers, grandparents and friends were also commonly missed. Around a third would have liked to see more of their mothers and the percentages were similar for the other roles just mentioned. A fifth would have liked to see more of another relative, and small but important minorities would have liked to see more of former foster parents, step-parents and other significant individuals. Only a quarter of the sample did not identify anyone of whom they wished to see more and on average the residents identified 2.3 such individuals. Any lingering presumption that family contact should mean contact with mother only should clearly be abandoned.

As can be seen from Table 10.3, we also asked the residents whether there was anyone of whom they would rather see less. A quarter said that

Table 10.3 People residents would like more or less contact with

	More contact		Less contact	
	(*n*)	(%)	(*n*)	(%)
Mother	81	36.3	19	8.5
Father	70	31.4	16	7.2
Step-parent	25	11.2	19	8.5
Grandparents	79	35.4	5	2.2
Brothers/sisters	114	51.1	6	2.7
Other relatives	48	21.5	3	1.3
Friends	64	28.7	3	1.3
Foster parents	18	8.1	1	0.4
Other	13	5.8	5	2.2

Note: The percentages do not add up to 100 as residents were able to indicate as many people as they wished.
Source: Resident interview.

there was. Mothers, fathers, and step-parents figured about equally in this list, a reminder that contact with relatives is not an unambiguous good.

In the penultimate question in this part of the questionnaire, we asked the residents whether Social Services had encouraged or discouraged family contact. In about half the cases the department was seen as having encouraged contact. In a small minority of cases it appeared to have discouraged contact either completely (3%) or in relation to certain individuals (8%). In a quarter of cases it was seen as neutral, neither encouraging nor discouraging, and there was a range of 'other' responses (10%).

Encouragement was associated with the area in which the young person had been placed in a home and (very strongly) with the purpose of their placement. In Areas 3 and 4, the two where residents reported the least satisfaction with their levels of contact, the departments were seen as having encouraged family contact in only around a third of cases. This proportion rose to a half in Area 1 and around two-thirds in Areas 2 and 5. Only 16% of those whose placement was for a long-term purpose believed that they had been encouraged to have family contact, as against 66% of those placed for treatment and half those placed for short-term purposes (a finding more in keeping with what we had expected than with the lack of association between time looked after and contact).

Finally we asked whether, in the context of the young person's wishes, the department had been helpful or unhelpful over contact. In just over half the cases the young person said it had been helpful, in just over a fifth that it had been unhelpful, and in just over a quarter that it had been neither. Encouragement was much more likely to be seen as helpful than the lack of it. However, contrary to what we now expected, departments did not differ significantly in how far they were seen as helpful (although the two areas with the least family contact did have higher proportions of young people who saw them as 'unhelpful'). Female residents were more likely to see the department as being unhelpful than male ones and those placed long-term or because they were 'victims' were also more likely to see the department as unhelpful (although these associations did not reach significance). Again, therefore, we have the finding that most young people want contact with their families even if they do not necessarily want to return home to live.

SOCIAL WORKERS

We asked the young people whether they had a social worker. All but seven said they had and of these five came from Area 4, which was under particularly heavy pressure. Mostly they said they got on with them.

Only one in 10 said that they got on 'not at all well', and a further one in six that they got on 'not very well'. By contrast, a quarter said they got on 'extremely well' and nearly half that they did so 'moderately well'. Satisfaction was not related to frequency of contact with either the young person or the family, as recorded by the social worker. Neither was it related to the 'harder' variables we examined (age, sex, authority and so on). It was, however, related to our measure of the activities that the social worker undertook on the young person's behalf—specifically, our measure of the number of activities undertaken, and a subsidiary measure of the amount of work undertaken with the family.

So the message seems to be that the young people value help in contacting their families, and work with the families by the social worker on their behalf. They do not value contact with the social worker *per se*.

CONCLUSION

School, work and leisure were all potential sources of pride and self-esteem for the young people. The majority of those participating in them found them enjoyable and were proud of at least some activity connected with them. It was unfortunate, therefore, that at the time of the interview nearly a third of those of school age were not at school and six out of 10 of those who had left school were neither employed nor receiving training.

As others have repeatedly found, contacts with families were also important and frequent although a third of the residents would have liked them to be more frequent still. The study again illustrated the complexity of the families from which the young people came, and the variety of relatives and friends with whom they would have liked contact. In keeping with American research (Zimmerman 1982), siblings topped the list of those of whom they would like to have seen more but parents, grandparents, other relatives and friends were also prominent. By contrast, however, a quarter of the sample mentioned someone of whom they would have liked to have seen less.

Social workers were also important to a minority of the young people. Contrary to our expectation, appreciation was not related to frequency of contact, but it was related to a measure of the different activities which the social workers reported themselves as undertaking and particularly to work with families.

As foreshadowed in the introduction to this chapter these findings do not contradict the received wisdom about the importance of schools or families. They may, however, elaborate them. A number of points can be made:

- On our evidence authorities and probably heads of homes can affect school attendance both by special schemes involving teachers seconded to the authority and through the thought-out policy of the head of home.
- A number of the young people wanted to change schools or were happy that they had done so. The policy of enabling residents to remain at their former schools has advantages but should not be followed uncritically.
- There was widespread disaffection with school. Around 50% were either not there (30%) or not enjoying it. The length of time for which the young people had not been at school, their age, and the very limited efforts that seemed to be made to enable them to catch up suggest that not too much can be hoped for, simply through a policy of getting the older adolescents back to school. If the intention is to help their future careers, they will require very serious help when they are there.
- Young people who were proud of something connected with their leisure were more likely to get work, although the causation may be varied. Every effort should be made to encourage any activity in which the young people can take a legitimate pride.
- The policy of encouraging family contact is clearly right but again, professionals need to be alert to the diversity of contacts which the young people seek and to the fact that some family contacts are not welcome.

11

THE RESIDENTS' WORLD—AMENITIES AND SOCIAL CLIMATE

INTRODUCTION

In the course of this book we have described the context of the home—the events which led up to the placement, the plans for what will follow and the social life (including work, education and family relationships) which surround it. We turn now to the residents' experience of the home itself. This chapter deals with the residents' general reactions to the home, their views of its regime and their relationship with the staff.

As already pointed out, early research (e.g. Tizard, Sinclair and Clarke 1975) documented major variations between homes on a great range of dimensions. Recent studies (Berridge and Brodie 1998; Brown *et al.* 1996), together with the data presented in this book, suggest that current children's homes are at least as varied. However, if we are to understand the causes of this variety we need first to describe and measure it. Against this background, the general aim of this chapter is to become more precise about the dimensions along which the residents evaluate their experiences and to develop measures which distinguish between homes.

GENERAL REACTIONS

We began our exploration of the young people's views by asking them whether they had been in any other children's home or foster home. Our idea was to see whether they had a standard of comparison. It turned out that only around a fifth (18%) had no other experience of the care system. Four in 10 had had experience of both forms of 'care' and the remaining two-fifths were evenly divided between those who had been in foster care only and those who had only been in residential care.

We then asked those who had been in foster care whether this had been better or worse than their current home. Around half (48%) said the current home was better and just over a quarter (28%) that it was worse. The remaining quarter said that it was either about the same (15%) or better in some cases and worse in others. As the young people were only likely to enter our sample from foster care if the latter had broken down, these opinions of foster care are likely to be much more negative than we would have obtained from a sample which was not biased in this way. Any fair comparison between foster care and residential care would need to take into account the very considerable variations in the quality of practice which exists in both sectors. Nevertheless, as already pointed out, it is important to recognise that for some young people residential care is clearly preferable.

We asked the young people why they preferred foster care or residential care, as the case might be, and their answers reflected the dimensions along which they evaluated these provisions. A quarter raised issues around rules and expectations (generally favouring a liberal approach); around a sixth mentioned the other young people (as either enhancing or diminishing their lives); between a seventh and a sixth mentioned the 'amenities' (particularly privacy or the lack of it), one in 10 mentioned relationships with adults, a small group (around one in 25) mentioned closeness to home, one in five gave a combination of these reasons, and one in eight gave a reply we found difficult to classify. Some examples may give the flavour of their replies:

More comfy and friendly—the staff are brilliant.

My foster mum was a bitch, I couldn't talk to her. She was dead tight, wouldn't give us the bus money to go and see my granddads.

Didn't get on with my foster mum—staff here are right easy to get on with.

People round my age in here. It's like living at home—like a family. When I was in the foster home I felt I was invading their home. Here I can do what I like.

There's never enough transport around here, we're not allowed to share the transport with other units—nor go on mixed unit trips.

In the foster home I had more privacy and could do my own thing.

They were more caring in the foster home and have got more time for you.

So foster homes can offer more privacy and more personal attention. But failure to get on with one of the adults there is much more serious than in a children's home, where there are more adults around, the young people may be tantalised by being part and yet not part of a family, and there may be no others of their own age with whom they can do 'their own thing'.

Around a quarter of those who had previously been in residential care had been in the same home. The majority of these, however, had also had experience of other homes—an issue which helped us in our desire to make comparisons but raises the issue of why those who had preferred these other homes had not been able to remain there.

The comparisons made by this group gave a very similar picture to that given by the earlier question on fostering. Half thought their present home was better, a fifth that it was worse and the remainder were evenly divided between those who said it was the same and those who said it was better than some and worse than others.

The reasons given were also similar. The key dimensions along which comparisons were made were once again the other residents (referred to by more than a third), the staff (referred to by more than a fifth), the rules (referred to by more than a sixth), the amenities and outings (referred to by more than one in nine) and—a new concern—the size and state of the home (referred to by one in 10). Some quotations may again serve to make clear the kind of thing the residents had in mind:

The homes are all the same, it's the staff that are different.

More homely here, you're able to make cups of tea. More choice in general and less strict atmosphere.

Staff here are better, more understanding, they join in the games and that. Girls are nicer to you too.

My last place was a smaller children's home—about seven kids—and I didn't get bullied.

The picture of the dimensions along which residents evaluated their placements remained essentially unchanged by the last two questions we asked in this part of the interview. These were simply what were the best and worst parts of their current home.

In terms of the best bits, the highest proportion of votes went to the staff (almost a third, not counting those who gave a number of reasons). A disturbing 11% could see nothing good about the home at all but the remainder gave the by now familiar list of reasons referring in proportions of around 10% to the other young people, the relaxed regime and, in around a fifth of the cases, to the amenities and outings.

Staff who are available to talk to you about your problems. Staff allow you to do what you want within the rules.

Staff are brill; get on with the girls really well.

If one resident wasn't here I would get on better with all the other residents and staff. Otherwise they (staff) have been helpful with clothing allowance and pocket money. I've also got my own space and freedom and my own room.

Staff take care and sit down and talk to you like an adult.

An encouraging fifth of the residents could see nothing bad about the home at all. The strictness or inconsistency of the rules were the focus of complaint for around a fifth of the residents and a further fifth complained of bullying and vandalism. The only other sizeable identifiable category concerned dissatisfaction with individual members of staff (found in 8% of the sample).

Not too much should be made of the percentages we give above. This is partly because they were in some cases underestimated because we used a category 'combination of responses'. More importantly, they were responses to open-ended questions and reflect the dimensions which were salient to the young person and which the interviewer chose to record. It may be assumed, for example, that all residents would prefer a place where they got on with the staff. The fact that they did not mention this in their answers may simply reflect the fact that they did get on well with the staff and wished to comment on some other aspect of their environment (e.g. bullying).

In general, therefore, the residents seemed to want what most people in their position would want—a home which was not vandalised or run down, where residents and staff got on, where there were adequate amenities and interesting things to do, and where the regime was relaxed and consistent, but also kept bullying and vandalism in check.

We turn next to some of our more detailed questions which bear on whether the homes were of this kind.

STAFF RELATIONSHIPS, REGIME AND AMENITIES

Relationships with Staff

The residents were asked to say how they got on with the care staff, the head of home and their keyworker. They were given three choices over their replies 'very well' 'so-so' and 'not at all'. Table 11.1 sets out their replies. As can be seen, very few said they got on 'not very well' to this question and in each case the majority thought they got on 'very well'.

Answers to the three questions tended to follow the same pattern for each resident and for this reason we decided to add them to form a 'pro-

Table 11.1   Getting on with staff

	Care staff (%)	Head of home (%)	Keyworker (%)
Very well	55.6	60.4	65.8
So so	40.8	28.8	22.4
Not very well	3.6	10.8	6.8

Source: Resident interview.

staff' score. This score proved to be unrelated to the standard variables (age, sex and so on) which we have been using or to measures of adjustment taken from the social workers' ratings. The score did, however, distinguish quite sharply between homes. Some homes scored on average much 'better' than others. As far as we could tell, this variation was not explained by variations in intake and the differences were statistically highly significant.

Amenities and Regime

We asked the residents how happy they were with various aspects of the regime. We chose these on the basis of earlier consumer research (particularly Fletcher 1993) and we asked the residents to rate how happy they were about each. As can be seen from Table 11.2, there was

Table 11.2   Residents' happiness with various aspects of living in the home

	Very unhappy (%)	Unhappy (%)	Happy (%)	Very happy (%)
Amount of privacy	13.0	14.8	54.7	17.5
Amount of choice over clothes, hairstyles, etc.	3.1	14.8	56.5	25.6
Inviting friends to home	12.5	26.5	50.2	10.8
Police checks on people you stay with	26.5	30.0	41.7	1.8
Rules and routines	17.1	30.9	44.4	7.6
Behaviour of other residents	13.5	35.4	49.3	1.8
The accommodation	8.2	16.1	59.6	16.1
The food	13.5	13.5	50.2	23.0
Arrangements for seeing family	7.6	14.3	58.8	19.3
Pocket money	16.1	24.7	48.4	10.8
Punishments	15.7	21.5	57.4	5.4
Outings/activities	3.1	14.8	52.5	29.6
Number of residents who come and go	3.1	14.4	77.6	4.9
Young people coming into home who are not residents	6.3	17.9	71.7	4.1

Source: Resident interview.

considerable variation in the proportion of young people who found different aspects of the regime unsatisfactory.

Half or more of the sample were unhappy about police checks, about the behaviour of other residents and about the rules and routines. These are among the almost inevitable 'pains' of care, although they may vary in severity. Homes may be more or less liberal, and their residents more or less friendly but there are inevitable disadvantages to living in a small institution, where the company is chosen for you and those in charge need to check up on the company you keep.

Somewhat fewer—about four in 10—were unhappy about the pocket money arrangements, the difficulty of having friends to the home, and the punishments. Satisfaction with two of these aspects of home life— punishments and pocket money—varied very significantly with age. Residents under 12 complained most about the punishments (perhaps because they were most often on the receiving end of them) and least about the pocket money (perhaps because it was geared to an older age range and so, in their eyes, generous).

Food, privacy and accommodation apparently troubled around a quarter of the residents, although by the same token three-quarters said they were happy or very happy with these aspects of residential life.

The highest level of satisfaction was with the outings and activities, the turnover of residents (which is presumably to say that most did not find this a major problem) and with children coming to the home who were not residents.

In general, residents who said they were happy about one aspect of a regime were more likely to say they were happy about other aspects. This suggested that the items could be added to form a simple scale of 'regime satisfaction'. The usual test for the reliability of such a scale relies on a statistic known as 'Cronbach's alpha' (α). The acceptable level for this measure depends on the purpose for which the scale is to be used. If it is intended to measure a quantity (e.g. 'intelligence') precisely, a value of greater than 0.8 is desirable. If the intention is to study the association between underlying dimensions (e.g. to see if 'intelligent' students get higher incomes in later life) a lower value is acceptable. In this case the value was 0.81, and so the scale seemed satisfactory for any purpose.

This measure of satisfaction suggested that residents were more satisfied with their care in some authorities than in others ($p < .05$). However, it did not differ significantly by age, sex, reason for admission or any of the variables concerned with care career which we have been discussing. The major difference was again by home, with the average level of satisfaction significantly higher in some homes than in others ($p < .03$).

SOCIAL CLIMATE OF THE HOME

A possible explanation for the variations between homes is that they depend on what we called the 'social climate' of the home. Our concept of social climate was taken from work by Heal and his colleagues (1973), who in turn took it from work by Moos (Moos 1968; Moos and Houts 1968). Basically the concept was concerned with resident perceptions of the way residents, staff and, to a lesser extent, visiting families treated each other within the home. Our hypothesis was that these perceptions would partly reflect factors special to the resident (e.g. their 'personality' or their particular friendships) and partly some common understanding among the residents of the way the home operated. By averaging responses between residents we would therefore be able to arrive at a picture of these shared understandings.

Operationally, we tried to assess social climate by means of a set of simple statements, for example, 'this home is a friendly place'. Both residents and staff were asked to say whether the statement was true, sometimes true, or not true. There were 29 of these statements but they were intended to tap a smaller number of conceptually distinct areas. These were:

- *Support from staff:* the degree to which residents felt that staff were committed to supporting them.
- *Staff expectations:* the degree to which residents felt that staff were consistent in their expectations which were that they should work hard and do well.
- *Staff strictness:* the degree to which residents felt that the staff were strict and prepared to use punishment.
- *Support from residents:* the degree to which residents felt that others were friendly and supportive.
- *Resident involvement:* the degree to which residents felt they had rights and were involved in the running of the home.
- *Resident behaviour:* the degree to which residents perceived others as involved in drug taking, bullying or fights.
- *Resident morale:* the degree to which residents were proud of the home and felt that being there was worthwhile.

In addition, there were questions about the treatment of 'black and ethnic minority' residents (frequently not applicable because there were none in the home) and about homework which were inapplicable to those not in school. Appendix C discusses the results in relation to black and ethnic minority residents.

We wanted measures which could be used with both residents and staff who were asked the same questions. We therefore developed the measures using the answers from the staff questionnaire. To do this we grouped the questions under the conceptual headings given above and then used Cronbach's alpha (α) to see if we could obtain a reasonable level of reliability. If we failed to do this, we dropped the questions which were least closely associated with the others and tested the scale again. We then applied the resulting scales to data from the resident interviews.

The following tables include data from both the staff and resident questionnaires. They show the reliability of the scores (strictly speaking the number of items in the score is low for an analysis of this kind, but we have included the value of α as an indication). The tables also show the significance level at which the scores distinguished between homes, and the correlation between the *average* resident score for the home and the *average* staff score on the same variables (a measure of the degree to which the staff and the residents see the home in the same way). All the tables are based on the resident interview ($n = 233$) and the staff questionnaire ($n = 304$).

Table 11.3 sets out the frequency distribution of the items in the staff support scale. As will be seen, most of the residents felt that staff were supportive (a fact which reflects the generally good relationships they said that they themselves had with them). We found that this more general measure of staff support did not distinguish between homes for the resident score although it did for the staff score. In keeping with this discrepant result the correlation between the two scores was low ($r = .13$).

Table 11.4 gives similar information on staff expectations. In general, staff were seen by the residents as expecting hard work and as being

Table 11.3 Staff and residents' views on staff support for residents

Items in scale		Yes (%)	Sometimes (%)	No (%)
Staff provide lots of	*Staff*	80.7	18.6	0.7
encouragement to residents	*Residents*	63.3	25.8	10.9
Staff go out of way to	*Staff*	69.9	29.5	0.7
help residents	*Residents*	57.5	30.7	11.8
Staff have time to spend	*Staff*	63.8	33.6	2.7
with residents	*Residents*	57.9	27.6	14.5

Reliability *Staff* $\alpha = .58$; *Residents* $\alpha = .68$
Distinguishes between homes *Staff* $= p < .01$; *Residents* = NS
Correlation between *Staff* scale and *Resident* scale = .13 (NS)

Sources: Resident interview; questionnaire to staff.

Table 11.4 Staff and residents' views on what is expected of residents

Items in scale		Yes (%)	Sometimes (%)	No (%)
Residents are expected	*Staff*	26.9	45.2	27.9
to work hard	*Residents*	49.3	26.7	24.0
Staff agree on what the	*Staff*	43.7	40.4	15.9
rules are	*Residents*	74.1	19.5	6.4
Staff expect residents to	*Staff*	46.5	36.2	17.3
work hard at school	*Residents*	66.4	17.5	16.1

Reliability   *Staff* α = .63; *Residents* α = .53
Distinguishes between homes   *Staff* = p < .01; *Residents* = p < .03
Correlation between *Staff* scale and *Resident* scale = .01 (NS)

Sources: Resident interview; questionnaire to staff.

consistent, although there was somewhat more doubt about this than about their supportiveness. This time the scale did distinguish significantly between homes and in the eyes of both residents and staff some homes had distinctively higher expectations than others. Unfortunately, however, there was almost no correspondence between staff and residents over which homes had the higher expectations. Moreover, residents were more likely to feel the staff had high expectations for them than staff were to feel that this was the case.

Table 11.5 deals with the degree to which the staff were seen as strict. These questions elicited more disagreement and a great many more 'no's

Table 11.5 Staff and residents' views on strictness in the home

Items in scale		Yes (%)	Sometimes (%)	No (%)
Residents in trouble if they	*Staff*	2.3	49.2	48.5
argue with staff	*Residents*	43.2	32.4	24.3
	Staff	5.0	71.3	23.7
Staff in this home are strict	*Residents*	11.7	39.2	49.1
There are lots of punishments	*Staff*	0.7	10.9	88.4
in this home	*Residents*	29.0	13.6	57.5
Residents in trouble if they	*Staff*	14.6	49.8	35.6
swear in front of staff	*Residents*	32.7	25.9	41.4

Reliability   *Staff* α = .49; *Residents* α = .63
Distinguishes between homes   *Staff* = p < .002; *Residents* = p < .0001
Correlation between *Staff* scale and *Resident* scale = .58**

** p < .01.
Sources: Resident interview; questionnaire to staff.

than those we have considered so far. Basically, very few residents saw the staff as strict but they nevertheless saw the home as stricter and more punitive than the staff. There was, however, a reasonable degree of agreement on which homes were less strict and which homes were more so.

Table 11.6 deals with the degree to which residents and staff felt that the homes were friendly places. In general it seems that they did. Residents, however, were much more likely to say that other residents laughed at those who talked about their feelings and that parents were uneasy on visiting. Despite adequate reliability, this scale failed to distinguish significantly between homes for residents but did so for staff. There was a very low level of correlation between the mean score for residents and staff, suggesting, perhaps, that staff are not always aware of the feelings of families or tensions in the resident group.

Table 11.7 contains a rather miscellaneous collection of items basically concerned with whether the residents had a say in running the home and the rights within it that current notions of good practice require. As can be seen, it was generally believed that the residents knew how to make a complaint, although, according to themselves but not to the staff, they generally lacked the facilities to make a private telephone call without permission. There was some disagreement on whether they had a say in the running of the home and over whether they could see their files. Not surprisingly, given this somewhat diverse selection of items, the

Table 11.6 Staff and residents' views on whether home a friendly place

Items in scale		Yes (%)	Sometimes (%)	No (%)
Families feel uneasy when	*Staff*	5.8	48.8	45.4
they visit here	*Residents*	47.2	30.1	22.7
Residents laugh if another				
resident talks about their	*Staff*	11.1	56.7	32.2
feelings	*Residents*	57.9	24.9	17.2
There's always someome to	*Staff*	57.6	41.4	1.3
have a laugh with here	*Residents*	73.9	19.4	6.8
	Staff	66.9	30.8	2.3
This home is a friendly place	*Residents*	51.8	36.5	11.7
Residents' families are made	*Staff*	89.9	7.9	2.3
welcome here	*Residents*	79.7	12.9	7.4

Reliability   *Staff* α = .44; *Residents* α = .57
Distinguishes between homes   *Staff* = p < .0001; *Residents* = NS
Correlation between *Staff* scale and *Resident* scale = .15 (NS)

Sources: Resident interview; questionnaire to staff.

Table 11.7 Staff and residents' views on rights and involvement of residents in running the home

Items in scale		Yes (%)	Sometimes (%)	No (%)
Residents can see their files	*Staff*	62.2	28.1	9.7
in this home	*Residents*	47.6	20.4	32.0
Residents have a say in	*Staff*	57.3	36.8	6.0
running the home	*Residents*	57.5	30.7	11.8
Residents know how to make	*Staff*	92.7	5.3	2.0
a complaint	*Residents*	87.2	6.4	6.4
Residents can make private				
'phone calls without	*Staff*	63.8	7.3	28.9
permission	*Residents*	33.9	7.2	58.8

Reliability	*Staff* α = .21; *Residents* α = .23
Distinguishes between homes	*Staff* = p < .0001; *Residents* = p < .03
Correlation between *Staff* scale and *Resident* scale = .50**	

** p < .01.
Sources: Resident interview; questionnaire to staff.

reliability of this scale was low (in other words, residents or staff who said 'yes' to one of these items were not much more likely than others to agree to other items in the scale). We kept this index because it dealt with items that most practitioners consider important, because it distinguished significantly between homes for both the staff and residents, and because the mean score for both the staff and residents was correlated.

The items on resident behaviour (Table 11.8) again attracted reasonably diverse responses, with residents seeing things rather more positively than the staff. The reliability of this scale was not particularly high, but once again it distinguished significantly between homes, and the mean scores for staff and residents were positively correlated.

Table 11.9 deals with the degree to which residents felt that it was worthwhile being in the home. Generally, residents saw matters more positively than the staff. The scale contained only two questions which were significantly and positively correlated. Both the staff and resident scales distinguished between homes at a significance level of less than 1 in 10,000, and the average staff/resident scores for the homes were significantly correlated. So in respect of morale the difference between homes seemed to be large and seen consistently by staff and residents.

These results show that in the eyes of both residents and staff the homes were almost certainly very different places. Even the scales which did not distinguish significantly between homes might nevertheless have done so if our hypotheses had been more precise (if, for example, we had

Table 11.8 Staff and residents' views on residents' behaviour

Items in scale		Yes (%)	Sometimes (%)	No (%)
Other residents sniff glue and	*Staff*	34.9	51.2	14.0
take drugs	*Residents*	38.2	24.0	37.4
	Staff	28.1	62.0	9.9
There are fights here	*Residents*	36.5	39.2	24.3
Residents who are weak are				
forced to give things to	*Staff*	25.8	54.3	19.9
stronger residents	*Residents*	28.2	23.6	48.1

Reliability $\quad$ *Staff* α = .51; *Residents* α = .35
Distinguishes between homes $\quad$ *Staff* = $p < .0001$; *Residents* = $p < .05$
Correlation between *Staff* scale and *Resident* scale = .33*

* $p < .05$.
Sources: Resident interview; questionnaire to staff.

Table 11.9 Staff and residents' views on whether residents' time in home worthwhile

Items in scale		Yes (%)	Sometimes (%)	No (%)
Residents are proud to live in	*Staff*	18.9	51.2	29.9
this home	*Residents*	34.7	30.1	35.2
Residents think it's a waste of	*Staff*	12.0	72.4	15.6
time being here	*Residents*	23.6	33.3	43.1

Correlation $\quad$ *Staff* r = .43; *Residents* r = .38
Distinguishes between homes $\quad$ *Staff* = $p < .0001$; *Residents* = $p < .0001$
Correlation between *Staff* scale and *Resident* scale = .41**

** $p < .01$.
Sources: Resident interview; questionnaire to staff.

been comparing the supportiveness of large and small homes). The majority of scales did, however, distinguish between homes, some of them at an extremely high level of significance.

CONCLUSION

The dimensions against which the young people evaluated the homes were far from surprising. They wanted a reasonable physical environment which allowed for privacy and was not run down, friendly staff who were prepared to listen, and residents who were friendly and who did not bully them or lead them astray. In general, the residents were appreciative of the care they received but there were wide differences between the homes in the way in which the young people perceived the regimes and in the behaviour and morale of the residents. Staff similarly gave very different accounts of the regimes in different homes.

These findings support those of Berridge and Brodie (1998) and Brown and her colleagues (1996), who have more graphically described the kinds of variations which we have documented above. As Berridge and Brodie comment, it is the *unevenness* of residential care for children rather than its average quality that is a problem. What this chapter has begun to do is enable us to put some figures to this variety. We shall look shortly at how this variation might be explained.

12

RESIDENTS' BEHAVIOUR AND SUBJECTIVE WELL-BEING

INTRODUCTION

One criterion against which the residents judged the home was that it should be a reasonable place for anyone to live. However, there was naturally a more personal agenda. They blamed the home if they felt that it had led them astray, or if they had been bullied, harassed or otherwise made miserable. Conversely, they sometimes praised it on the grounds that it had, as they saw it, helped them settle down or improve their relationship with their families, or get on better at school. This chapter deals with these more personal reactions to the home. We will focus on three main areas:

- The temptations and pressures the residents experienced.
- The degree and kind of help they received.
- Their subjective well-being and self-respect.

In the main, we will explore these issues by looking at what the residents said. We will also create a 'help' score designed to see whether some homes are experienced as giving more help than others, and look for statistical relationships between our measure of subjective well-being and aspects of the residents' past and current experience. We begin, however, with a topic which, as we have seen, was of considerable concern to social workers, parents and residents alike—the young people's involvement in delinquency. For this we draw on the 'resident log' completed by the head of home.

DELINQUENCY

We asked the heads of home to list all the residents who had been in the home over the previous year and say whether they had been convicted or cautioned before coming to the home. This was partly for reasons of history. We wanted to know whether the homes were sheltering residents who would have gone to Community Homes with Education (CHEs) prior to the latter's demise. It was also because we suspected that delinquent behaviour would be an issue for the homes, as it was for social workers, parents and residents (see Chapters 2–5).

Overall, just under half (49%) the male residents and a quarter (23%) of the female ones were said to have a prior conviction or caution. The likelihood of this rose with age. For example, only 30% of boys aged 13 or under as against 60% of those aged 16 or more had had such brushes with the law. The comparable figures for females were 9% and 38%.

A more important question was whether the residents were convicted or cautioned after arrival. Table 12.1 examines the proportion of current and past residents who were adjudged to have been involved in delinquency through a caution or conviction, and running away, (an unauthorised absence overnight) whilst in the home. As can be seen, the likelihood of conviction in the home rose with the length of time spent in the home. This is an almost necessary consequence of an increased period 'at risk'. Young people who were only resident for a week were obviously far less likely to be convicted of an offence while in the home than were those who were in the home for a year. It was also not surprising that young people who had been previously convicted were more likely to be reconvicted than those who had not been. We cannot be sure that convictions relate to offences committed while in the home, rather than to previous offences which came to light or resulted in a conviction subsequent to arrival. However, the steady rise in convictions with length of stay,

Table 12.1 Residents running away or convicted while in home—by length of stay

	(n)	Less than 1 month n = 335 (%)	1 month n = 164 (%)	2 months n = 112 (%)	3 months n = 72 (%)	4 and 5 months n = 112 (%)	6 months or more n = 295 (%)
Convicted—by length of stay (%)							
Previous convictions	416	7	18	50	52	64	73
No previous convictions	674	2	12	23	33	24	40
Run away—by length of stay (%)							
Previous convictions	416	71	51	81	81	88	87
No previous convictions	674	18	43	57	63	62	63

Percentages rounded.
Source: Resident Log.

together with the fact that very few remands were said to be convicted while in the home, strongly suggests that the great majority of these offences occurred while the young people were resident.

These figures were a surprise to us. Nearly four in 10 of those who had no previous criminal record got one if they stayed for six months or more. Nearly three-quarters of the residents who had had a previous conviction or caution and who stayed for at least six months in the homes had another such contact with the police before they left. These proportions look high in comparison with reconviction rates for prisons or the former Approved Schools, even when these were calculated over years rather than months. Similarly, the 'running away' rate given in the second half of Table 12.1 looks high in comparison with Approved School or Probation Hostel absconding rates from the 1970s (Clarke and Martin 1971; Sinclair 1971).

As the research in the 1970s and as yet unpublished research by Biehal and her colleagues would lead one to expect, there was a strong association between conviction in the home and running away. Roughly half those who ran away, as against only one in 10 of those who did not, were also convicted or cautioned for an offence while at the home. This association remained very strong when account was taken of time at risk. For example, among those who stayed for one month or less, a third of those who ran away but only 4% of those who did not were also convicted or cautioned for an offence.

As can be seen, there was a high rate of running away in the early months among those who had previous convictions. It is important to remember that homes are open establishments. Thus, despite their relatively short length of stay, half those remanded to homes also ran away. A fifth of them were convicted or cautioned for an offence while at the home but in this respect they were, after allowing for length of stay, no more delinquent than other residents.

These figures do not necessarily mean that the homes were causing the young people to offend (e.g. through contamination). As we have seen, some residents said that they had indeed been led into offending, whereas others said that they had stopped offending as a result of their experience. As we will also see, the young people were as likely to report that they had been encouraged to take part in delinquency or drug taking before they entered the home as they were to report these temptations while they were there. A more serious possibility is that some homes were inhibiting delinquency, whereas others appeared to foster it. The conviction rates of residents who had been in the home over the past year varied widely between homes, ranging from 0 (two homes with 11 and 14 residents) to 74% (one home with 19 residents).

In considering these figures we need to bear in mind that some rates are based on small numbers (two of the homes had only taken six residents). We also need to take into account variations between the homes in the average number of previous convictions among their residents and in the length of time for which they stayed. As with the other variables we have been discussing, individual homes varied considerably in the degree to which they took young people with previous convictions or cautions. Two took none and two three-quarters or more; the average for all homes was a third. As it happens, the correlation between this measure and the conviction rate for the home, though positive, was not significant ($r = .17$, ns). The correlations for proportion of females and average age with conviction rate were similarly low and non-significant. There were, however, significant associations between conviction rate and the proportion of short-stay residents ($r = .43$, $p < .01$) and the proportion of long-stay residents ($r = .39$, $p < .05$).

So the question of the relationship between convictions and the characteristics of the home is a complicated, if vital, one. We will return to it with a more complicated analysis in the next chapter. Immediately, however, we turn to the question of whether the residents themselves felt they were being encouraged to be delinquent or become involved in drink or drugs.

TEMPTATIONS AND PRESSURES

At the time of developing our questionnaire, one of us was living in the same house as a recent resident in a children's home. In commenting on an initial draft of the questionnaire, he pointed out that it would easily give an unfair picture of what life in the homes was like. At that time we asked questions about the temptations and pressures to which the young

Table 12.2 Pressures experienced before and during time in home

Type of pressure	Before (%)	During (%)
Bullied	41.4	43.9
Offered cannabis	42.9	39.5
Offered heroin/cocaine	12.3	6.7
Offered other drugs	32.9	31.9
Encouraged to get drunk	43.8	47.1
Encouraged to sniff glue	16.4	18.1
Taken sexual advantage of	22.6	13.4
Encouraged to steal	37.7	30.9

Source: Resident interview.

people were subject in the home but not about the temptations they had experienced before. So by asking, for example, about drugs in the home we could easily have been given the impression that these were a unique feature of home life and not freely available on the school playground. In the light of these comments, we modified the questionnaire to include comments about the residents' previous experience. As can be seen from Table 12.2, according to their accounts, on average experience in the home was very similar to experience before it.

Table 12.2 compares proportions, showing, for example, that 43% said they had been offered cannabis before admission and 40% that they had been offered it after. In the case of many variables there was, as we will see, substantial continuity at the level of individuals. Over two-thirds of those who said they had been offered cannabis before said that they had been offered it while at the home. By contrast, less than a fifth of those who said they had not previously been offered cannabis said they had been offered it since arrival. In part this highly significant association may reflect a willingness to admit to such approaches. If you admit to it before, why not admit to it during your time in the home? However, it is also true that young people are not only subjected to temptations, but also put themselves in the way of them. Those who enjoyed cannabis and who knew where it was to be found in the local town would be likely to ensure that someone offered it to them after their arrival. That said, the data packed into Table 12.2 are worthy of more detailed analysis and we explore them below.

Bullying

Farmer and Pollock (1998) studied a sample of children and young people who had been involved with sexual abuse, either as active abusers or through being abused themselves. The children were looked after in varying settings but roughly half their sample had either bullied others or been bullied themselves. Bullying appeared to be a particularly serious problems in children's homes, where it often continued over a long period without detection. These findings support the impression from our earlier chapters that bullying in homes may be widespread and we asked the young people about it.

Questions about bullying presuppose some common definition of what it is. Does physical violence have to be involved or are threats and systematic humiliation sufficient? Our own question referred, in fact, to *attempts at bullying*—an experience which is likely to be highly uncomfortable but which may not necessarily be as serious as the horrific examples provided by Farmer and Pollock. For ease of expression we have sometimes shortened this expression to 'bullying'.

As can be seen, four in 10 said they were bullied before arrival and just over four in 10 said that they were bullied after it. At the level of individuals there was some continuity. Just over half those bullied before but only just over a third of those not bullied before were, according to them, bullied after. This association does not seem to reflect the fact that many of the residents continued in the same school after arrival—residents were equally likely to cease to be bullied or become so whether or not they changed schools. Some individuals, therefore, seem to be particularly vulnerable to bullying (or at least to attempts at it).

Age and reason for admission seemed to be particularly important (and statistically significant) in explaining who was and was not bullied in the home. Seventy per cent of those aged 12 or under, nearly half of those aged 13 and 14, but only just over a third of the remainder said that someone had tried to bully them after arrival. Half the 'victims' but only a quarter of those in trouble outside the home said that this had happened to them—all of which might suggest that in some homes there is the kind of culture depicted in *Lord of the Flies* or, from a research perspective, by Polsky (1965), in which older, more delinquent young people establish a hierarchy and humiliate or bully younger, less 'streetwise' residents. Certainly, a number of the heads of home commented on the importance of the 'pecking order' and of the struggles to adjust it which occurred on admission.

In relation to 'being bullied', change for both good and ill was particularly common among 'victims'. For around a quarter of these, life got better in this respect and for around a quarter it got worse. So it seems that what may be important for them is the nature of the home in which they find themselves. This is also true for 13 and 14 year-olds, who experienced as a group quite considerable changes in their 'bullying status'. For those under 13, however, the situation was more bleak. One in 10 ceased to be bullied, and over a quarter (28%) were bullied when they had not been before.

So the situation seems to be that care needs to be taken when placing 'victims' and 13 or 14 year-olds. They are vulnerable to bullying and, whereas placement in a home may improve things in this respect, it can also make things worse. With younger children the risk of bullying (or at least attempted bullying) is very high and should presumably always be weighed in making a placement. As we will see later, the prevalence of bullying varies between homes, and it almost certainly affects both immediate well-being and long-term behaviour for the worse.

Drug Use

According to the British Crime Survey (Ramsey and Percy 1997) nearly half (45%) of young adults are prepared to admit that they have tried an illegal drug at some time in their lives. Much of this drug use seems to be episodic and experimental and much of it is restricted to cannabis, which over a third of the sample admitted they had tried. By contrast, only 11% of the sample admitted to trying 'hallucinants'—amphetamines, LSD, magic mushrooms, ecstasy and poppers—and only 5% admitted to have tried any of methadone, cocaine, heroin or crack.

Even given the widespread availability of drugs, there is particular anxiety about their use among young people who are looked after (Social Services Inspectorate 1997). It seemed important to discover whether there were particular problems relating to them in homes where older residents could induct younger ones. We examined this issue in relation to different kinds of drug.

In keeping with other research (Newcombe, Measham and Parker 1995), we found that age was strongly related to whether or not the young people said they had been offered cannabis before entry. Only 7% of those under 12, as against 40% of those aged 13 or 14 and 54% of those aged 15 or over, said they had been. There was no evidence that older residents tried to induct the younger ones. None of the under 13s said they had been offered cannabis since arrival. The small number (10%) who said that they had been offered cannabis since arrival but not before were found entirely among the 13, 14 and 15 year-olds, particularly the former. This suggests that, in these localities and for this kind of sample, recruitment into cannabis use occurs around 13 or 14. By the age of 16 the young people may be users or inoculated against it.

As might be expected, the numbers who said they had been offered heroin or cocaine either before or after admission were much smaller (15% before and 7% during). These numbers were too small for much statistical analysis. However, it was of interest that all the 15% who had been offered it at some stage were aged 13 and 14 or above, but that within this age range there was no trend over time. Again, this would suggest that recruitment is targeted at the 13 and 14 year-old age group. Overall, only four of those who said they had been offered one of these drugs since arrival had not been offered any before. By contrast, 10 who had been offered such drugs before had not been offered any since.

Other illegal drugs (most commonly amphetamines and ecstasy, but also LSD, magic mushrooms and others) had apparently been offered to a third of the sample before arrival (21% of those aged 12 or under, 28% of those aged 13–14 and 39% of those aged 15 or over). A third (but only one in seven of those aged 12 or under) said that they had also been offered such drugs during their time in the home. As usual, there was very considerable continuity with most of those who had been offered the drugs before saying they had been offered them since. A few (all but one aged 13 or over) had been offered the drugs for the first time since arrival but their number was almost exactly balanced by those who had been offered these drugs before but not since.

Overall, only one in nine of the sample said they had been offered any illegal drug since entering the home of a kind they had not been offered before. Only one of these was aged under 13. Sixty-one per cent of the residents (70% of those aged 15 or over) said they had been offered some illegal drug at some stage. There is no evidence that the homes were in themselves an important source of recruitment into the drug culture. However, it is clear that illegal drugs were readily available and that many residents knew a lot about drugs.

Drinking

Drinking is another aspect of young people's lives about which there is considerable concern (Social Services Inspectorate 1997). There was, however, no evidence that the homes either increased or protected against the pressure to get drunk. Almost the same proportion (43% as against 45%) said they had been encouraged to get drunk before entering the home as said they had after it. The under 13s were least likely to say that this had happened to them at either stage, but interestingly there was otherwise little difference by age. In this sample, once someone is a teenager, others seem to have little inhibition in encouraging her/him to drink to excess.

Interestingly, female residents were again more likely than male ones to say that others had encouraged them in this way. Conceivably this had to do with the way we phrased the question—males may have felt that they needed no encouragement. Alternatively it may be that the females were more exposed to this pressure from boyfriends.

Overall, 12% said they had been encouraged to get drunk after arrival but not before. Half of these were aged 13 or 14 and it seems likely that, as in the case of drugs, they had reached an age when others took it upon themselves to offer such an encouragement and that this would have happened whether they had been in the home or not.

Glue Sniffing

The proportions of those who said they had been encouraged to sniff glue before and after admission were roughly the same—somewhat less than a fifth. Eight per cent of the sample said that they had been encouraged to do this for the first time after arrival at the home. All but three of these were aged between 13 and 15.

Taken Sexual Advantage Of

Farmer and Pollock (1998) have highlighted the problems of young people continuing to abuse or be abused while looked after. Children's homes, in their study, commonly sheltered the abused and the abusing and also posed awkward questions about apparently consensual sexual relationships between teenagers.

In keeping with such concerns, we asked the young people whether anyone had tried to take sexual advantage of them, and if so whether this had happened before or during their time in the home. In our minds, this rather indirect phrase referred to unwelcome sexual advantage and as far as we know this was the way it was interpreted by the young people. The way we phrased the question left room for doubt over the exact nature of these experiences, but data reported later strongly suggest that they had a negative impact on the young people. A number of the young male residents implied that any such event would have been far from unwelcome, but this was by way of a joke.

Not surprisingly, the answers varied sharply by sex. Over a third of the female residents (37%) but only one in nine of the male ones said that this had happened before admission. Nearly a quarter (23%) of the females and 7% of the males said that it had happened after.

As in the case of drugs and delinquency, there was continuity. In the case of both male and female residents, those who reported that this had happened before admission were more likely to report that it had happened after. Nevertheless, there was also change. Twenty-one female residents reported no such affronts while they were in the home although they had experienced them earlier. By contrast, nine who had not previously had such experiences said that they had had them since arrival. The comparable figures for male residents were five and 11. It would seem, therefore, that as many male as female residents were exposed to unwelcome sexual invitations for the first time in the home.

Stealing and Taking Cars without Consent

As we have seen there is considerable anxiety that homes may 'contaminate', and lead residents into delinquency. So we asked the residents whether anyone had tried to get them to steal something or get into a car which was stolen. This seemed to be a reasonably frequent experience, with nearly four out of 10 saying that it had happened to them before coming to the home and nearly a third saying that it had happened since. In contrast to the situation with drugs and drink, the experience was not, in this sample, related to age. The under-13s were as likely to report such encouragement as their older peers.

Encouragingly, it was not usually an experience which residents met for the first time in the homes. Only one in nine reported that it had only happened to them since their arrival. Young people placed for short-term purposes were also significantly less likely to report such temptations than others. Conceivably they did not think it worthwhile joining any delinquent culture the home may have had. Moreover, delinquent acts while the young person is being assessed may be more likely to have adverse consequences than at other times.

HELP AND IMPROVEMENT

Any discussion of the pressure of residential life needs to be balanced by an account of the help the homes can offer. We explored this at various points throughout the questionnaire, where we asked the residents about problems they might have and whether they felt that the home had helped them over them.

Early in the interview we asked the residents three questions about whether they had had any help over difficulties at school, finding or keeping a job, or planning for their education or work. Seven out of 10 said that they had been helped in at least one of these ways and half that they had been helped in two or more. Asked about what kind of help they had received, they mentioned contacts with the school to sort out problems (the most common), practical help over getting a job or training course, a chance to talk over problems and their future, and help with school work:

Staff have helped in a way by making me go to college and I help myself by going. They've given me lots of support.

They talk to me about school and make telephone calls to the school. At the moment they're trying to get me into a different school.

Yes—the staff help me with homework and talk to me about the qualifications I'll need if I want to train as a nurse.

Later in the interview we asked if they had any worries about health, school or work, leaving, or getting on with other young people of their own age. Table 12.3 sets out the results. We had expected from other research (Whitaker *et al.* 1985) that the residents would be concerned about their futures. Who would not be in their situation? However, the table reveals what was to us a disturbingly high level of anxiety about

Table 12.3 Worries about health, education, leaving home and getting on with others

Worries	Yes, a lot (%)	Yes, some (%)	No (%)
Health	74.3	21.2	4.5
Education/school	66.2	19.7	14.1
Leaving here	55.5	30.5	14.1
Getting on with peers	81.4	14.9	3.7

Source: Resident interview.

subjects on which we had thought the residents would have few worries (e.g. their health).

Our naivety was perhaps shared with others, resulting in a low level of help with many of these problems. Only 18% said that they had had any help over their worries over health (mainly counselling or work in collaboration with a medical professional). Only a quarter said that they had help over their worries about school, and the proportion was similar in relation to leaving. Only 4% said that they had any help over what was the most common worry—their relationship with others of their own age.

These figures are lower than those suggested by our earlier question about help would indicate. The home was perhaps seen as helping with problems with which adults are concerned—suspensions, school reports and lodgings. Adolescent agonies over appearance, weight, love and loneliness may have remained unrecognised and unaddressed.

This rather gloomy assessment was modified by a question which asked young persons whether being in the home had helped them get on better with their families or in other ways, and if so, how. Nearly half said that they had definitely been helped, nearly a quarter that there had either been no change or a change for better and worse, and the remainder were evenly divided between those who gave no reply and a small group (13%) who said that things had been made worse. The areas in which these changes had occurred were various. The most common was behaviour (17%); others included attitudes, family relationships, and depression (all around 12%).

Later on in the interview we dealt with moods and personal problems. As described in the next section, we asked a series of questions concerned with how the resident was feeling. We then asked how the home had affected these feelings. The replies illustrated the complexity of the topic we were trying to probe. About a quarter implied there had been no change, about one in seven that the home had affected their feelings for the better, nearly as many (one in nine) that the home had made things worse and the remainder (about half) gave mixed replies, or replies which could not be coded one way or the other.

This open-ended question was followed by questions which offered a limited range of replies and produced a decidedly more optimistic picture. Six out of 10 said that the home had helped with their feelings and the remainder were evenly divided between those who said that it had made no difference and those saying that it had made things worse. Asked whether they had been helped in relation to a range of particular areas (see Table 12.4) the residents were optimistic, the proportion saying that they had had some help varying from 36% to 51%. Overall, more than eight out of 10 residents said they had been helped in some way, most commonly through talking things over (instanced by 35% of the sample) or through a combination of methods (instanced by a quarter).

So the upshot would seem to be that about half the residents feel that they have been helped in a way which was important enough for them to mention it in a reply to an open-ended question. Even more feel that they have been assisted in ways substantial enough to count as help but not necessarily particularly important to themselves. The kind of help, however, is extremely various and the residents' problems extremely serious and diverse. Thus, the homes were undoubtedly seen as helpful places but many of the residents' worries may have been untouched.

As we had asked a large number of questions about help, we decided to combine them into an overall score. Basically the score represented the number of areas in which a resident said that he/she had been helped. We found that this score was significantly correlated with:

- The residents' reports of their relationships with their social workers.
- The residents' reports of their relationships with their keyworkers.
- Our assessment of the degree to which the head of home said that he/she had thought through ways of helping the residents.

These findings are encouraging, for they suggest that residents believe that they have been helped in the ways that others set out to help them.

Table 12.4 Whether help given by home

Help with	Yes (%)	No (%)
Personal problem(s)	48.2	51.8
Temper and moods	45.2	54.8
Family problems	41.2	58.8
Things that have troubled me in the past	50.7	49.3
Planning for future	35.6	64.4
Looking after myself	41.0	59.0

Source: Resident interview.

The association between help and good relationships is perhaps suspect, in that residents who got on with their social worker or keyworker may have been motivated to give as favourable a picture as they could. However, our assessment of the head of home's methods (a measure we describe in more detail later) was made blind to what the residents had said. So it seems likely that heads with worked-out philosophies did have an effect.

SUBJECTIVE WELL-BEING

The Happiness Score

Part of the difficulty, but at the same time interest, of this research lies in the variety of outcomes against which the homes could be evaluated. Some of these do not have to do with the residents and include, for example, the role which the homes may play in relieving pressure in other parts of the care system, servicing the courts, or raising or lowering the costs of departments. However, even those which have to do with individual residents are various. So we need to take into account the criteria suggested by the *Looking After Children* project, the degree to which the various stakeholders (young people, parents, social workers and staff) approve of the quality of what they get and the degree to which what they get is what they would have chosen. We also need to distinguish between immediate outcomes while the resident is being looked after and outcomes in the longer term.

These considerations may cast light on many of the measures we have discussed earlier in the book. However, there is one to which we attached importance in planning the research and which is yet to be introduced. Briefly, we wanted a measure which would encompass the subjective well-being of residents—a broad and somewhat imprecise term under which we included depression, anxiety, self-esteem and morale. Our view was that any operational measures of these latter concepts would be likely to be highly inter-correlated. For this and other reasons, we would be unlikely to be able to make precise statements to the extent, for example, that homes were effective in reducing depression but not anxiety. So we decided to tackle the simpler question of whether homes made residents feel better in a variety of ways, and for this we needed a broad-brush measure.

We took our measure from questions used by Arnold and his colleagues (1987) at the Institute of Psychiatry in a survey of teenagers. Unfortunately we did not feel that we could include all their relevant questions and keep the interview to a reasonable length. We therefore 'cherry-picked' questions which we particularly liked. Table 12.5 sets out the questions and the distribution of the answers. The questions were embodied in the form of statements which were put on a card given to the resident. The interviewer then read out the statements and asked the resident whether each was true or false for them in the last month. As can be seen, the 'face validity' of our questions looks high and the results disturbing.

On most of the questions, between a third and two-thirds of the residents gave answers suggesting that they were worried, depressed, had a low opinion of themselves or felt they were going nowhere. Eight out of 10 felt that they easily became upset or angry. Hardly any described themselves as often happy, and a staggering four in 10 had apparently considered killing themselves in the last month.

These answers bring out the misery, pain and anger with which staff deal on a daily basis. They may also explain why it is not always easy to listen to residents. Two nights before this paragraph was written there was a news item about a young man who had killed himself. Staff in social services had read his notebook, which said that he wanted to die, but had taken no action, apparently because they did not consider him a suicide risk. These figures illustrate how easily such things can happen. Nearly half (48%) of those who said 'Yes' to our question on suicide were said by their social workers to have harmed themselves or attempted suicide. The comparable figure for those who said 'No' was only 26%, a highly significant difference. Nevertheless, nearly half of those who had harmed themselves did not say 'Yes' to this question, and half of those who said 'Yes' had not at the time harmed themselves.

Table 12.5 How residents are feeling at the moment

'During last month I have felt or thought'	True (%)	False (%)
Worried a lot of time	52.3	47.7
Miserable or unhappy	65.8	34.2
I'm a good person to have around	38.0	62.0
Often lonely	49.1	50.9
Sometimes I'm no good	56.3	43.7
Often happy	16.4	83.6
Blame myself for things not my fault	48.2	51.8
Thought about killing myself	38.7	61.3
I'm getting somewhere in my life	35.0	65.0
Easily upset and angry	82.4	17.6
Nervous	59.8	40.2

Source: Resident interview.

The implication of this result is, perhaps, that thoughts of suicide should always be taken seriously—if not for the intent then for the misery that lies behind them. Staff should also consider whether they should sometimes raise the issue with residents. Concern was expressed when we decided to do so. However, we argued that if one has thoughts of suicide it may be reassuring to know that others are willing to listen to such thoughts and do not regard those expressing them as mad or deeply different from ordinary people. These arguments still seem to us valid. However, we do not have to live with the young people and suspect that if we did we would often prefer not to know how miserable they were.

To return to our analysis, the next step was to test the reliability of a simple scale formed by adding up the items given in Table 12.5, giving '1' for an answer suggesting unhappiness or upset and '2' for an answer suggesting the reverse. The α (see earlier explanation, Chapter 11) was 0.73. This is slightly low for a scale designed to measure a concept precisely (e.g. to enable a doctor to pick out someone who is depressed) but certainly adequate for a scale intended to make comparisons between groups (e.g. to say that this group is on average 'happier' than that one). All the items contributed to this reliability, except the one concerned with whether the resident was getting anywhere in life. If we had dropped this item, the reliability of the scale would have risen to 0.74. This did not seem much of a benefit, so we left the item in. It seems, however, that it is tapping a slightly different dimension and so we have sometimes analysed it on its own.

The Happiness Score and Abuse

For brevity we will call our measure of subjective well-being 'happiness', although the reader should bear in mind that the meaning of this concept is defined by the statements given in Table 12.5. If this measure is valid as well as reliable, it should relate in sensible ways to other variables. As we will see, it does, and given this, an immediate question is: what influences it? Are the residents' miserable or happy because of things that are going on currently or because they dwell on things that have happened before?

A useful way of approaching this question is through issues of bullying and sexual abuse. For ease of exposition we divided the sample into those who had scores at or above the median on the happiness scale (happy) and those who scored below it (unhappy). Table 12.6 gives the proportion of those who were happy, depending on whether they said others had tried to bully or take sexual advantage of them in the past or now. As can be seen, there were strong and highly significant relationships with all four variables.

Table 12.6 Happiness—by whether bullied and harassed

| | | | Happiness score | |
| | | | Low | High |
		(*n*)	(%)	(%)
Bullied before	Yes	91	62.6	37.4
	No	128	39.8	60.2
Bullied during	Yes	97	62.9	37.1
	No	123	39.0	61.0
Harassed before	Yes	46	71.4	28.6
	No	170	42.5	57.5
Harassed during	Yes	29	86.2	13.8
	No	186	43.5	56.5

All differences significant at .001 level.
Source: Resident interview.

It will be remembered that past attempts at bullying or sexual abuse were associated with current ones. So the question arises of whether it is the past that influences present feelings, or whether it does so through its association with the present. There could, of course, be a more complicated relationship. For example, it could be worse to be bullied now if you have been bullied in the past—you may feel it will never end. Or it could be better because you have become inured to such things.

One way of approaching such questions is through more complicated cross-tabulations. For example, it is of interest that only four of those who said that someone had tried to take sexual advantage of them in the home were 'happy', and all of these said that they had had such attempts on them before. This would suggest that in these four instances past experiences had no impact on the present or, if anything, had inoculated and resident against further attempts. However, examination of the table where no resident claimed that anyone in the home had tried to take advantage of them showed that happiness was significantly less likely if there had been previous attempts at abuse.

In many ways, the easiest way to examine such issues is through a two-way analysis of variance which uses the 'happiness score' as the dependent variable and previous/current attempts at bullying or abuse as the independent ones. The aim of this analysis is to apportion the apparent impact on the dependent variable between the two independent variables and their interaction (the more complicated kinds of relationship illustrated above). Some readers may be unfamiliar with this technique and so we give the results in English. These were:

1. Previous attempts at sexual abuse were significantly associated with unhappiness ($p < .05$).
2. Current attempts were more strongly associated ($p < .001$).
3. There was a significant 'interaction'—residents were (on average) happiest if they reported no attempts and next happiest if they reported two, i.e. a previous and a current attempt ($p < .01$).
4. Previous attempts at bullying were significantly associated with unhappiness ($p < .05$).
5. Current attempts were more strongly associated ($p < .001$)
6. There was no significant interaction (i.e. the effect of current bullying did not depend on whether the resident had been bullied in the past).

All of this suggests that, although the past may have an effect on the happiness score, current events are of even greater importance.

THE CORRELATION OF HAPPINESS

We wished to see what variables were associated with our happiness score in the hope that we would be able to identify some which could be seen as causing high or low scores and which might be influenced by the home. We began with our standard list of variables (age, sex, reason for admission, age at first admission, length of time 'in care' since the last admission, and purpose of placement). Of these only sex was significantly associated with happiness, with female residents being on average less 'happy' than male ones. This association was partly but not fully accounted for by the fact that female residents more frequently reported harassment.

We next looked at the way the residents spent their time. This analysis was remarkable for suggesting that school had almost no relevance to whether the residents were happy. Those who were of school age were not significantly happier or unhappier if they said they were at school, suspended from school or waiting to go to one. Their happiness or unhappiness was unrelated to whether they said they enjoyed their time at school or whether they were proud of anything they did there. These findings were repeated when we related our question about 'getting somewhere in life' to our school variables and found no associations. These findings are also something of a challenge to those who put their trust in the school system for the salvation of young people 'in care', or indeed of disaffected youth.

For the 52 young people who spent their time in the home, rather than at school, what they did, and how they enjoyed it, were related to happiness. Those who said they enjoyed this time were on average 'happier'. Those who said that they were proud of something they did there were not happier but were much more likely to feel that they were getting somewhere in life.

Work was similarly salient. Those in work or on schemes were much more likely to feel they were 'getting somewhere', although the small numbers prevented this association from reaching significance. For those of working age, pride in their achievements and enjoyment of working time were strongly associated with happiness and belief in the future.

Leisure activities were also associated with belief in the future, although not, contrary to what we had expected, with happiness. Those who were proud of something they did in their leisure time were much more likely to feel they were 'getting somewhere'.

This suggests that schools were less relevant to self-belief than work or alternative programmes in the home or leisure. The moral, however, is probably not that school should be given less importance, but rather that attention should be paid to all aspects of residents' lives which may act as sources of self-respect.

We next examined the relationship between happiness and what the residents had told us about their family and friends. The associations were as predicted and very strong. Residents were less happy if they had left behind an 'important friend' ($p < .0003$), happier if they were going around with a particular group of friends ($p < .004$), and less happy if they wanted to see more of their family ($p < .0001$).

The relationship between happiness and attitudes to 'care' were again as predicted. Those who had felt that coming into care was a good idea were happier than those who had had mixed feelings, who in turn were happier than those who said they had thought it a bad idea ($p < .05$). Those who said that residential care would have been their first or second choice were very much happier than the others ($p < .0004$). There was a significant, although not very strong, correlation between happiness and the degree to which the residents said they were happy about the plans that had been made for them.

Contrary to our prediction, residents were not happier if they said they got on well with the staff or if they reported that they had had a lot of help from the home. The variables that seemed to matter in the home were their attitude to the overall environment (as expressed in our 'facilities' score) and their perceptions of the residents as friendly and as reasonably behaved (all $p < .01$).

The most likely explanation for these associations is that the staff are generally kind and well-intentioned (although no doubt, like everyone, they have their off days). This kindness is, as we have seen earlier, appreciated, but as it is generally available it is not this that makes the difference between those residents who are unhappy and those who are not. Rather, it is the resident group and how they get on with them.

PREDICTING HAPPINESS

We were interested in using these results to predict happiness on the basis of a number of variables analysed together. There were four reasons for this.

First, we wanted to predict happiness on the basis of variables which did not specifically relate to time in the home (sex, whether a special friend had been left behind, etc). We could then see whether, having taken this prediction into account, the homes differed significantly in terms of their average happiness. This was a weak test (because we were not trying to see whether specific kinds of homes did better in this respect) and we did not find a significant difference.

Second, we wanted to see whether variables that did refer to time in the home (e.g. the perception of the other residents as friendly, or reports of attempted bullying) added to the prediction. They did.

Third, we wanted to arrive at a parsimonious predictor of happiness and see what variables went into it. Various equations were produced using multiple regression, but the simplest contained five variables, all of which were associated with happiness at a very high level of significance ($p < .002$ to $p < .0005$). These variables were sex, whether the residents reported attempts at bullying since arrival, whether the residents reported attempts to take advantage of them sexually since arrival, whether the residents said they were friendly with a particular individual or group, and whether the residents said that residential care would have been their first or second choice at the time of arrival. The multiple correlation of these variables with happiness was 0.52. Higher correlations were obtained but the equations were longer and more complicated.

Fourth, we wanted to see whether we could significantly improve our prediction by adding information on what the keyworker, social worker or other professionals were doing. It will be remembered that we had some measures of their activities from the social worker questionnaire. To our disappointment, we could find no associations between these measures and our happiness score, either before or after allowing for other variables. As far as these particular data go, counselling by social workers, keyworkers and other professionals is neither targeted on those who are likely to be miserable, nor affects the misery of those who receive it. The same is true of frequency of social work visits, as reported by the social worker, to either the young person or the family.

CONCLUSION

Policy on children's homes has been heavily driven by scandals and the consequent fear that staff will physically and sexually abuse residents. By contrast, the evidence in our study was that current physical and sexual harassment of which the residents complained had to do with the young people associated with the home. There were strong associations between reports of both bullying and harassment and the residents' statements that they were unhappy about the other residents. These experiences were also significantly more common among those who said that they were unhappy about other young people coming into the home. By contrast, these reports were not associated with the residents' reports of school (e.g. whether they wanted to leave school) or of how they got on with keyworker or head. 'Bullying' was associated with getting on poorly with staff in general but this may have reflected their inability to stop it.

It would be foolish to use these facts to minimise the risks of abuse by staff. Like Berridge and Brodie (1998), we would be amazed if such abuse were widespread. However, abuse is commonly hidden and is appalling, however infrequent. Where policy can be criticised is in its failure to pay more attention to problems which are more easily apparent: the prevalence of misery and delinquency and the risks of exposure to drugs and delinquent behaviour. The bullying and harassment which stems from the young people and their visitors makes many residents very unhappy. We will see later that it probably has long-term negative affects. If these are matters that are, as it were, under our noses, why are so few enquiries devoted to them? Certainly there are risks that need to be weighed if there is a possibility of increasing the number of children's homes (Utting 1997).

So, if these are problems, what might be done about them? Our discussion of measures which might inhibit delinquency needs to wait for the next chapter. Our discussion of measures against misery can take place now but needs to be tentative, for we have found no evidence of practice by social workers or staff that successfully counteracts it. What we have found are the correlates of misery and by tackling these we may have the best chance of reducing misery itself. So staff need to develop ways of tackling:

- Bullying and sexual harassment (perhaps drawing on programmes that have been successfully developed in schools).
- Home-sickness (residents who missed their families or a particular friend were more unhappy than others).
- Relations with the resident group (residents who did not have a particular friend or who thought the other residents were a problem were less happy).

- The residents' success or otherwise in social roles.
- Listening to common worries (residents valued listening but were unlikely to say that staff had helped them with a number of very common worries).
- The arrangement of therapeutic help for residents who had previously been bullied or sexually abused (both experiences associated with current misery).
- Choice (residents who did not want to go into residential care were less happy than others).
- The placement of children under twelve and victims of abuse, both of whom seemed more vulnerable to bullying than others.

Issues Relating to the Residents' World

In many respects the reactions of the young people to the homes were hardly surprising. They were happier if they had friends and they missed important people whom the had left behind. The wanted to see more of a wide variety of different members of other families. They got on with their social workers and sometimes valued them highly. Within the homes they complained of the consequences of group living and official constraints—the behaviour of other residents and police checks. They valued homes where the staff listened, the regime was not restrictive, the residents were friendly and there were interesting things to do.

In many respects the overall evaluation of homes depends on whether one wishes to call the glass half-empty or half-full. Perhaps the most encouraging aspect was the residents' evaluation of the staff. Generally they spoke well of them and felt that their relationship with them was good. A majority felt that they had been helped in one way or another, most commonly because the staff had listened and enabled them to talk things over.

A less positive feature of the homes was the degree to which they seemed to embody a delinquent culture. Nearly a third of those of school age were not going to school and intensive efforts to remedy their educational deficiencies were rare. Delinquency, bullying and harassment were widespread, and the offer of various kinds of drugs commonplace. These things had also characterised the residents' lives before they entered the homes. Criticism, if it is merited, is that the homes had not protected the residents against the local delinquent culture, not that they had increased its temptations.

A second disturbing feature was the widespread misery the residents experienced, and the degree to which key concerns (most notably their worries about their relationship with their peers) had not been addressed.

The misery was associated with the residents' previous experiences but more strongly with current events—bullying, sexual harassment, lack of friends and being in an environment which they had not chosen. It is not a situation of which the adult world can be proud. So it is ironic that the 'official' analysis of what is wrong should concentrate so heavily on the wrong-doing of staff—a group with whom residents typically get on well.

As in the last main section of this book, a striking feature of these data was the degree of variation between homes they revealed. Homes were seen very differently by both staff and residents; they differed also in the prevalence of delinquency and running away and in the degree to which residents said they had been helped. Our next two chapters are concerned with whether these differences can be explained and, if so, what lessons this explanation might bring.

13

OUTCOMES— VARIATIONS IN IMMEDIATE IMPACT

INTRODUCTION

The next two chapters are the culmination of the report. We have seen that homes differed widely in their structure (e.g. their staff ratios) and their processes (e.g. the rules and regulations). Our interviewers also reported that the atmosphere in different homes was very different, and we have found wide variations in both apparently hard measures (e.g. the proportions convicted while in the home) and reports by residents of how they treat each other and get on with the staff. These variations are in keeping with those noted in the research prior to 1975 (Bullock, Little and Millham 1993a), as well as more recent studies (Berridge and Brodie 1998; Brown *et al.* 1996). We need now to tackle two questions. First, can we develop reliable and valid measures of home outcomes? Second, can we identify links between this measure and the measures of structure and process on which the homes also differ?

In this chapter, our measure of outcome will be at a group rather than an individual level, and it will be heavily focused on delinquency. We will be examining rates of conviction and running away, and 'average' perceptions of the homes' social climates, not the convictions and perceptions of individuals. Partly for this reason, we will be concerned with what can loosely be called the 'resident culture'. The importance of this has been apparent in our data. We have seen that the friendliness of the residents and the nature of their behaviour was related to resident happiness and misery, while relationships with the staff were not. We have also seen the stress placed in the interviews with the head of home on the importance of establishing a culture whereby certain things are acceptable and others not—for once bullying and sexual exploitation become the norm, the most inoffensive young person may get swept along with the crowd, if not from the cruelty latent in us all, then from a prudent desire to be a member of the pack rather than the quarry.

There are four steps in our argument:

1. We develop a measure of culture and test its reliability.
2. We examine the measures' validity, exploring the degree to which it relates in an apparently sensible fashion to other measures which might be used in evaluation (e.g. staff morale).
3. We look at how far the measure relates to our measures of structure and outcome, taken one at a time (for example, at whether homes with a high proportion of 'trained' staff tend to have apparently better outcomes).
4. We try to develop a simple model which can explain variations in our measure in terms of measures of structure and process. The question is whether the statistical associations we find are simply associations or reflect some underlying structure of cause and effect.

In the following this argument readers need to bear in mind—but also, we hope, take in their stride—the serious errors of interpretation which can easily be made and which we list below:

1. There is the familiar danger that correlation does not mean causation. For a while the number of road accidents per year rose in parallel with the import of bananas. The reason was not that pedestrians slipped on banana skins.
2. There is a particular version of this danger which arises because we are considering variations in rates and averages when our real interest is in individuals. It may well be that football teams with the most expensive goal-keepers tend to score the most goals. It would however, be an error to suppose that it was the goal-keepers who were doing the scoring. In the end, such hypotheses have to be tested by going down a level and looking at individuals rather than groups.
3. We have shown earlier that, whereas there is a large group of homes which, to the outside eye, are performing much the same function, there are also a highly diverse group of more specialised homes (e.g. a home providing secure accommodation, or a home specialising in homes for young girls who have been sexually abused). It is possible, although no evidence has so far suggested it, that the relationships between structure, process and outcome are different in different kinds of home. An analysis which lumps all homes together could therefore be misleading.
4. The numbers on which our measures are based vary very considerably between homes. A running away rate based on 80 or so residents is,

from a purely statistical point of view, a much more reliable measure than one based on 10.

In listing these problems we risk inviting the reader to dismiss the chapter out of hand. In our view this would be a mistake. The dangers of misinterpretation call for caution, not total scepticism. One of the potential strengths of our study is that we have tried to look at the same question in a number of different ways, including—centrally—the kind of analysis embodied in this chapter.

DEVELOPING THE MEASURE AND TESTING ITS RELIABILITY

As we noted above, our measure of resident culture was heavily focused on delinquency. This may seem somewhat old-fashioned or even, given the welfare perspective of the Children Act, misguided. However, delinquent behaviour was a serious concern to social workers and parents. Residents also, in retrospect, commonly felt that they had been led into trouble and blamed the homes for their acquisition of a record. Moreover, we shall see below that delinquent behaviour outside the home was associated with a youth culture within the home that few would see as desirable.

Our measure of the resident culture had 10 components. Eight of these were taken from our measures of social climate. As will be remembered, we asked residents and staff to respond to a series of 28 statements and we used these to develop a variety of scores. The scores which we used in our measure were:

- Resident Friendliness (staff score).
- Resident Friendliness (resident score).
- Resident Behaviour (staff score).
- Resident Behaviour (resident score).
- Resident Involvement (staff score).
- Resident Involvement (resident score).
- Resident Morale (staff score).
- Resident Morale (resident score).

Each home for which data was available was given an average score for each of these variables, with the score for 'behaviour' reversed so that a 'high' score suggested a low level of fighting, drinking, and so on.

We also used two further measures, both derived from the heads of homes record of whether a young person who had been in the home over the previous year had run away or been convicted of an offence while there. It will be remembered that there were very wide variations between homes in the proportions who had been involved in these forms of behaviour. However, the likelihood that young people would be convicted in the home or run away was strongly related to the length of time for which they were in the home and whether or not they had had a previous conviction. For these reasons, we needed measures which took account of variations in the backgrounds of the young people and in the length of time for which they stayed.

We approached this problem in two different ways. The first involved predicting the likelihood of running away (and also of being convicted) on the basis of all the information available on the residents' backgrounds and on their length of stay. We then added information to the effect that a resident had been in a particular home rather than any of the others. This step made it possible to see whether information on the identity of homes significantly improved the predictions (which it did). It also provided a measure of the degree to which the home had fewer or more runaways and convictions than would have been expected from its intake and turnover. We had one measure for runaways and one measure for convictions and we added them together.

Our second approach made use of the relationship between absconding and offending on the one hand, and length of stay and previous conviction on the other. Thus, for those staying six months or more and having a previous conviction, the probability of being convicted while in the home was 0.73. The probability for those staying less than a month and not having a previous conviction was almost negligible. We calculated how far a home was doing better than expected in terms of offending by giving each resident a score of '1' if they offended and '0' if they did not, and then subtracting this score from their probability of getting into trouble. For example, if the probability was 0.73 and the resident did offend, he/she was given a new score of –0.27, whereas if he/she stayed out of trouble against the odds, his/her score remained at 0.73. The home's 'average' was based on these new scores for both offending and running away, which we again added together.

We included our two 'adjusted delinquency' scores with the eight based on the social climate scale in our overall measure. We made sure that a high score was *prima facie* 'good' in every case. We also standardised the scores to ensure that they were similar in their variability and had averages of zero. Table 13.1 sets out the correlations between these indices of the way the home functioned and, as can be seen, all were positive. In the light of this relatively high level of inter-correlation, we felt justified in adding the scores together on the grounds that it was tapping some underlying dimension.

Table 13.1 Correlations between suggested indices of delinquent culture in 39 homes

		1	2	3	4	5	6	7	8	9	10
1	Friendliness (res. score)	1.00									
2	Involvement (res. score)	.20	1.00								
3	Behaviour (res. score)	.25	.29	1.00							
4	Morale (res. score)	.53**	.24	.21	1.00						
5	Friendliness (staff score)	.15	.30*	.29	.21	1.00					
6	Involvement (staff score)	.22	.50**	.05	.31*	.55**	1.00				
7	Behaviour (staff score)	.11	.01	.33*	.26	.43**	.05	1.00			
8	Morale (staff score)	.17	.20	.17	.41**	.59**	.49**	.57**	1.00		
9	Adjusted delinquency (1)	.11	.40*	.33*	.30*	.36*	.09	.36*	.10	1.00	
10	Adjusted delinquency (2)	.26	.32	.44**	.44*	.39*	.09	.44**	.23	.85**	1.00

* $p < .05$.
** $p < .01$.
Sources: Resident interview; questionnaire to staff; Resident Log.

We called the resulting measure 'Goodhome' for convenience. From a statistical point of view, it was encouragingly normal. It varied from a low of −16.2 to a high of 12.5. It had an average of 0, a median of .4 and a standard deviation of 6.1. Fifty per cent of the homes scored between −4.6 and 4.1. Sixty-seven per cent fell within one standard deviation of the mean. We tested the inter-item reliability of this measure using Cronbach's alpha (α: see earlier explanation, Chapter 11). The value was 0.76 and certainly high enough for our purposes. We were afraid that this high value reflected the high correlation between our two measures of 'adjusted delinquency'. However, we found that dropping one or other of these variables made little difference to the overall reliability. We had enough information to calculate the measure on 39 homes.

TESTING THE VALIDITY OF GOODHOME

We are afraid that the last section may have alienated some readers, who may feel that the analysis was unnecessarily complicated and that they are being asked to accept a measure whose meaning has been obscured by a statistical fog. Hopefully, however, they will accept that the test of the measure is whether it relates sensibly to other information about the homes, and whether it picks out homes which are recognisably different in other ways.

At this point it may be useful to turn back to the description of two homes at the end of Chapter 7. These were, as it happens, the highest and lowest scorers on the Goodhome measure. Clearly they were very different places. Moreover our measure distinguished between them as it should have done.

The next step was to examine whether Goodhome related to other *prima facie* measures of quality. Table 13.2 gives the correlations between Goodhome and variables selected to reflect some of the major concerns of our earlier chapters. The outcome score is simply based on adding up the ratings of the head of home interview, which were based on asking her/ him how successful the home had been in particular areas (e.g. in relation to promoting good health).

Table 13.2 Relationship between Goodhome measure and other variables

	Correlation coefficient r
Home in a 'stable state' *(Details of Home Questionnaire)*	.43**
Home in a 'stable state' *(Rating of head of home interview)*	.47**
Positive staff/resident relationships *(Interviewer rating)*	.63**
Outcome Score *(Head of home interview)*	.37*
Staff morale score *(Staff questionnaire)*	.68**
Low proportion of reported bullying *(Interview with residents)*	.33*
High resident satisfaction with regime, etc. *(Interview with residents)*	.47**
High average 'happiness' score *(Interview with residents)*	−.26
Low proportion 'run away' *(Resident Log)*	.65**
Low proportion 'convicted' *(Resident Log)*	.58**
Residents report high average level of help *(Interview with residents)*	.38*

* $p < .05$.
** $p < .01$.

The major discrepant note in Table 13.2 is struck by the negative correlation between the happiness score and Goodhome. At the level of the individual, 'happiness', as we measured it, it was significantly related to attempts at bullying (or rather their absence) and perceptions of friendly relationships among residents. The corresponding group measures are either correlated with Goodhome or are components of it. So why was Goodhome not correlated with 'happiness'?

Part of the explanation for this anomaly lies in the background factors which predict a high 'happiness' score. A modified score based on the degree to which residents were happier than their sex, previous history, etc. would have predicted, have no correlation with Goodhome either way. The explanation for the remaining anomaly is likely to lie in the difference between the levels of analysis. Bullying almost certainly makes those on the receiving end very unhappy, but not necessarily the perpetrators. Indeed, they may well flourish. Thus, bullying may redistribute happiness within a home rather than alter its total quantity. That said, the remaining variables are significantly (generally highly significantly) correlated with Goodhome. Table 13.3 presents these associations in a different way for the variable 'Staff Morale', for the benefit of those to whom correlations are unfamiliar.

In Table 13.3 the range of scores for Staff Morale and Goodhome have been reallocated for the sake of simplicity into either 'low' or 'high', to demonstrate the relationship between the two variables. So, for example, 17 of the 21 homes which scores 'low' on the measure of Staff Morale also scored 'low' on the Goodhome measure; conversely, only four of the 21 scored 'high'. A similarly strong association can also be seen when it came to the 'high' scores for Staff Morale, where 16 of the 18 homes scored 'high' on the Goodhome measure and only two scored 'low'. It will be remembered from Table 13.1 that the correlation coefficient for the association between these two variables was 0.68 and significant in statistical terms at least at the .01 level.

Table 13.3 The relationship of Staff Morale to Goodhome

	Goodhome		
	'Low' (n)	'High' (n)	Totals
Staff Morale—'low'	17	4	21
Staff Morale—'high'	2	16	18
Totals	19	20	39

Difference significant at .0001 level.
Sources: Interview with residents; questionnaire to staff; Resident Log.

It is, of course, possible to replicate this type of presentation to demonstrate the relationship between Goodhome and a range of other measures, but space prevents us from doing so. Suffice it to say that we carried out several similar tests and each reflected a strong, statistically significant association and provided further confirmation of the validity of the Goodhome measure.

Some of the measures with which Goodhome was correlated came from instruments which also provided components of Goodhome. The correlations might for that reason be regarded as potentially suspect. For example, staff with high morale might be more likely to present the resident culture in a favourable light and their assessment of social climate is included in the Goodhome score. Other correlates of Goodhome, however, came from independent instruments, and the degree of inter-correlation is striking. A components analysis which used Goodhome and all the variables in Table 13.2 extracted 42% of the variance with the first component, on which the loading of Goodhome was 0.87.

The high level of inter-correlation no doubt partly reflects the way in which within a home one thing leads to another. Difficult behaviour by the residents may lead to poor morale on the part of the staff, which may make them less helpful. A lack of helpfulness on the part of the staff may then make the residents less amenable. It could therefore be that in a sense there is no reason for the large differences in our Goodhome score. In some homes a chance spark ignites the explosive mixture. Others are more fortunate.

This kind of explanation will need to be examined. For the moment we have shown that Goodhome correlated significantly with a large number of important variables. It seemed to us a reasonable 'all purpose' measure of the 'culture' of the home. In the rest of this chapter we will be concerned with explaining its variations.

THE CORRELATES OF GOODHOME

Structure

Children's homes are variable and sometimes explosive social entities. However, some aspects of them—size, staffing ratios, buildings and so on—remain fixed, at least over the short term. As we have argued earlier, these structural features are important partly because of their association with costs and partly because they are, over time, amenable to managerial control. How far can structure explain the variations in Goodhome discussed above?

In recent years, three structural features have been the focus of management attention. Homes have become smaller. There has been concern that staff in the homes are under-qualified, accompanied in some authorities (e.g. our Area 2) by attempts to improve their status and qualifications. There has been a sharp rise in staff ratios. So the official philosophy seems to be that homes will do better if they are small, professionally staffed, and have relatively high numbers of staff. Such a policy is expensive and we need to explore its impact.

Table 13.4 sets out the average Goodhome score by different levels of size, training and staff ratios. We present the data in this way rather than through correlation coefficients, partly because it is less vulnerable to 'outliers' (e.g. a very large home would have a major impact on any correlation involving size) and partly because it allows for the fact that the association between, for example, size and Goodhome may not be the same over the whole range. The figures presented in Table 13.4 look startling. They provide strong support for the policy of reducing the size of homes, and none at all for the policy of seeking qualified staff or of increasing staff ratios.

BBBBTable 13.4 Goodhome scores by size, training and staff ratios

Variable	Number of homes	Goodhome score
Size of home		
6 and under	19	2.7
7–9	13	–0.5
10 plus	7	–6.4
Percentage of trained staff		
0	11	1.0
4–12	15	0.1
13–50	10	–1.2
Percentage with relevant training		
0–10	25	0.6
11–20	5	–1.7
21 and over	6	0.8
Percentage with any training		
0– 17	11	0.2
18– 27	11	0.7
27–100	14	–0.6
Whether head trained		
No	16	1.5
Yes	23	–1.0
Staff hours to residents ratio		
23– 39	8	–0.8
40– 68	19	0.6
69–144	12	–0.3

Sources: Interview with residents; questionnaire to staff; Resident Log; Details of Home Questionnaire.

The first question is whether the negative findings on hours and training are in some way explained by the positive finding on size. It could be, for example, that the results were being skewed by a small number of large establishments with low staff ratios and under-qualified staff. If this was so, staff ratios and the proportions of staff with different kinds of training should vary with size. However, there was no relationship between size and staff qualifications or staff ratios.

The next question was whether unusual homes or extreme values of Goodhome were in some way distorting the results. We therefore analysed the data after dropping the 10 single-sex homes, the large home which had secure accommodation, and the home which had the most extreme value on Goodhome. We then repeated this analysis, dropping in addition homes where the average age was less than 13. In both cases the correlation with size (i.e. numbers of 'beds') remained highly significant, while those with staff training and staff ratios remained small and negative. There was therefore no evidence that our results were distorted by unusual homes or extreme values.

This analysis made it important to try and allow for differences in intake. Here we had two which seemed appropriate. The first was the proportion of residents who had a previous conviction or caution. The second was the average 'Adjustment' rating for the residents, which, as described earlier, was based on information from the social worker questionnaire. In some ways the former measure was the most suitable, since it reflected behaviour before arrival. By contrast, the social worker's view of the young person was likely to have been influenced by his/her behaviour in the home, which in turn was likely to reflect the home environment. Nevertheless, it seemed better to err on the side of caution and use both.

The proportion of young people with previous convictions was unrelated to our measures of staff training. It was positively associated with size ($r = .3$) and staff ratio ($r = .21$) and negatively associated with Goodhome ($r = -0.23$) but the associations were not significant. Our Adjustment measure was unrelated to staff training and negatively but not significantly related to staff ratio ($r = -0.18$). It was significantly associated with Goodhome ($r = .36$, $p < .05$) and negatively associated with size ($r = -0.36$, $p < .05$: statistically minded readers may wish to note that the latter correlation was done using the square root of size to diminish the influence of the small number of large homes). In other words, intake was unlikely to account for our failure to find an impact of training or staff ratios on Goodhome. However, smaller homes had better adjusted residents and better scores on our Goodhome measure. So intake might account for the apparently better results of smaller homes.

We tested this latter possibility taking into account previous convictions and average adjustment. We did the analysis taking account of each separately and then in combination. As might be expected, the correlation between size and Goodhome fell. Nevertheless, it remained obstinately significant ($p < .025$).

We made one final, speculative, attempt to find some impact of staff training and staff ratios. We reasoned that our Goodhome variable was strongly influenced by the way the residents were behaving and that, whereas trained staff might be no better than untrained ones at inducing good behaviour, they might be better at listening to residents, and that this might influence the level of happiness in the home. The data provided no support for this hypothesis.

Before leaving this section on structure we should note that we looked at the influence of building on outcome. We did not expect to find any associations. In fact, however, the interviewer rating of the degree to which the building looked 'institutional' was associated with a low Goodhome score almost at a significant level ($p < .06$). This, however, turned out to be an effect of size (for the more institutional homes were larger).

Our data would have allowed us to look for numerous other relationships (e.g. the possible effect of the proportion of women staff, of higher proportions of long-staying staff or of proportions of part-time staff). About the effect of such variables we had, however, no clear hypotheses, and 'fishing trips' to look for significant relationships, while beguiling, could have yielded a misleading number of significant results. In two respects, however, we had clear leads from Berridge and Brodie (1998), who found that homes with low staff turnover and homes where the head had a clear philosophy both produced higher quality care. As will be seen in the next chapter, we found that heads with a clear philosophy did appear to produce better long-term results. We did not, however, find that either of these two variables had the immediate effect we expected on our Goodhome measure.

In summary, the natural interpretation of the findings seems to be that if Goodhome is a measure of a home in reasonable 'control', it is promoted by keeping the numbers low, but not by insisting on a high proportion of qualified staff or particularly favourable staff ratios.

PROCESS VARIABLES AND GOODHOME

External Management

For reasons laid out in Chapter 7, we expected the success of the home to be greater when the head of home had a clear remit and reasonable autonomy to operate within that remit. Reorganisation was likely to interfere with the clarity of the remit and—temporarily perhaps—lower the home's success.

We tested these hypotheses using four variables:

- *Clarity*—the degree to which the head of home felt he/she had a clear remit, had thought how to fulfil it, and could see no particular difficulties in doing so.
- *Autonomy*—based on the head of homes' ratings of the autonomy they had in specified areas.
- *Empowerment*—a measure based on the components analysis described in Chapter 7, of which the first component (used here) was interpreted as indicating that the head of home felt empowered in specified ways by the management.
- *Reorganisation*—whether the home was said to have had a major change of function in the past year.

Table 13.5 sets out the correlations between these variables and Goodhome. The second column gives further information on their relationship with empowerment. There was no relationship between Goodhome and Autonomy. With this exception, Goodhome related to the selected variables as expected, although the relationship with Clarity was not significant. Empowerment was significantly related to Clarity but not—contrary to our expectations—to Reorganisation.

As before, we wanted to know whether the relationships between Empowerment, Reorganisation and Goodhome reflected the influence of some other variable. We therefore tested the association between Goodhome and Empowerment, holding steady our measure of intake (Adjustment) and size. The correlation with Empowerment remained significant ($r = .51$, $p < .002$). The correlation with Reorganisation sank ($r = -.25$, $p < .09$). For the moment, therefore, we can accept Empowerment, as we measured it, as a key influence on Goodhome.

Table 13.5 Correlation between remit variables and Goodhome and Empowerment

	Goodhome (r)	Empowerment (r)
Clarity	.32	.45**
Autonomy	.04	.14
Empowerment	.48**	1.00
Reorganisation	−.34*	−.07

* $p < .05$.
** $p < .01$.
Sources: Interview with residents; questionnaire to staff; Resident Log; interview with head of home.

Intake

As we have described, the heads of homes felt strongly that inappropriate admissions were a major source of trouble in their homes. In particular, they argued that their inability to reject admissions meant that difficult young people were admitted when the home could not cope with them or when their needs clashed with those of others. A more specific hypothesis was that remands caused difficulty because their needs were so different from those of other longer-stay residents. These hypotheses were supported by Whitaker and her colleagues (1998), whose work was based on staff accounts, and by Berridge and Brodie (1998), who found that a home's ability to influence its intake was associated with a high quality of care. For these reasons we examined the relationship of Goodhome with:

- The apparent difficulty of the intake as measure by the proportions with a previous conviction and the average level of Adjustment.
- The head of home's assessment of their ability to refuse admissions.
- The proportion of remands.
- The proportion of emergency admissions.

As already described, there was a significant correlation between our measure of Adjustment and Goodhome. This, however, dropped below the level of significance when we took account of the fact that the less well-adjusted seemed to go to the larger homes. Home size seemed to be a more potent influence on Goodhome than the level of Adjustment *per se*. The correlation between proportion with a previous conviction or caution and Goodhome already fell short of significance. It fell to almost nothing when account was taken of size.

We asked the heads of home whether they had a lot of freedom to refuse admissions, some or none. The relationship between this variable and Goodhome was not significant, and in any case in the reverse direction to the one we had predicted. The small number of heads who said they had a lot of freedom to refuse admissions had on average worse Goodhome scores than those who said they had some, who scored only slightly better than those who said they had none.

Homes that had had no remands in residence in the past 12 months did 'better' than homes that had had up to 10%, which in turn did 'better' than homes that had taken 10% or more. Once again, if size was taken into account, this association dropped below significance. Indeed, it was interesting that a small (six-bed) home had a particularly high proportion of remands but a high Goodhome score nonetheless.

As we predicted, there was a negative association between the proportion of emergency admissions and Goodhome. The correlation was, however, low ($r = -.17$), and was not significant whether or not size was taken into account.

In short, our investigation of the effects of intake and admission policy did not suggest that these had a strong effect on our Goodhome score. In so far as there was an association, it seemed to arise from the effects of size. Large homes differed in their intakes from smaller ones, but it was their size rather than their intake that seemed to be the important factor.

REGIME AND RELATIONSHIPS

Sinclair (1971, 1975) found that the proportion of residents leaving probation hostels because they had offended or run away depended essentially on three things—the degree to which the person in charge (warden) expressed warmth, the strictness of the regime, and the extent to which the warden and matron (always at that time the warden's wife) agreed over the way the hostel should be run. The strongest correlate of the absconding and offence rate was disagreement (measured by the number of questions to which the warden and matron gave different answers in a questionnaire they filled in independently). Strictness, it turned out, was associated with relatively low absconding and offence rates, not because it was valuable *per se* but because it was associated with agreement. These findings suggest that regime (and in particular the liberality of the regime) needs to be looked at in conjunction with staff consistency and the relationship between staff and residents.

Unfortunately, we have no satisfactory independent measure of staff 'warmth'. Good relationships between staff and residents, as rated by interviewers, were significantly correlated with our measure Goodhome. This association, however, did not show what produced good relationships between staff and residents—merely that they varied with Goodhome.

In practice, no-one in their right mind is going to doubt that warmth is a 'good thing' and any researcher who found otherwise would be rightly suspect. It is of more interest to discover whether Permissiveness is positively associated with Goodhome, as the residents would undoubtedly expect, or negatively, as Sinclair's earlier study would have suggested. Either way, it is important to assess the effect of staff agreement.

We took as our measure of Permissiveness the component given this name in Chapter 7. We had two measures of Staff Agreement. In the head of home interview, we rated the importance the head of home attached to Staff Agreement, the degree to which she/he had thought out ways of achieving this, the difficulties there seemed to be in achieving it, and the success apparently achieved. We added these together to give a measure of Staff Agreement as the head perceived it. In addition, the interviewers rated Staff Agreement on a four-point scale, ranging from 'friendly and cohesive' to 'tension and hostility'. Table 13.6 sets out the correlations between Permissiveness, the two measures of Staff Agreement, Size (or rather, for statistical reasons, its square root), Empowerment and Goodhome.

As can be seen, both our measures of Staff Agreement correlated with Goodhome, but disappointingly they did not correlate significantly together. A different method of analysis (analysis of variance, ANOVA) did in fact show a linear association between the two methods of assessing Staff Agreement, which just reached significance. Possibly our measures were tapping different but related concepts—the degree to which staff were agreed on the home's philosophy and the extent of interpersonal tensions among them. It therefore seemed that both our measures might have a contribution to make and we decided to simplify our analytic task by combining them (by standardising each and then adding them). The new measure of Staff Agreement correlated .52 ($p < .01$) with Goodhome. Before seeing what we can make of Table 13.6, we should look at the correlations between our regime variables and the two variables we have used to represent Intake (average level of adjustment and proportion of residents with previous convictions, Table 13.7).

Taking the two tables together, we can see that size is not correlated with any of the regime or management variables but is significantly associated with Adjustment and Previous Convictions. Larger establishments took more difficult young people, but, as we have already discussed, this did not fully explain its association with Goodhome. Size, it seems, is likely to play an honoured part in any explanation of Goodhome's variations.

Table 13.6 Correlation matrix for Goodhome and other key variables

	Good- home	Size	Em- power- ment	Staff 1	Staff 2	Permis- sive- ness
Goodhome	1.00					
Size (sq root)	−.46**	1.00				
Empowerment	.48**	−.04	1.00			
Staff Agreement 1						
(rated by interviewer)	.38**	.17	.29	1.00		
Staff Agreement 2						
(head of home interview)	.44**	.08	.44**	.29	1.00	
Permissiveness	.37**	−.13	.14	.29	.41**	1.00

** $p < .01$.
Sources: Interview with residents; questionnaire to staff; Resident Log; interview with head of home; interviewer rating.

Table 13.7 Correlation between regime variables and 'Average Adjustment' and percentage of Previous Convictions

	Average Adjustment (r)	Percentage of Previous Convictions (r)
Goodhome	.37*	−.23
Size	−.35*	.31*
Empowerment	.20	.01
Staff Agreement	.21	.03
Permissiveness	.54**	−.26

* $p < .05$.
** $p < .01$.
Sources: Interview with residents; questionnaire to staff; Resident Log; interview with head of home; interviewer rating.

It was interesting that Sinclair's 1971 findings on Permissiveness were reversed. Staff Agreement was more, not less, likely in permissive homes and such homes were less, not more, troubled with difficult behaviour. The reason perhaps had to do with the differences in the managerial environment. In the 1960s, Home Office regulations made Permissiveness difficult to achieve with any consistency. Social Services departments in the 1990s encourage a more relaxed approach.

In one respect, however, Sinclair's results were confirmed. The effects of Permissiveness or the lack of it almost certainly depended on the level of Agreement which the policy commanded. The association between Agreement and Goodhome remained very highly significant if we controlled for Permissiveness. However, the association between Permissiveness and Goodhome fell below significance when we controlled for Agreement. Thus, permissive establishments where there was little Agreement did no better than strict ones where the staff were similarly at odds. Neither, if they achieved agreement, did they do significantly better than strict establishments where the staff were agreed.

The correlation between Permissiveness and Goodhome also shrank below significance if we took into account the fact that permissive homes had, on average, better-adjusted residents (the latter perhaps a reflection of the fact that the better adjusted the residents, the easier it is to run a relaxed regime).

Did intake similarly account for the apparent effects on Goodhome of Empowerment and Agreement? The answer is apparently 'no'. Both associations remained significant when we took account of our measures of Previous Convictions and of average level of Adjustment. More surprising, perhaps, was the fact that the association between our measures of Intake and Goodhome dropped below significance when we took account of Size. As far as these statistics go, homes with difficult intakes do badly because they are large, not because their intake is difficult.

So what about the relationships between our remaining three variables (Size, Empowerment, and Agreement)? If we take any two into account, does the relationship of the other one and Goodhome drop below significance? The answer is 'no'. So each of these variables seems to have an independent effect on Goodhome.

A multiple regression using Goodhome as the dependent variable and Size, Empowerment and Staff Agreement as the independent ones produced a multiple correlation coefficient of 0.7, (although the regression coefficient of Empowerment fell short of significance—$p < .08$).

SUMMARY

There are five main groups of findings in this chapter:

1. The homes varied widely in the degree to which their residents ran away or got into trouble with the police and these differences did not seem to be accounted for by differences in intake or in time 'at risk'.
2. These differences are strongly associated with the degree to which residents and staff see the home as containing a 'delinquent' culture marked by difficult behaviour, unfriendly relationships between residents, a feeling on the part of residents that they had little say in how the home was run, and low resident morale.
3. A measure, Goodhome, based on these associations, was strongly related to other desirable features of the homes (e.g. staff morale and the degree to which residents felt they had been helped).
4. Staff:resident ratios and the proportion of trained staff were unrelated to this measure.
5. Goodhome was positively associated with Staff Agreement, Size and Empowerment of the head. These associations were not explained as far as we could see by Intake.

Two points should be covered before we draw implications for practice: the degree to which we should trust the negative findings on staff qualifications and staff hours; and the degree to which our findings match or contradict the findings of Brown and her colleagues (1996) and Berridge and Brodie (1998).

Our confidence that the existence of a qualified head and the proportion of qualified staff did not in themselves have a good effect on outcomes is bolstered by two observations. First, this conclusion is in keeping with that of Berridge and Brodie (1998), who similarly decided that a qualified staff group was not a key to a high quality of care. Second, it is in keeping with our own finding that both a qualified head and a relatively high proportion of qualified staff were positively associated with low morale among staff. On these grounds we think it highly unlikely that a high proportion of qualified staff will, under present conditions, have the good effect on homes that is expected of it.

There are similarly two reasons for thinking that a favourable staffing ratio is not the key to a smooth-running home. First, Berridge and Brodie again concur—indeed, they suggest that a large number of staff may on occasion have a negative effect, as they may tend to gather in the office and talk to each other in preference to talking to the residents. Second, more complicated analysis of our own suggested that a high staff ratio might, other things being equal, have a bad effect. As we noted earlier, larger homes tended to have a lower ratio of staff to residents up to a size of 14, after which homes tended to be subdivided into sub-units. As smaller homes do better, one would expect that over this range, homes with higher staff ratios should do better. This association did not occur because of a countervailing tendency. After allowing for size, a high staff ratio was significantly associated with a worse Goodhome score. We can believe that this is a statistical chance. However, it seems very unlikely that high staffing ratios were having a good effect.

So what of our agreement or disagreement with the other recent studies that have been concerned with differences? For us, the agreement is far more striking than the difference. Both the two studies emphasise the importance or staff unity and Brown and her colleagues place considerable stress on coherence—between the official basis of the homes, the external management, the goals of the home, the beliefs of the head, and the culture of the staff (measured in their case by similar responses to questions about what should happen around certain key events). These conclusions are eminently in keeping with ours. If staff unity is the key, a mismatch between the head of home's beliefs and those of external management is likely to disturb it, offering a different definition of what the home is about which may be seized on by dissident members of staff. Hence, perhaps, arises the different association between permissiveness and staff unity in this study and that found in Sinclair's study in the less permissive 1960s.

These considerations may cast light on the key topic of the relationship between the home and its external management. The fear is that autonomy for the home may enable poor practice. However, a strategy of ensuring compliance through frequent inspections and the like may be counter-productive. The present study suggests that what is required is agreement. Autonomy *per se* does not seem to matter. Rather, it is the sense that the head of home knows where he/she is and can therefore act confidently and creatively, certain of what the home is about and what her/his management expects.

There are three groups of findings where our results appear to conflict with those of Berridge and Brodie. In the case of two of these, we would much rather have confirmed their conclusions. They suggest that a high quality of care is more likely where the head has a clear philosophy and staff turnover is low. Both these factors are likely to produce a more cohesive staff group and would therefore fit our overall conclusion. Our failure to replicate their results may reflect the different way we measured outcome—their measure, for example, included aspects of practice and morale which may have been more affected by the head's views and staff turnover than was Goodhome.

Berridge and Brodie found no association between size and quality of care. They suggest that the positive association between Goodhome and Size in our study may arise because we, unlike them, had a number of large homes. In practice, however, the association is still significant if homes taking more than 10 residents are omitted. We think it more likely that the difference between the two studies arises because their study included different kinds of home (e.g. homes for disabled children). The association between size and outcome may be easier to detect in homes that are serving similar populations.

Finally, to any readers who are not used to statistics and who have struggled this far, it is, hopefully, encouraging that the message from these statistics seems simple. Homes are more easily kept in reasonable shape if:

- They are small.
- The head of home feels that its roles are clear, mutually compatible, and not disturbed by frequent reorganisation and that he/she is then given adequate autonomy to get on with the job.
- The staff are agreed about how the home should run and are not at odds with each other.

The message is perhaps even simpler. The problem is to get agreement among the residents on what is acceptable behaviour. The solution is to have small homes where staff and management are agreed on what the home is about.

14

OUTCOMES—
VARIATIONS IN LONG-
TERM IMPACT

INTRODUCTION

We are almost now at the end of our empirical journey. Our last task is to try to make some statistical sense of the outcomes which the young people sketched out for us six months after we first interviewed them.

As researchers we approached this task with guarded optimism. Few studies of the long-term effects of residential care have been encouraging. Some have emphasised the confusion engendered in both staff and residents by treatment approaches and their hostility towards them (Ackland 1982; Kendrick and Fraser 1992; Polsky 1965; Walter 1977), others the concentration of residential staff on immediate concerns rather than long-term change (Millham, Bullock and Cherrett 1975; Petrie 1980; Walter 1977); others the way in which changes that take place in residential care tend to be nullified by the environments to which the residents return (Allerhand, Weber and Haug 1966; Coates, Miller and Ohlin 1978; Lewis 1982; Petrie 1980; Sinclair 1971, 1975; Taylor and Alpert 1973). Nevertheless 'cross-institutional' designs of the kind used in this study have been able to identify some differences between establishments in their effects on longer-term outcomes (Dunlop 1974; Sinclair and Clark 1973). So we had some grounds for thinking that we might be able to do the same.

Our task could be broken into two sub-tasks. First, we needed to develop measures of outcome. Second, we needed to explore their relationship with the kind of home in which the young people had been. Both purposes required us to amalgamate data from different surveys. This naturally increased the number of missing cases. Analyses that are based on linking the first and second social worker questionnaires are based on 122 cases and those which linked the first social worker questionnaire to the resident survey on 113 cases. We compared these two samples with the original resident sample on a wide number of variables. In almost all respects they were very similar. There was no reason to think that the ways in which they differed were likely to affect our conclusions.

DESTINATIONS

Table 14.1 sets out where the residents were according to the social workers and their own accounts. The third column is based on a combination of the two accounts, giving priority to information from the residents where this was available.

As can be seen, there was little difference in the overall frequency of the destinations described by social workers and residents. 'Destinations', indeed, is a somewhat misleading word because the most common outcome, applying to 50–60% of the sample, was that the young people stayed in residential care, the majority of them in the same home. Approximately equal numbers (around 15%) went to family or relatives as went into some form of independent living. The remainder were roughly evenly divided between foster care and 'other'.

These destinations matched to some extent the earlier expectations of social workers and young people and the young people's aspirations when they had been interviewed around six months earlier. To compare plans and outcomes, it is necessary to omit those still in residential care—for these must include many for whom the plans were not yet fulfilled. Comparisons between actual and expected destination is still not easy (e.g. because at the first stage no plans had yet been formulated). If these 'don't knows' and 'other' destinations are ignored, almost exactly half the remainder had gone where the social worker had expected and just over half where the young person had expected (albeit 28% of the residents

Table 14.1 Resident destinations according to residents and social workers

Destination	Residents n = 141 (%)	Social workers n = 141 (%)	Combined n = 163 (%)
Same home	52.1	39.0	48.6
Another home	10.7	10.6	9.0
Birth parent(s)	11.4	12.8	11.9
Other relatives	3.6	4.3	3.4
Foster parents	4.3	8.5	5.6
Hostel	2.9	5.7	4.5
Flat	5.7	5.7	5.6
Lodgings	4.3	6.4	5.1
Somewhere else	5.0	7.1	6.2

Sources: Follow-up questionnaire to residents; follow-up questionnaire to social workers.

had had no expectations). On the same basis, just over half the residents had achieved the destination they wanted.

The relevant social workers were able to consider where the young people in the sample were now and assess whether this was what had been intended six months previously. They said that 43% of the residents were not where it had been expected they would go. Events, it seemed, were often out of the control of either the young person or the social worker:

Went home but thrown out, then requested local authority accommodation but this refused. He was encouraged to stay at a hostel with a view to independent living but went home. There was a breakdown at home and he is now at a hostel.

No-one professionally can provide for young person's needs as all services refuse responsibility. Spent one month in hospital, caught between adult services, who said he was not mentally ill and was on no medication, and the young person's unit, who would not take him in for proper assessment as requested. He falls between resources and at the moment I can find no resources for him. He is currently on remand for armed robbery.

Describing another unsettled young person, the social worker noted that 'She has drifted from one crisis to another at a great cost to herself, her family—and her social worker!!!'. Clearly such cases put great strain on all involved. Yet in fairness, their vivid stories need to be balanced against those of others who pursued a quieter course:

Young person has continued to need support, both practical and emotional, after leaving 'care'. This has been reduced as appropriate and he is now living independently fairly successfully—this has increased his self-esteem.

Before when I came in this home I felt unhappy because I was getting bullied. But the Staff have changed that for me. Now I am very happy. I love it here (young person).

Things have turned out very well for me. I have moved into another children's home, but there are fewer children so I get the individual attention that I needed. I am very pleased with the way that social services pushed to find me an environment that would suit me and help me (young person).

Any evaluation should include such positive stories and also take into account the troubled starting point from which the young people began their time in care. Moreover, as will be apparent from some of the above quotations, the success of a placement in residential care often depends in the final analysis not on the home but on the actions of others after the resident has left. In order to assess the impact of the home on these events, we need first of all some measures of outcome.

DEVELOPING MEASURES OF OUTCOME

At the time of the first interview, we asked the social worker how happy they were that the current placement was the right one. We asked them again at the follow-up to rate the success of the placement on a four-point scale ranging from markedly successful to markedly unsuccessful. These measures have the disadvantage of subjectivity, but the advantage that the social worker was presumably measuring success in the light of what was possible and the particular aims that the placement was intended to achieve. We therefore included them among our measures of success.

We balanced these questions to the social workers with a similar one to the residents at follow-up when we asked them, 'Do you think it was a good thing that you went to that home?'. This question had the disadvantage that it implicitly involved two questions, not one: first, whether the residents thought that 'care' had been a good idea at all, and second, whether, given that they were going into care, they thought that the home had been the right placement. Despite this disadvantage, the question seemed to tap some overall evaluation of whether their experience had been a good one and we included it as an evaluative measure.

We took one other measure from the resident follow-up questionnaire. This was our Happiness scale, which contained the same questions as those we used in the resident interview but with one exception—we did not ask the residents whether they had thought of killing themselves in the last month. It seemed wrong to raise this issue out of the context of an interview.

Our final set of measures was taken from the social worker follow-up questionnaire and was based partly on the ratings of Development, which we had used at the time of the first interview, and partly on a list of Problem Behaviours. We scored these in the same way as previously and produced measures of:

- Adjustment.
- Occupation (involvement in work/education).
- Relationships.
- Skills at looking after self.
- Problem Behaviours.

Relationship Between Measures

This gave us a rather large set of 10 outcome measures and we were anxious to reduce this number, if we could. For this reason we looked for inter-correlations among them and began with the Development and Problem Behaviour measures taken from the second social worker questionnaire. Table 14.2 sets out the inter-correlations between them.

As can be seen, there were high correlations between all our Development and Behaviour measures. This could have occurred because of a 'halo' effect. Social workers who thought the resident was doing well in one area of life may have felt that they were doing well in all. However, it is also likely that these outcomes were characterised by benign or vicious circles. Young people who were well-adjusted, behaving well and competent at looking after themselves were likely to please their families and get on at school or work. Success at school or work would have pleased families and increased a young person's self-respect. Family support and increasing self-respect were likely to improve Behaviour and Adjustment. So the potential benign circle was obvious enough and the potential vicious one could be easily imagined.

Ideally, we would have included all these areas in a composite measure. However, as we have seen, social workers were more ready to rate the young people than to list their problem behaviours. Inclusion of the Problem Behaviour variable would therefore have unacceptably lowered the numbers available for analysis. For these reasons we computed a new variable based on all the variables in Table 14.2 except for Problem Behaviour, standardising them and adding them as usual. The reliability of this variable, which we called Doing Well, was 0.76, which we considered satisfactory.

We next examined the relationship between Doing Well and our other outcome measures. Table 14.3 sets out the results. As can be seen, there were positive and significant relationships between most of the

Table 14.2 Inter-correlations of development and behaviour measures

	Adjustment	Occupation	Support	Skills	Behaviour
Adjustment	1.00				
Occupation	.35**	1.00			
Family's Support	.62**	.20*	1.00		
Skills	.63**	.35**	.50**	1.00	
Problem Behaviour	−.66**	−.28**	−.47**	−.42**	1.00

* $p < 0.05$.
** $p < 0.01$.
Source: Follow-up questionnaire to social workers.

Table 14.3 Inter-correlations between Doing Well and other outcomes

	Happiness	Doing Well	Good idea	Placement right	Placement a success
Happiness	1.00				
Doing well	.24**	1.00			
Home good idea	.04	.11	1.00		
Placement right	.08	.26**	.28**	1.00	
Placement a success	.16	.36**	.21*	.28**	1.00

* $p < 0.05$.
** $p < 0.01$.
Sources: Follow-up questionnaire to residents; first questionnaire to social workers; follow-up questionnaire to social workers.

variables in Table 14.3. The exception was Happiness, to which only Doing Well was significantly related. The inter-correlations in Table 14.3 were lower than those in Table 14.2 and so we decided not to amalgamate the variables involved in some composite measure of outcome.

It is interesting that the resident's positive evaluation of the placement was associated neither with Doing Well nor with current mood (Happiness). It is as if the young people were regarding the placement as disconnected from their current experience and as good or bad in its own right, rather than because of its subsequent effects. We will return to this speculation below.

GOODHOME AND MEASURES OF OUTCOME

We have argued earlier that the 'culture' of the home had a major impact on the young people's behaviour and that the homes could be usefully described in terms of our measure Goodhome. We wanted to see whether being in a Goodhome was associated with our outcome measures. Table 14.4 sets out the relevant correlations.

The message of these correlations seems simple and discouraging. Goodhome was significantly correlated with the social workers' first evaluation

Table 14.4 Correlations between outcome and Goodhome

Outcome	r
Happiness	−.05
Doing well	−.06
Placement a success	.05
Placement right	.26**
Placement a good idea	.22*

* $p < .05$.
** $p < .01$.
Source: Follow-up questionnaire to social workers.

of the placement, and with the young person's retrospective view of it. It was quite unrelated to the current measures of outcome, whether these were based on the social workers' assessment of success, reports of Happiness on the part of the resident, or the social workers' ratings which made up our Doing Well score. The impact of the home may have been powerful at the time and a source of pleasure or displeasure in retrospect. It seemed to have very little relevance in the medium term.

One possible explanation for this result was that if the home could have a powerful impact, so too could a new environment to which the residents went. If this was so, we would expect to get more meaningful results if we took into account whether the residents had stayed in the same home or moved somewhere else. There was some evidence that this was so. If we considered only those residents who remained in the same home, the correlation between the resident's evaluation of the placement and Goodhome rose to 0.33, a highly significant correlation if hardly a large one. We also rated the young people's accounts of how they were doing and found a highly significant correlation between this and Goodhome ($r = .34$). The correlation with the social worker's estimate of the success of the placement and Goodhome remained insignificant. Where the young people had moved from the home, none of these correlations reached significance or even approached it.

The effect of movement on Happiness was also interesting. The happiest young people were, on average, those who had been in a home with a below-average Goodhome score (a Badhome) and who had subsequently moved from it. The next happiest group were those who were in a goodhome and had stayed there. The two unhappiest groups were those who had been in a Goodhome and left it and those who had entered a Badhome and stayed there. This statistical 'interaction' was significant ($p < .03$). From a less statistical point of view, the result recalls the comments of the young people quoted earlier, both those breathing relief that a bad experience was over, and those expressing sadness that the support they had received in 'care' was no longer theirs.

In contrast to happiness and the resident's subjective evaluation of the placement, Goodhome appeared to have no relationship to Doing Well, either for good or ill.

EXPLAINING THE OUTCOME MEASURES

Environmental Effects

The results reported above suggest that a young person's immediate environment can have a major impact on them but that this is often transitory. Further evidence for such an effect came from an analysis of the association between our Happiness Score and whether the young person had reported that someone had tried to bully them or sexually abuse them in the home. It will be remembered that unhappiness had been strongly correlated with these variables. Their correlation with unhappiness at follow-up was low and not significant. In fact, improvement in the Happiness score was significantly associated with reports of attempted sexual abuse in the home at the first interview.

Our next enquiry focused on the possible impact of environment on the young person's behaviour and adjustment. We had two measures of the young people's involvement in their current environment, one relating to school and work, and one relating to their family. We began by seeing how far these measures could predict our measure of Adjustment. As might be expected from the findings in Table 14.2, they could do this quite well. This, however, did not take us very far, since the causation could run in either direction. A young person might be maladjusted because he/she was not involved in work or school, or not involved in work or school because he/she was maladjusted. To try to disentangle cause and effect, we did a rather more complicated analysis which took account of what we knew about the young person at an earlier point. We tested three main hypotheses.

Our first hypothesis was that the current environment accounted for adjustment completely. If this was so, one would expect that any apparent association between a young person's previous adjustment and their subsequent behaviour would occur because their previous adjustment had affected their subsequent environment (for example, by behaving in a criminal way they had got themselves into prison, where they had taken on prison ways). This rather extreme hypothesis was false. There was a strong correlation ($r = .54$) between previous adjustment and subsequent adjustment after taking account of the subsequent environment (involvement in school and involvement in relationships). So the effects of individual characteristics on subsequent behaviour were not mediated solely by their impact on the subsequent environment.

Our second hypothesis was that a young person's environment when we first encountered them (i.e. their involvement in school or work and with their family) would have a lasting effect on their subsequent adjustment irrespective of the subsequent environment. This hypothesis was also false. There was no association between subsequent adjustment and the previous environment after taking account of the subsequent environment.

Our last hypothesis was that subsequent environment (involvement in school and work, and involvement with family) would have an impact on subsequent adjustment even after taking previous adjustment into account. We found this to be so for both school/work and family relationships. So subsequent adjustment partly reflects subsequent environment.

These findings suggest that homes need to operate on two fronts. First, they need to try and improve the adjustment of the young people in them, for this may have an effect on the young people's adjustment in the long term. Second, they need to operate on the young people's environment in the longer term, for this too is relevant to long-term adjustment.

CHANGING THE INDIVIDUAL

The previous sections are testimony to the power of the previous environment but also to its short-lived effects. The section may also suggest that individuals also have enduring personal characteristics and may make their histories as well as respond to them. Is there anything that the homes can do about changing the individual so that he/she is different in the long term?

Social Work

Social work was one possible way of achieving individual change which we considered. As Chapters 5 and 10 made clear, it was an area of work in which the young people saw much variability and for which they were sometimes very grateful. We were not able to consider the effects of social work after the young person had left the home and so we looked at our measures of social work in the home to see if they were associated with outcome on leaving it.

We looked at the association between all our measures of social work involvement and found that, if anything, they were associated with negative outcomes. It seemed more likely that this arose because social workers concentrated on the more difficult cases, rather than that the social workers were making their clients worse. By taking account of various background characteristics, we managed to lower most of the correlations to insignificance. Two, however, obstinately remained. Current mood (as reflected in our Happiness score) and the social worker's estimate of the placement success were both 'worse' when the young person had received social work counselling of some kind as we measured it and also when the social worker had been comparatively heavily involved in making arrangements. This remained true even when we took account of mood at the time of the first interview (when the counselling would have been given). There were similar associations with the social worker's assessment of the success of the placement.

There are a variety of possible explanations for these findings. A fall in our Happiness score could reflect a greater willingness to acknowledge problems which had been encouraged by counselling. It could reflect a drop in support. Just as young people who had left Goodhomes were sadder than those who had left Badhomes, so those who had received intensive counselling might be sad when it stopped. It could reflect disappointment that social workers had embarked on activities for which they had neither the time nor the skill. Or it could simply be that there is some correlate that we have failed to identify. Whatever the explanation, the main point is that it is very unlikely that social work at the first point in time made much positive difference to the young people six months later. (This says nothing, of course, about the disadvantages or advantages of intervention at the time of follow-up. According to the young people, some social workers were worth their weight in gold at this point.)

If social work at the time the young person was in the home appears to have relatively little effect, what about the home itself?

OUTCOMES AND HOME EMPHASES

As a check on the possibility that the home might be having effects in specific areas, we looked at the average outcomes for each home in each of our dimensions of outcome. We then related them to the questions we had asked of the head of home. It will be remembered that in our interview we concentrated on what the home was trying to do, what means it used to this end, what the difficulties were, and what degree of success was thought to be achieved. We rated each of these areas and we will look in turn at how ratings were associated with the outcomes.

Before presenting the results we should give two caveats. First, it was not possible to take account of 'input' to the degree to which we would have wished. It might appear that one could use the information gathered at the time of the first interview and allow for this in assessing outcome at the second. Unfortunately, at the time of the first interview the homes were already having an important effect. By following the procedure just suggested, we could apparently prove that being bullied was good for mental health, for attempted bullying around the first interview was associated with an improvement in Happiness at the second.

Second, we will be presenting a large number of correlations (32 for each area of questioning). When so many correlations are carried out, at least one is likely to be significant at the 5% level. So it is more than usually important to look both at the level of significance and at the degree to which they make sense, and 'hang together'.

Problem Behaviour

Table 14.5 sets out correlations between eight possible measures of outcome and the heads' aims (expectation), means, difficulties and apparent success in the area of Problem Behaviour. (In examining outcome, we used both our overall measure Doing Well and the four measures of which it was comprised.)

The correlations in Table 14.5 suggest that the head's approach to Problem Behaviour was important—for success in this area had two significant correlations with measures of outcome. However, it is dubious whether these correlations represented successful efforts on the part of some homes. It may simply have been that residents who were 'easier' made the heads of homes feel that they were being successful and then went on to do well in the future. Aims and means were uncorrelated with outcome, and the one significant correlation with a low level of difficulty may well have reflected the advantages of having an easy intake.

Some correlation to these rather negative conclusions was provided by a further analysis which we carried out at the level of the individual and which looked at change in adjustment. In carrying out this analysis, we associated each young person with the head's score on means for improving behaviour. We also took account of the resident's Adjustment score at the time of the first interview (for it is likely that residents with very good or very poor scores at first interview will have been caught at a particularly good or bad time and will tend to get more average scores at

Table 14.5 Correlation of outcomes and head of home's response to Problem Behaviour

| Outcome | Head of home interview: Problem Behaviour | | | |
	Aims (r)	Means (r)	Difficulties (r)	Success (r)
Doing well	.05	.08	.02	.22
Skilled for age	.08	.14	.13	.38*
Involved in school or work	.14	.03	−.07	−.05
Adjustment	−.13	−.03	.03	.21
Relationships	.05	.10	−.01	.19
Placement good idea (young person)	.26	.24	.32*	.43**
Placement a success (social worker)	−.01	−.06	−.14	−.12
Young person happy now	.05	−.10	−.15	−.02

* $p < .05$.
** $p < .01$.
Sources: Follow-up questionnaire to residents; first questionnaire to social workers; follow-up questionnaire to social workers; interview with head of home.

follow-up). This analysis showed that on average there was very little change in Adjustment between the first and second interviews. However, there was an almost significant tendency ($p = .06$) for residents to improve more (or deteriorate less) if they were in homes where the head had a well-developed philosophy on how to deal with behaviour.

Emotional Problems

Table 14.6 sets out similar correlations in the area of Emotional Problems. Two points about it are of interest. First, aiming to deal with emotional problems was negatively associated with a number of dimensions. It is to be hoped that this reflected the effects of intake rather than of ill-judged efforts in the wilder reaches of psychotherapy or behaviour modification. Second, our ratings of means as opposed to aims were positively associated with most areas of success, and significantly so in the case of relationships.

It is possible to take these findings a little further and examine the relationship between 'means' and Doing Well while holding 'aims' steady. When this was done, 'means' related significantly to Doing Well, Skilled for Age, and Relationships. All this suggested that after allowing for the effect of 'aims' on intake, a thought-through approach had an important impact.

Family Relationships

Table 14.7 gives the correlations for the area of Family Relationships. The correlations were in the expected direction, but only the one relating to

Table 14.6 Correlation between outcomes and head of home's response to Emotional Problems

	Head of home interview: Emotional Problems			
Outcome	Aims (r)	Means (r)	Difficulties (r)	Success (r)
Doing well	−.31*	.24	.15	.06
Skilled for age	−.26	.25	.26	.13
Involved in school or work	−.27	.06	−.07	−.11
Adjustment	−.34*	.10	.18	−.01
Relationships	−.22	.32*	.13	.16
Placement good idea	−.13	.18	.27	.18
Placement a success	−.03	−.04	−.05	−.26
Young person happy now	.10	.03	−.02	.27

* $p < .05$.
Sources: Follow-up questionnaire to residents; first questionnaire to social workers; follow-up questionnaire to social workers; interview with head of home.

Table 14.7 Correlation between outcomes and head of home's response to Family Relations

	Head of home interview: Family Relationships			
Outcome	Aims (r)	Means (r)	Difficulties (r)	Success (r)
Doing well	.05	.28	.22	.16
Skilled for age	.02	.22	.21	.22
Involved in school or work	−.04	.24	−.02	.02
Adjustment	.15	.23	.26	.16
Relationships	.06	.30	.32*	.13
Placement good idea	−.04	.01	−.08	.13
Placement a success	−.02	.08	.18	.07
Young person happy now	.03	.13	.11	.21

* $p < .05$.

Sources: Follow-up questionnaire to residents; first questionnaire to social workers; follow-up questionnaire to social workers; interview with head of home.

level of difficulty actually reached significance. So as far as this table goes, homes which put a high level of effort into this area of work probably did not do much better than others.

Subsequent analysis at the level of the individual again gave a more positive impression. As in the case of behaviour, this analysis associated each individual with the 'family means score' of their head, was concerned with the change in relationships, and allowed for the initial state of these relationships when we first met the young person (the degree to which heads had thought through their approach to their area of work). What we found was that the family means score appeared to have no effect on the frequency with which the young person saw her/his family, but did appear to have a marked effect on family ties as the social workers assessed them. After allowing for the initial strength of these ties, the apparent effect of the family means score on change for the better was very highly significant ($p = .0007$).

Education

Table 14.8 looks at the relationship between an emphasis on education and our measures of outcome. As can be seen, a high rating for 'means' correlated significantly with five of our measures of outcome and with four of them at a high level of significance.

Paradoxically, one outcome with which this measure did not correlate was Involvement in School or Work. This raises the question of whether what was involved was the emphasis on school *per se* or whether this was a proxy for a more general emphasis on responsible social behaviour. In

Table 14.8 Correlation between outcomes and head of home's response to Education

	Head of home interview: Education			
Outcome	Aims (r)	Means (r)	Difficulties (r)	Success (r)
Doing well	.18	.42**	.10	.29
Skilled for age	.30	.50**	.15	.33*
Involved in school or work	.01	.09	−.01	.30
Adjustment	.15	.32**	.10	.15
Relationships	.18	.47**	.18	.26
Placement good idea	.23	.42**	.41**	.50**
Placement a success	.15	.01	−.19	.02
Young person happy now	.05	.15	.01	.24

$*\ p < .05.$
$**\ p < .01.$
Sources: Follow-up questionnaire to residents; first questionnaire to social workers; follow-up questionnaire to social workers; interview with head of home.

this case, analysis at the level of the individual did not give more positive results. We return to this issue later.

Moving On

Table 14.9 looks at the relationship between outcome and the home's reported work in the area of Moving On. The relationships here were not surprising. The only ones which reached significance had to do with difficulties. Success in Moving On depends on a number of factors which are probably beyond the homes' control. Heads of homes rated as reporting a high number of difficulties were significantly more likely to find problems with the care planning system, and with local employment and housing opportunities. So it is not surprising to find that a low level of difficulties over Moving On were positively related to most of our outcome variables, and significantly so in the areas of Doing Well, 'Skill' and the young person's evaluation of the Success of the Placement.

Work

Table 14.10 deals with the emphasis on Finding Work. Thought-through means of doing so correlated positively with all but one of our measures of success, but not significantly so. The positive correlation of reported success in this area with Skill for age and the young person's positive evaluation of the Placement reinforce the presumption that work is important. It is not, however, clear that the homes had a major impact in this area.

Table 14.9   Correlation between outcomes and head of home's response to Moving On

| | Head of home interview: Moving On | | | |
Outcome	Aims (r)	Means (r)	Difficulties (r)	Success (r)
Doing well	.01	.08	.37*	.25
Skilled for age	−.03	.05	.33*	.33*
Involved in school or work	.06	.02	.29	.13
Adjustment	.02	.11	.28	.12
Relationships	−.03	.14	.26	.19
Placement good idea	.16	.13	.35*	.24
Placement a success	−.08	.16	.06	.04
Young person happy now	.03	.15	.11	.20

* $p < .05$.

Sources: Follow-up questionnaire to residents; first questionnaire to social workers; follow-up questionnaire to social workers; interview with head of home.

Table 14.10   Correlation between outcomes and head of home's response to Finding Work

| | Head of home interview: Finding Work | | | |
Outcome	Aims (r)	Means (r)	Difficulties (r)	Success (r)
Doing well	.08	.30	.30	.27
Skilled for age	.13	.33	.27	.36*
Involved in school or work	.02	.31	.35*	.24
Adjustment	.21	.29	.24	.13
Gets on with family	−.03	.14	.14	.17
Placement good idea	.15	.26	.34*	.49**
Placement a success	−.11	.18	−.06	−.05
Young person happy now	−.02	−.27	.20	−.16

* $p < .05$.
** $p < .01$.

Sources: Follow-up questionnaire to residents; first questionnaire to social workers; follow-up questionnaire to social workers; interview with head of home.

THE ASSOCIATION BETWEEN MEANS AND OUTCOME

Introducing 'Goodmeans'

In interpreting these results we have put considerable emphasis on the significance of our rating of means. A rating of high success presumably implied that the residents behaved, went to school or got work, as the case might be, but not necessarily that these outcomes were due to the home. A high rating for 'difficulties' may have implied that circumstances or intake conspired against success. Similarly, our rating for 'aims' was concerned with intention rather than achievement. Our rating of means, however, suggested that the home was (or was not) doing something which might conduce to success.

A natural first question is whether these varied means needed to be seen, as it were on their own, or whether they were manifestations of some overall style of work, something which reflected a greater or lesser drive to enable the young person to survive in the outside world. A second question was how these means related to the Goodhome variable which was the focus of much of earlier analysis.

To our disappointment, there was no significant correlation between Goodhome and any of our means ratings. The means ratings for Behaviour and Education approached a significant relationship but fell short ($r = .3$ and $r = .27$, respectively).

By contrast, the correlations between the means variables themselves were positive and a number of them were significant. The means rating for Moving On was an exception to this rule and not significantly related to any of the others. The remainder, however, might plausibly be seen as reflecting some underlying component, perhaps the degree to which the home emphasised adult values, consistently trying to produce young people who behaved themselves, did not have obvious emotional problems, went to work or school and kept in touch with their families. A components analysis on the means variables reflecting these values supported this idea, producing only one component which accounted for 50% of the variance. This component was the basis for a score which we called Goodmeans and which aroused all the questions which surfaced around Goodhome.

Goodmeans and Intake

The first question was whether any association between Goodmeans and outcome was explained by intake. As a first step, we looked at the association of Goodmeans with the average number of preconvictions ($r = .06$, ns), average level of adjustment at first interview ($r = .14$, ns) and the head's rating of the severity of the problem posed by difficult residents ($r = -.41$, $p < .05$). This last association does not necessarily mean that difficult residents cause a low Goodmeans score. It could be that heads who had not thought through their means of achieving good outcomes found their residents difficult. Nevertheless, it seemed better to err on the side of caution and assume that the heads who found their residents difficult genuinely had ones who were.

Table 14.11 sets out the correlations of Goodmeans with our outcome measures, with and without taking account of difficult residents. By taking account of the difficulty of the residents, we did not reduce the correlations as much as we had expected. Indeed, we raised involvement in school/work to the level of significance, while the social worker's rating of success almost reached significance ($p < .06$). The association between the young person's rating and outcome dropped below significance, but only just ($p < .07$).

These findings made it unlikely that the effects of Goodmeans were entirely explained by intake. However we checked this conclusion in two ways.

First, we argued that if the aspect of homes measured by Goodmeans was having an effect, this should be more pronounced in long-stay than in short-stay homes (because the residents were exposed to these benign pressures over a longer period). It will be remembered that we had divided our homes into those which were on average short-stay, medium-stay, and long-stay. We now also divided them according to whether they scored above or below the average on our measure Goodmeans. Our prediction was that the longer the residents stayed on average the stronger the association should be between a high Goodmeans score and a high average Adjustment score at follow-up. This was borne out (i.e. there was a statistically significant interaction) both when we allowed for previous average adjustment and when we did not. To put it bluntly, a high Goodmeans score seemed to make little difference to subsequent Adjustment when the residents stayed for a short time. It did seem to make a difference in relatively long-stay homes.

Table 14.11 Correlation of Goodmeans with outcomes, taking account of difficult residents

	Correlation 1+	Correlation 2++
Doing well	.42*	.43**
Skilled for age	.42*	.40*
Involved in school or work	.21	.32*
Adjustment	.31*	.31*
Gets on with family	.44**	.42**
Placement good idea	.40*	.27
Placement a success	.10	.28
Young person happy now	−.03	−.06

+ 1st order correlation: Goodmeans with outcomes
++ 2nd order correlation, allowing for resident difficulty
* $p < .05$.
** $p < .01$.
Sources: Follow-up questionnaire to residents; first questionnaire to social workers; follow-up questionnaire to social workers; interview with head of home.

Our next step was to check these findings on adjustment against our data on individuals. We gave each of them a score corresponding to the Goodmeans score of their home and then explored the association between this score and their previous and subsequent Adjustment. Details of this analysis are available from the authors, but basically it confirmed the findings at the level of the home. The young people in homes with high Goodmeans scores became in their social worker's eyes significantly more adjusted over time. This finding held for those who remained in residential care. There was also a significant association between the Goodmeans score and improved Adjustment among those who went into independent living ($r = .49$, $p < .05$), although this finding dropped below significance when allowance was made for other variables. There was no association between the Goodmeans score and improvement among those who returned to their families.

An interesting and important feature of this further analysis was that it highlighted bullying as a probable cause of poor adjustment in the longer term. Those who said that someone had tried to bully them were significantly more likely to be judged less adjusted at follow-up. Comments from parents and social workers suggested that young people subjected to bullying sometimes became bullies in their turn. So although the misery produced by bullying may cease with the bullying itself, its malign effects may still persist into the future.

As a final step, we explored whether the variables which seemed to produce Goodhomes might also explain Goodmeans. First, we wanted to know whether it related to any of our key structural variables. It was, after all, plausible to think that time spent in finding work or getting young people to school would require a reasonable staffing ratio, or that trained staff would be needed to get young people back to their families. However, it was unrelated to these variables or to size.

More encouragingly, Goodmeans was associated with Empowerment ($r = .53$, $p < .01$), and Staff Agreement ($r = .34$, $p < .05$). So in these respects a policy designed to encourage 'good homes' should also encourage Goodmeans.

CONCLUSION

This chapter has not been an easy read. Those who are unused to the kind of statistics used may have found it turgid. Those accustomed to such analyses may have wanted more detail than we have given (if so, further details are available from the authors). Both groups may experience a feeling of unease—a sense that somewhere in the calculations a false step may have been made or an inference too easily asserted. We sympathise with such feelings as we have had them ourselves. That said, we have come to feel confident that the conclusions outlined above are, in broad outline at least, correct.

One reason for thinking this is that findings from different sets of data have related in sensible ways. Changes in the strength of family ties, as rated by the social workers, were strongly associated with our ratings of the degree to which the heads of homes had thought through ways of achieving this, even though the two ratings were made blind to each other. There was a similar coherence between our measure of means and changes in adjustment, and between accounts of attempted bullying (from the residents) and changes in adjustment.

A second reason for believing our findings lies in their internal coherence. In general they suggest that young people's future behaviour is influenced by their past behaviour and by their future environment. Young people's happiness, as we measured it, showed some continuity over time, but was also heavily influenced by their immediate situation—those who were bullied or harassed when we first interviewed them tended to become happier over time (presumably because the situation changed); those who were in 'bad homes' at first interview became happier if they left. The adjustment of young people receiving more intensive social work tended to drop—presumably because the level of support was not continued. The young people rated their experience more highly if they had been in a good home—but only if they had not left it. A thought-through approach seemed to influence adjustment, but the effect was only apparent when the young person did not return to his/her family, where presumably family influences predominated for good or ill. Overall, therefore, there was some continuity of mood and adjustment but considerable evidence that the next environment had a major impact on both.

A third reason for trusting the findings lies in their coherence with other research. The importance of the head fits with findings on other small institutions such as probation hostels and private old people's homes (Gibbs and Sinclair 1992; Sinclair 1971, 1975). The apparent importance of a coherent philosophy of care fits with Berridge and Brodie's (1998) finding that a high quality of care was more common where the head could express one, and is at least compatible with Brown and her colleagues' (1996) emphasis on coherence. The findings on the importance of the immediate environment fit with early studies, which emphasised both the great impact of residential care while the residents were there and, almost as a corollary, the corresponding impact of the environment to which the residents left (e.g. the studies in Allerhand, Weber and Haug 1966; Coates, Miller and Ohlin 1978; Lewis 1982; Petrie 1980; Sinclair 1971;

Taylor and Alpert 1973; Tizard, Sinclair and Clarke 1975). Conversely, the suggestion that behaviour within the institution can be changed in such a way as to link with behaviour outside it fits with studies of establishments for delinquents in the 1960s and 1970s (Clarke and Martin 1971; Dunlop 1974; Millham, Bullock and Cherrett 1975; Sinclair 1971; Sinclair and Clarke 1973).

So if the findings are in broad outline to be trusted, what might be their practical implications? We think there are at least five:

1. The time a young person spends in the home should generally be used both to enable change in behaviour and for work on the environment to which they return (or their relationship with others in that environment). Our findings suggest that limited success in both areas is possible.
2. Good order (as measured by our Goodhome score) is not sufficient to ensure long-term change, although policies designed to develop 'good homes' would also tend to develop effective homes (as defined by our Goodmeans score).
3. It is very important to appoint heads who have reflected on their experience of residential care and have developed a coherent philosophy of how they will achieve their ends.
4. Such reflective practice may well both enable and benefit from the kind of relationship between the head and external management for which we argued in the last chapter (for there was a reasonably strong correlation between our measure of Goodmeans and our measure of Empowerment).
5. Given that successful 'treatment' is likely to be both personal and social, a major limitation on the effectiveness of residential care is likely to lie in its inability to control either the school system or employment. The lack of association between an emphasis on education and an improvement in the residents' involvement in school may reflect the fact that change had taken place before the first interview. Probably it does (see Chapter 10). It may also reflect the fact that the homes could influence return to school but not the young people's school experience. A policy which emphasises return to school needs to go hand-in-hand with strenuous efforts to involve them once there.

ISSUES IN THE EVALUATION OF HOMES

The Conclusions of this chapter and the last one have covered the main points in our evaluation. The homes differed widely in their impact on the residents at the time of our first interview, and, to a much lesser extent, in their impact six months later. These effects were not fully explained by differences in intake. The apparent effects could, however, be sensibly linked to size, staff agreement and 'empowerment' of the head (in the case of immediate impact) and to the philosophy of the head (in the case of medium-term impact). Heads were more likely to have a coherent philosophy where they were 'empowered' and where the staff were agreed.

Three points are common to the two chapters. First, the expensive measures on which policy makers have relied for improving the homes (staff training and increasing staff ratios) were unrelated to our measures of outcome. Second, the head of home and the degree to which he/she was 'empowered' seemed to play an important role in success in both the short and medium term. Third, there was considerable evidence of a powerful environmental effect on the behaviour and happiness of the residents. These points will play an important part in the analysis in our final chapter.

15

CONCLUSION

INTRODUCTION

This conclusion considers the relevance of our findings to the dilemmas currently facing children's homes and examines possible ways forward. There are three questions:

1. Why do we need children's homes?
2. What kind of homes do we need in terms of:
   (a) their functions.
   (b) their clientele.
3. How can they be made as effective as possible?

WHY DO WE NEED CHILDREN'S HOMES?

The young people, their parents and their social workers in this study generally felt that a children's home placement was not ideal. Roughly two-thirds of each group would have preferred the young person to have remained in the community or to have been looked after somewhere other than in their current children's home. The social workers were the most explicit about the alternatives. Typically, they wanted more foster carers able to take difficult teenagers, more resources for preventive work and some therapeutic residential care.

This sense that residential care should be avoided if possible was probably shared by the authorities' treasurers. Currently, the estimated cost of a residential place is £61,000 per year (Carr-Hill *et al.* 1997). Social services spend approximately two and a half times as much on residential care as they do on disabled children and those on the child protection register put together. Taken as a whole, the sector costs nearly 50% more than foster care, which provides roughly six times as many placements (Carr-Hill *et al.* 1997; Department of Health 1997). A possible reason for the use of residential care is that it can change behaviour. We suggest below that this argument has some force. The heads of homes did seek to enable their residents to change. However, their accounts of their methods were more likely to feature the resident group (the distinctive feature of residential care) as a problem than as a resource. Bullying, sexual harassment, delinquency and the offer of drugs were all commonplace in residential homes. All these things had occurred before placement with roughly equal frequency. Nevertheless, it was not surprising that, as judged by social workers, the young people's adjustment over the period did not on average change.

Undoubtedly the main reasons for placement are pragmatic and relate to the residents. To judge from this research, the 'typical' young person in a residential home had changed little since the system was last described (Berridge 1985; Fisher *et al.* 1986; Garnett 1992; Rowe, Hundleby and Garnett 1989). He (rather more commonly) or she is 13–16 years old and from a disrupted family, has serious and complex difficulties with parents or step-parents and has entered the care system in his/her teens for this reason, often compounded by difficult behaviour outside the family. A minority of residents are looked after because of abuse, because they are remanded or, rarely, because they have committed serious crimes. Those who are abused have often entered 'care' at a younger age. There are now no 'easy' young people in children's homes. Taken as a whole, the clientele is even more difficult than it was when Berridge first described it (Berridge and Brodie, 1998).

The arrival of these young people in the home is usually precipitated by an emergency, either in the community or, almost as frequently, in some other placement which has been tried and broken down. For the social workers, the young people represent an awkward dilemma. They cannot go home—their parents will not have them or they will not return. They cannot be fostered—they are unwilling, they are seen as too difficult or too damaged for a substitute family, or there are no suitable foster placements available. Residential care seems to be a requirement.

For their part, residents and parents generally seem to agree with this assessment. Only a minority of the residents said that 'care' had been a bad idea, although around half the remainder had mixed feelings about it. Just under half of those who did not wish to be with their parents would have opted for a residential placement. However, given a choice of placements, residents were around four times as likely to choose residential care as foster care, where they might fall out with the foster carers or feel excluded. Most parents felt that the situation at home had become intolerable and that placement was necessary. They, too, were more likely to choose residential care than foster care, largely on the grounds that the former would provide better control.

Parents and young people also accepted that in the majority of cases the outcome would be that the young person would not return home. This acceptance was in both cases strongly related to age. Where the resident was under 12, the general wish on both sides was that he/she should return home. Where the resident was 15 or over, the usual wish was that the placement should lead to independent living. At least on the residents' side, however, this was generally accompanied by a wish to have frequent contact with their parents. Parents also did not wash their hands of the young person and welcomed the period apart as offering a chance for tempers to cool, for absence to make the heart grow fonder and for fences to be mended (cf. Bullock, Little and Millham 1993b; Fisher *et al.* 1986; Packman *et al.* 1986).

Against this background, the homes seem to serve five main purposes (cf Rowe, Hundleby and Garnett 1989). They receive *emergencies from the community* and return them as soon as possible to the front line of family warfare. They provide a *'decompression chamber'* for those who may not return home or whose placements have broken down, giving them time to 'get their heads together' so that a considered choice can be made over what should happen next. They provide *treatment* for those whose behaviour needs to change if they are to go to another placement. They offer *long-stay shelter and up-bringing* for the seriously damaged. They provide *training in the skills of independent living* for those expected to live on their own.

These roles can be played by foster care (Rowe, Hundleby and Garnett 1989), albeit not necessarily with as difficult a clientele. The question of how far residential care should play them must depend in part on the authority. Some have more residential care than others; some find it easier to recruit foster carers than others; some have a higher proportion of difficult teenagers who may overload the foster-care system; and there are differences in the price of property, the dispersal of the population and the size of the authority. All of these factors are likely to affect the pragmatic case for residential care—the perception that in the circumstances of the authority there is no alternative. For basically, the answer to the question of why residential care is needed is that—to a degree that varies with the authority—it is not possible to get away without it. And the reason for this has to do with its perceived capacity to contain or at least tolerate difficult adolescents.

WHAT KINDS OF RESIDENTIAL CARE ARE NEEDED?

One of the key recommendations of Sir William Utting's recent report is that the system for looking after children should allow more choice. It would be a pity if this was necessarily interpreted to mean an expansion of residential care. This would indeed require more homes from which to choose. However, many of those in residential care would rather be somewhere else: choice should be choice for them as well.

That said, there may well need to be a greater variety of residential care and hence of different kinds of home. Homes may be classified in terms of the purposes they serve or their clientele. Before considering what kinds of home are needed we need to look at the general principles which might determine how this question should be answered.

An important point is that the classification of homes should allow a more rational allocation of staffing ratios. It is easier to justify a high staffing ratio for homes which serve short-term purposes only or which provide specialised treatment for a highly disturbed clientele. By contrast, homes which are intended to keep residents for a long or varying length of time should have a low staffing ratio. If they do not, there will be pressure to move residents on before they are ready. This principle will raise unease. However, it should be remembered that we found no relationship between staffing intensity and the roles of the home. Neither did homes which were more intensively staffed do any 'better' than those which were not.

It is also important that the geographical imperative which requires that children are placed close to their homes should be loosened. There is evidence from other studies (Dharamsi *et al.* 1979; Kendrick and Fraser 1992) that the continuing involvement of residents in their local culture can be a problem. Gibbs and Sinclair (in press) found that residents in private homes were much less exposed to invitations to take drugs than they had been before entry or than their peers were in this study. Case studies in Farmer and Pollock's (1998) research similarly suggest that young people involved in prostitution may find it easier to desist if away from their local networks. We argue below that local placement is desirable for some purposes. So any classification should allow for differences in geographical location.

Breaking the requirements for local placements should enable greater specialisation. This is desirable for reasons connected with the running of the homes. If heads of homes are to exercise effective leadership, they need to understand and agree with their remit. This is more likely to occur if the remit is clear. This, in turn, is more likely to happen if there is more specialisation than at present. Too often homes have to be all things to all people in their local area.

Greater specialisation may involve a blurring of the distinction between specialised foster care, supported lodgings, residential care and various ways of providing an emergency response in the community. Residential workers are expected to be skilled, to tolerate difficult behaviour, to integrate their work with that of the Social Services department and to operate on the basis of 'professional altruism' rather than their own psychological need. In return, they expect to be properly paid, trained and supported. These requirements will apply equally in placements which can be seen as alternatives to residential care (e.g. treatment foster care). There is a case for having all such placements staffed by individuals on the same grading, for managing many of them within the same structure, and for reviewing the relevant regulations so that flexible, 'hybrid' provision is not prevented by the regulatory framework.

What Kind of Role Could Different Homes Play?

Reducing the size of the residential sector has not greatly reduced the proportion of local authority expenditure devoted to it. It has, however, had consequences for the ease with which homes can be run. On the positive side, homes are now smaller—a development which, on our evidence, should make them easier to manage. On the negative side, a reduction in the number of residents has meant that only the very difficult are admitted (Berridge and Brodie 1998); staff jobs are threatened as homes are closed, and the fewer the number of homes the greater the pressure for them to be all things to all children. Increases in the difficulty of running homes have been met by an increase in staffing ratios and hence in costs. This has led to a pressure to move residents on from homes even before they may be ready to leave. As costs and difficulties rise and concerns over scandal persist, the pressure to cut the number of homes increases, until a point may be reached where the system becomes unviable.

This point, which was reached—perhaps by accident—by Warwickshire, may result in a decision to provide no residential care within the authority (all authorities seem to make use of some, even if only on an 'out-of-county' basis). This position also has its drawbacks. It is difficult to provide a choice of foster parents, young people may enter long-term placements with little time to reflect and choose where and with whom they want to live, and fostering breakdowns, which can be acutely painful to both sides, may increase (Cliffe with Berridge 1991).

What kinds of residential care are needed if these drawbacks are to be avoided? This research suggests that matters will go more easily if staffing ratios (and hence costs) are relatively low; if the homes are more specialised, and if they are closely integrated with other provisions (a requirement if the young people are to be able to move on to an adequately supported environment). The seven kinds of home suggested below are intended to put some flesh on these bones. They are intended not as blueprints, but rather as possible examples of the way these principles could be worked out.

First, it may be useful to 'split off' the role of children's homes as a resource in community emergencies. Some homes might act essentially as back-up to other services, supporting carers, offering foster carers relief, and providing emergency placements to tide adolescents over a brief period while matters are sorted out. Such homes would be closely integrated with local services and might not in time resemble homes at all (e.g. one or two emergency beds and a 24-hour back-up service for professional foster carers could be offered from a family centre) although they would call for the skills needed by residential staff. By offering the resource through a centre which provided other services or through specialised short-stay foster carers, it should be possible to reduce the staffing ratio per bed and hence costs.

This provision would need to be closely integrated with a social work service. Packman *et al.* (1986) found that parental requests for accommodation for their children were variously accepted and refused. She did not find that either response was associated with a better outcome. However, parents who were refused were commonly offered very little else and felt very let-down. A rapid and responsive social work service backed by a small number of short-term beds might avoid this danger, while making the financial savings commonly claimed for the American 'family preservation' projects (Stein 1985; Reid, Kagan and Schlosberg 1988; Wells and Biegel 1992) which operate on this 'crisis intervention' model.

A further feature of such back-up provision would need to be the development of purposive and intensive education for adolescents who are not at school. This could be provided in various ways, might draw on the experience of authorities such as Area 4, who have shown that it is possible to get children in homes back to school, and might need to be complemented by out-of-school provision during the holidays. Parents, foster carers and residential staff all suffer from adolescents who do not go to school and who may have fallen so far behind that there seems little point in their going anyway. On the evidence of this study, educational provision for these young people in homes tends to be extremely limited and sometimes non-existent. Determined and successful efforts to relieve this problem should ease the staffing pressure on homes, provide back-up to foster carers and parents, and offer the young people a genuine way out of their current educational predicament.

A second locally-based form of provision might correspond to supported lodgings (a form of care which seems under-researched). If an enhanced form of such provision (e.g. staffed by residential staff on appropriate salaries and with cover) could contain those young people who are currently placed in homes to be trained for independence, it might offer more realistic preparation (the lack of realism of current independence training was sometimes criticised in this research). It should make easier a move-on which was timed to suit the needs of the young person, rather than the need to maintain an age range within a residential home on the current model. If staffed, albeit professionally, on the model of supported lodgings, it could lower the ratio of staff to places and hence costs and the pressure to move young people on. Integrated with after-care services, it could provide a point of contact for the young people after they have left. In this study, a quarter of the residents said that if they got into trouble after leaving, they would turn to the staff in the home in preference to anyone else.

A further advantage of providing 'independence training' on a local basis is that it would allow the young people to develop supports in the community and, in particular, relationships with their families. The point of encouraging contact with families is that both sides want this, not that it will necessarily result in the resident returning home. There is evidence that in some circumstances adolescents 'in care' do 'worse' if they return home than if they do not (Minty 1987; Quinton and Rutter 1984; Sinclair 1971; Zimmerman 1982). This study suggests that what most residents want is to live near their families but not with them. While at the home they wanted to have more contact with, on average, two relations or friends—most commonly siblings, but also fathers, mothers, grand-parents, friends and other relatives. A system which provides them with a variety of adults to whom to turn is less likely to fail them than a system in which they are dependent on one (cf Triseliotis *et al.* 1995). Such a system is more likely to discharge them from a placement local to where they are going.

A third form of residential care might aim to contain emergencies, enabling young people with serious difficulties with their families, or whose placements had broken down, to think through their next moves so that a considered choice can be made. Berridge and Cleaver (1987) found that foster placements made from residential care, and not made in a hurry, were less likely to break down. In this study, most of the young people entered the homes as 'emergencies' and often without feeling that they had the time to make a considered choice, or indeed to visit the home beforehand. This practice is generally deplored but may be inevitable. The important point may be not that emergencies are abolished—a desir-able but probably impossible aim—but rather that the homes allow the next step to be made after due reflection. This would imply for us that the homes were in reasonable control and hence, probably, that they were not local. Although the cost per place of such homes is likely to be high, the cost per placement would be lower. If such homes lowered the number of foster care breakdowns, they could well be cost-effective.

This third form of residential care would be very similar to that which is provided at the moment. It would face three problems: the accommodation might 'silt up' as placements proved difficult to find; the range of young people looked after and the varying lengths of stay might mean that the homes lost their sense of purpose and became very difficult to control; the evidence from Berridge and Cleaver (1987) could be explained in other ways and there is no proof that specialised foster care could not do the job as well. Thus, there is a need to ensure that any such provision is backed by an adequate variety of placements to which to discharge; that the homes are very well managed; and that there is comparative research on the capacity of foster care to carry out this function.

A fourth form of residential care might aim to 'treat'. This would not be geographically based, would be specialised, and might consist of residential homes or specialised foster care provided by salaried staff. American and British research (e.g. Reddy and Pfeiffer 1997; Meadowcroft *et al.* 1994; Colton 1988) suggests that foster care is at least as effective in producing change over a wide range of difficulties, cheaper and avoids the dangers of bullying and sexual harassment by other residents or involvement in a delinquent culture. It seems possible that there may be an upper limit of difficult behaviour beyond which foster care is unable to go, but further research is required to determine what this is.

There is also a need for research into the key ingredients in successful treatment. In the past, residential care has variously relied on individual or group therapies, strong relationships with members of staff, the ability of staff to use day-to-day interactions in a purposeful way, social treatments (e.g. Outward Bound) and the resident group. Of these ingredients, specialised therapies and use of day-to-day interactions are also possible in foster care. The increased size of the staff group and the fact that staff now live out probably makes strong staff–resident relationships less likely than in foster care. Social treatments are rarely available to either foster or residential care. Only the resident group, with its capacity to mould attitudes and offer opportunities for mutual help and encouragement, seems to be a potential advantage for residential care. It remains to be proved that residential staff can enable the resident group to be a force for good rather than ill.

If treatment is to be attempted, it is important that plans which are conditional on changes being made by the young people or their parents are clear. In this study, parents were generally vague about the care plans and in more than half the cases the social workers and young people seemed to disagree quite seriously about what they were. Clearly, young persons' decisions over whether to return home or move out on their own is of major significance to them and so there may be need for an acknowledged vagueness as decisions are arrived at over time. Vagueness may also arise because of a difficulty in arranging foster care or other resources. Vagueness which reflects a failure to agree on what precisely is required by way of change on the part of parents or young people is less forgivable.

A fifth kind of home, possibly smaller, and certainly less generously staffed than current models, might act as some hybrid of the family group home and the 'super' foster carer. This home would cater for at least some of the 20% of residents who are currently in homes for 'up-bringing' and who have often entered the care system when relatively young and had foster placements which broke down. The home would make perhaps less intense emotional demands than an 'ordinary' foster home. It would, however, approximate more closely to an ordinary home than current residential care. In such homes it would be particularly important that the residents were reasonably compatible. The aim would be that they only left when they were ready to do so.

Sixth, there would need to be secure accommodation (for some young people have committed such serious crimes or are so prone to running away, bringing risk to themselves or others, that no alternative seems possible). In our view, this would need to be linked to other less intensive provision to which the resident could be discharged in her/his home area. In this way it might be possible to combine the advantages of both security and of discharging a young person from a placement near to where they are going to live.

Finally, there may be a need for some form of residential education. For younger adolescents, the latter would provide relief from home circumstances which were not going to improve, the maintenance of a relationship with home, and a reasonable education. The main defect of this arrangement is that it would be intended to last for a considerable time and might therefore be very costly. This disadvantage might be overcome by combining foster care with a day school some way from the young person's home.

What Kind of Residents Would the Homes Take?

The different kinds of home sketched above were created by separating out the roles which most homes play simultaneously. Most homes also take a wide variety of residents. So there is an issue of whether they specialise by resident as well as by function. The 'typical' resident is white, aged between 13 and 16 and is looked after because of poor relationships with her/his family. There are four minority groups of residents: black and ethnic minority residents; younger residents (under-13s); young people on remand; and 'victims', young people who have been neglected, or physically or sexually abused.

Appendix C brings together data from different sources on black and ethnic minority (which in our terminology includes Asian and dual-heritage) young people. It identifies two basic problems. First, although the proportions of staff and residents who were black and ethnic minority were almost identical (7% and 7.5%), it had proved very difficult to ensure that homes with a high proportion of black and ethnic minority residents had a similarly high proportion of black and ethnic minority staff. Second, the young people as a group were significantly less at ease than their white counterparts—they were more likely to have problems with the food, less happy about police checks, less likely to see residents as friendly and the staff as supportive, and more likely to feel that families were uneasy when visiting the homes. Around half felt that the homes were better for white young people than for black and ethnic minority ones.

These problems clearly call for a sensitive response from the homes. Nevertheless, they are going to be extremely difficult to tackle in authorities where the proportion of ethnic minorities is low and which aim to place young people in homes near to their families. Some black and ethnic minority young people may well be at easy in predominantly white children's homes. Others, however, may be better placed with professional foster carers who can match their ethnic origin or in specialist homes which would necessarily be at some distance from their families.

In relation to younger residents, our data suggest that they should either be kept away from residential care altogether or placed in homes specially catering for them. In our study they were far more likely than other age groups to be bullied and more likely to wish to be in another residential home. Their parents were also more likely to feel that the regime was wrong for them. Further grounds for considering special care for this group are that they are at an age when their education might be remedied by placement in a residential (EBD) school, an option which recent research by Triseliotis and his colleagues suggests may have much to recommend it (Triseliotis *et al.* 1995). In keeping with these arguments, some of our authorities either made very little use of residential care for this age group or placed them in particular homes.

Our data also suggest that young people on remand should be kept out of the care system or segregated within it. The homes were open institutions from which such residents ran away frequently. Heads of 'ordinary' homes rarely welcome them—seeing them as difficult young people with their own preoccupations who did not fit easily into the routine. In keeping with this view, the level of trouble within the home (as measured by our Goodhome measure) increased with increasing proportions of remands. To be fair, it was not the young people on remand *per se* that were the cause of the difficulty, but rather the fact they tended to be found in larger homes. One home which took a relatively high level of remands seemed, nevertheless, to maintain a satisfactory level of order. However, caution would suggest excluding young people on remand from children's homes and instead expanding remand fostering, bail support- and specialised provision, perhaps with secure accommodation. Any such step would obviously require the endorsement of local courts. It was interesting that one of our authorities appeared to place almost no-one on remand in its homes—presumably because the courts felt that such measures were not required.

The question of whether homes should cater for young people who are victims of abuse as well as for those who are at odds with their parents is more complicated. In our study, around three out of 10 of the current residents fell into this category and, on the face of it, homes are not very desirable places for them (a view reinforced by our reading of Farmer and Pollock's (1998) study of abused and abusing young people). Just over half of these young people said that someone had tried to bully them since arrival at the home and nearly a quarter of them said that someone had tried to take sexual advantage of them. Only just over a quarter of them said they would ideally have gone into a children's home of any kind when they were first placed in their current one.

Unfortunately, the placement which the victims of abuse most frequently said they would have liked was with their own family. There may of course have been good reasons why this should not have happened and, presumably, why they could not have been placed with relatives (another quite popular choice). Among the remainder, foster care was not more popular than residential care, and those who chose residential care of some kind very rarely said that they would have liked a home other than their present one.

So, whereas residential care may be in a sense a second-best option for these young people, it is not clear that it is second-best in the context of the options likely to be available. Those who have suffered abuse may well find living in a family difficult. If, in addition, they have had a foster placement breakdown, they may well appreciate a time in residential care in order to 'get their head together'. 'Victims' were likely to report attempted bullying on entering the home when they did not report it as happening before. However, they were more likely than other groups to say that someone had tried to bully them before entry but not since. Thus, the lesson may be not that 'victims' should be excluded from residential care but rather that the latter should be sufficiently well-managed and diverse to accommodate them.

HOW CAN HOMES BE MADE AS EFFECTIVE AS POSSIBLE?

The effectiveness of homes depends on their ability to manage the resident group and their work with individual residents. Both kinds of effectiveness depend on certain preconditions (e.g. the quality of the head of home and of the management arrangements). We will discuss these preconditions before the work with groups and individuals.

The Preconditions for an Effective Home

A variety of mechanisms might help to produce effective homes. These include the selection of a good head of home, development of a coherent staff philosophy, high staffing ratios, training, and 'empowerment' (a hackneyed term which we have defined for our purposes earlier). We will consider these mechanisms below.

Research on residential care suggests that the head of home can have a great impact on the quality of care. Sinclair (1971, 1975) produced very strong evidence that, in the model of probation hostel then current, the head of home (or rather the husband and wife team that ran the establishment) had an almost overwhelming impact on the delinquent behaviour of the residents. Gibbs and Sinclair (1992) found that in private old people's homes, ratings of the leadership exercised by the head of home made by one inspector correlated significantly with the ratings of quality of care in the home made by another. In as yet unpublished research, Godfrey (1996) has found that the attitudes of heads of private homes to training correlate with the attitudes of their staff.

These same researchers, however, have all found less powerful effects of heads of home in other institutions. Sinclair, in unpublished work, found that the absconding rates of approved schools, unlike those of probation hostels, did not change with change of head. Gibbs and Sinclair found no significant association between their measure of the leadership exercised by the heads of old people's homes in the public sector and the quality of care in the homes. Godfrey found a small negative correlation between the attitudes to training of heads of public sector old people's homes and the attitudes of their staff.

So it seems that in small establishments, particularly those where the head hires and fires and plays a key role in day-to-day care, the atmosphere stems from the top. There are, however, larger, more complex establishments, where the head does not live on the premises, and may have heavy administrative responsibilities, and where there may be powerful sub-groups of staff with views of their own. In such places the head may be of less predominant importance or may exercise influence through a relationship with key members of staff.

The question to be answered is whether children's homes are establishments where the head is very important. Authorities would be prudent to behave as if this was so. In our study, heads who could give a coherent account of the means by which they sought to achieve certain ends were more effective. Berridge and Brodie (1998) concur. It is possible that the heads were mouthing philosophies developed by others. However, it seems more likely that the philosophies were their own and that their ability to get their staff behind them was a key factor in the home's success. So authorities might be wise to insist on evidence that the head has performed analogous roles successfully (e.g. when acting up as a deputy). They should give great attention to supporting the head but should be ready to move her/him sideways if things do not work out.

Our study suggests that the relationships between the head and the external management are very important. Heads need to know where they are, so that they can exercise creative leadership within an agreed framework. These findings are in keeping with those of Berridge and Brodie (1998) as well as Brown et al. (1996), who emphasise the importance of 'coherence' between all levels of management. The findings support, albeit with qualifications, the findings from the 1970s on the importance of giving autonomy to staff (Tizard 1975; Heal and Cawson 1975). They are not an argument for a lack of external management interest (something which Berridge and Brodie criticise) or for excessive efforts to control through procedures and regulation.

Our findings on staff qualifications were a disappointment to us. As far as we could see, they tended to lower morale for both the individual and the staff group. They had no bearing on any of our measures of effectiveness. The implication, however, is not that training needs to be abandoned—it is potentially a key mechanism for improving quality of care. However, we cannot assume that just because a certain proportion of staff have got some kind of qualification, a home's effectiveness has been enhanced (if anything is achieved, it seems on the evidence of this study more likely to be staff disunity). The effort that is put into training should be matched by efforts at developing and evaluating it, and the latter should continue until it is quite clear that a form of training is available that works. In this respect, useful leads (for example, on the potential advantages of group training to develop staff agreement and on the importance of supervision) may be derived from this research.

A further negative finding was that a high staff ratio did not have any apparent impact on results. If anything, the reverse was the case. Homes that had fewer than 14 beds tended to have higher staff ratios if they were relatively small. A small size was associated with good order, although not good long-term effects. However, if allowance was made for the effects of size, the higher the staffing ratio, the greater the degree of disorder. Berridge and Brodie (1998) similarly found that staffing ratios were unrelated to good results. It is perhaps natural to assume that better order can be achieved by having more staff. However, our study suggests that it depends not on numbers but on establishing a culture of what is and is not acceptable. This suggests that there may be scope for a more cost-effective use of resources, and this thought lies behind some of the suggestions made earlier.

In this latter respect we found that staff unity was crucial. This finding again chimes with those of Berridge and Brodie (1998) and of Brown and her colleagues (1996). We deal with these points in more detail below.

Managing the Resident Group

Issues of order and behaviour are central in children's homes. In part this has to do with behaviour outside the home. Nearly three-quarters of those with a previous conviction who stayed in the homes for at least six months were reconvicted during the period that they were there. Four out of 10 of those who had no previous conviction also fell foul of the law if they remained that long. Parents, young people and social workers all complained that in some homes the young people were led astray.

One of the key findings of the study was that there were major variations between the homes in the way the residents behaved. This seemed to be true of running away and getting into trouble with police after allowance had been made for intake and for length of time in the home. It was equally true of the behaviour, general friendliness and morale of residents, as these were perceived by both staff and residents. In some homes bullying was endemic, in others it was rare. In some homes, more than three-quarters of those resident in the course of the year had a conviction. In one home no-one had been convicted.

These findings are reminiscent of studies carried out in the late 1960s (Tizard, Sinclair and Clarke 1975), which found equally wide variations between residential establishments in almost all the aspects the researchers chose to measure and which equally could not account for them in terms of intake. A new feature in the current study was the degree to which the various measures of 'trouble' were correlated together and were in turn correlated with measures of the relationship between staff and residents and with staff morale.

One reason for this high degree of inter-correlation must lie in the fact that homes are potentially explosive places in which one thing leads to another. Thus, the arrival of a particularly difficult resident may lead to an outbreak of stealing among the young people, which may in turn lead to a drop in the morale of staff and a breakdown in the relationship between staff and residents. Such matters were again documented in the 1970s (Millham, Bullock and Cherrett 1975; Sinclair 1971, 1975), when the evidence suggested that, although epidemics of trouble occurred, they were more frequent or more serious in some establishments than others. It is important, therefore, to know whether there are some aspects of homes which tend to reduce the incidence of 'trouble' and are potentially under managerial control.

We used the high degree of inter-correlation between our measures of resident morale and behaviour to create a measure, Goodhome, which can be roughly equated to a measure of the degree to which the home is in reasonable order. We considered a variety of possible explanations for homes scoring high on Goodhome. These included the characteristics of the head of home, the home's size and staffing ratio, the proportion of its staff who were trained, the characteristics of the intake, the degree to which the head was given autonomy and 'empowered', the regime and the degree of agreement among the staff. We have discussed the results of these analyses in our previous section. Our overall conclusion was that the most important thing in establishing reasonable order in an establishment is to get an acceptance among the residents of what is and is not reasonable behaviour. Such an agreement feeds on success—for both good and bad behaviour is 'catching'. However, it is easier to produce it where establishments are small, the head of home feels clear about what he/she is doing, and the staff are on good terms with each other and agree on the home's philosophy of care.

Enabling Change in Individuals

The residents present to themselves or others four major problems. First, they are extremely unhappy or moody. The great majority said they had felt angry or upset in the previous month and four out of 10 had considered killing themselves. Second, the great majority are liable to behave in a disturbed or delinquent way—for example, by harming themselves, running away from home or 'care', attacking adults or other young people, or putting themselves or others at risk through their sexual behaviour. Third, they are poorly integrated into education or work and their prospects for long-term secure employment are generally dismal. Fourth, the great majority come from disrupted families with whom they are almost always at odds.

In this section we will concentrate on unhappiness and behaviour. Our findings on schooling and family relationships were few, if positive. We showed that one area had almost certainly succeeded in getting many of its residents back into school. We also showed that heads of homes who had a thought-through philosophy for dealing with family relationships were more likely to have residents whose relationships with home improved. We did not, however, show how these results were obtained. So we will concentrate on issues where we have more to discuss.

Happiness

Young people were more unhappy than their peers if they missed their family or a particular friend, or if they reported attempts at current or previous bullying or sexual abuse. On leaving care they were, on average, more unhappy if they came from a 'good home' (which perhaps they missed), just as they were, on average, more unhappy if they had stayed on in a less than 'good home'. These findings are arguments for determined efforts to maintain the young people's contacts with those they miss (where these are other than clearly a bad influence) (cf. Aldgate 1980; Bullock, Little and Millham 1993b). They also emphasise the overwhelming importance of efforts to stamp out bullying and sexual abuse and to have some appropriate therapy available for those who have been abused. Finally, they emphasise the need to continue to support young people who have had a good experience in their residential home and are now coping with a lonely and perhaps dangerous bedsit (Stein and Carey 1986; Biehal et al. 1995).

All this, however, is about minimising the bad effects of the care system. If one is to look for further leads, they are perhaps to be found in three areas. First, there was the importance of listening. There is no evidence that this would reduce misery but it was certainly appreciated (Farmer and Pollock, 1998, may have evidence that listening is effective as well). Second, there were areas of the young people's lives—most crucially their relationships with others of their age—where the young people almost universally had worries and equally universally felt that no-one had tried to help them. Third, pride in work was correlated with happiness, as was pride in leisure activities. So the message may be that adults should listen harder, pay attention to those things which trouble the young people, and recognise and encourage those activities in which they take a justifiable pride.

Behaviour

In relation to behaviour, the findings suggest that in one respect this is very much a creation of the immediate environment. This was particularly true of delinquent behaviour. The readiness with which young people became involved in delinquency varied greatly between different homes. So, too, did the readiness with which they became involved in running away.

These findings encourage a certain caution over aspirations to modify behaviour in the longer term. If behaviour is so responsive to the immediate situation, it will respond to cues from the new situation when the resident leaves. The likelihood of this, however, may suggest the strategy that should be followed in trying to ensure reasonable behaviour in the longer term. Sampson and Laub (1993) have recently suggested a model of delinquency in which environment (family and employment) is both influenced by and influences delinquent and difficult behaviour. Their model is completely compatible with the findings of this research and would suggest that one role of residential care is to enable young people to get settled in environments (work, school, lodgings) which will support social behaviour after the resident has left.

Such a model would be strengthened by an acknowledgement that the environments to which the young people go may well break down (Biehal *et al.* 1995). Placements in lodgings have been notoriously unstable; young people returning home often fall out with their families; work, even for the most motivated, no longer provides a job for life. So as the middle classes stand behind their volatile but frequently talented young until such time as the latter are—hopefully—settled, so perhaps there is a role for children's homes in standing behind their less fortunate charges as they claw their way back into the mainstream of life. After-care was a role which staff typically wished was theirs and which, if they had it, was associated with high morale. In keeping with this aspiration, Biehal and her colleagues (1995) suggest that children's homes can play a useful role as part of an integrated leaving care service (cf. our suggestions on 'supported lodgings').

This model strengthens the case—if this was needed—for efforts on the part of the home to ensure that the young person becomes integrated into school and work. Our measure of Doing Well reflected the fact that most of the aspects of doing well which social workers would consider important were inter-correlated. The strongest association with 'good adjustment' on discharge was not the home's reported emphasis on ensuring good behaviour but rather the degree to which the head had thought through ways of getting the young people involved in education. Paradoxically, this measure was more strongly associated with good adjustment than it was with involvement in education itself. So what may be at issue here is not a particular means of ensuring a good outcome—if the young person goes to school all will be well—but rather the effect of a general insistence on a respectable way of life.

This finding is again reminiscent of research in the 1970s. It was a commonplace then that absconding (as it was then known) was associated with future delinquency. It seemed highly likely that the effect was in some ways a causal one (Clarke and Martin 1971; Sinclair 1971; Sinclair and Clarke 1973) and mediated in part by the way in which the young person and others perceived the significance of absconding (Sinclair 1971). Even more relevant, perhaps, may be Dunlop's (1974) finding that approved schools which emphasised work had, after allowing for the effect of intake, lower reconviction rates than others. The natural explanation for this result was that the young people got work and thereby lowered their likelihood of offending. There were, however, two objections to this view. First, the training was not sufficiently realistic to make the young people very employable. Second, within schools, those young people who were committed to the work training were no more likely to stay out of trouble than those who were not. It seemed therefore likely that what Dunlop was detecting was the effect of some general emphasis on adult values, and this was in keeping with her other finding that schools which emphasised responsibility were more successful than those which did not.

This discussion leaves open the precise question of how long-term change is achieved. It could reflect a change in the way that young people view themselves, or in the way others relate to them, or in their situations (e.g. because they see themselves as workers, because others relate to them as workers or because they get work). Most probably a variety of interacting mechanisms are involved and practically it may not matter much exactly how the effect occurs. One lesson of this research seems to be that a thought-through and coherent approach on the part of the head of home can be effective.

There is, however, another and more disturbing implication. The impact of this coherent approach only seemed to be apparent for those young people who remained in the children's homes or who left them but did not return to their own families. Our suggested explanation for this finding was that for long-term change to occur, both the young person and the environment must generally change. Thus, homes can be more or less effective with young people going into independent living. What they do makes a difference, and the task here is to ensure that all homes achieve the same results as the best. By contrast, it is very doubtful whether homes do differ in their effects on young people returning to their own families.

CONCLUSION

These suggestions arise from an overall appraisal of current residential care. The arguments for such care are pragmatic—it is the only form of provision which seems capable of containing some extremely difficult young people, many of whom prefer it to foster care. On the other hand, it is extremely expensive, lacks a treatment rationale which might give it an apparent advantage over foster care, may expose vulnerable young people to bullying, sexual harassment and delinquency, and turns them out into the community when many are not ready to leave. The quality of care it provides is currently, and perhaps inherently, uneven (cf. Berridge and Brodie 1998).

Faced with this situation, local authorities need to decide how much residential care they should provide, what kinds of home are needed, and how these homes can be as good as possible. In considering these questions we would suggest that local authorities need to consider all their 'heavy end' resources for young people and the way in which the budget should be distributed among them. The resulting system will need to be both more specialised and more closely integrated and may well call for the skills of residential staff in areas where they are not now employed. It should also in our view provide a system which is better value for money, better able to move young people on at a pace that suits them, and less liable to disruption.

Our own answers to the specific questions would be as follows:

- In relation to the *size of the residential sector*, we do not think it should be increased—if anything the reverse. In this study, two-thirds or more of the residents and of their social workers and parents thought that a residential placement was not ideal and that something else would have been preferable. Choice for them is probably better and more cheaply provided by directing extra resources to other kinds of provision. The strong arguments for residential care are that there is no alternative—if local authorities are managing with a given level of residential care they would need very strong grounds to expand it.
- In relation to *the kinds of homes which are needed*, we agree with Utting that the geographic imperative should be loosened. This would allow for a diversity of homes, some closely integrated with local services and some more specialised and at greater distance. Basically, we have argued above for smaller homes, some much more generously staffed than others, for blurring the distinction between residential care and alternative provisions such as foster care and supported lodgings, and for closer integration between residential care and other provisions (e.g. after-care). In this way the problems of high costs, delinquent subcultures and pressures to move before the resident is ready might all be reduced. It is likely, however, that some high-cost treatment homes and some high-cost homes concerned with choice and assessment would be retained, albeit subject to continuing evaluation.
- The task of *ensuring that the homes are as good as they can be* depends, on our evidence, on a number of factors. The home should be small. It should be clear what it is supposed to do. The head is almost certainly vital, and he/she needs to have a clear philosophy on how the home

can achieve its ends. The external management of the home should neither be 'hands off' nor rely on close procedural control to achieve its ends. Rather, there needs to be agreement between the head and the management on what the home is to do and how, thus providing a framework within which the head can provide leadership. The staff should not be at odds personally and should agree on what the home is about. Practice likely to inhibit agreement—a heavy reliance on relief staff, bringing a group of staff from a previous home into a current one, frequent changes of function—should be avoided.

We end with a dilemma. This book suggests that change is needed in residential care. It also suggests that frequent reorganisation is harmful. This dilemma will only be overcome if the book is seen not as a blueprint for action but as informing a debate whose particular conclusions will vary with the circumstances of each local authority. If all concerned have thought through the implications of change, then change should be less harmful: if the book has provoked thought on the part of those who must take decisions over residential care, it will have justified its writing.

Appendix A

REPRESENTATIVENESS OF THE SAMPLES

INTRODUCTION

In this Appendix we demonstrate, first, that the study included a sample of young people in residential care similar in their basic characteristics to those found at national level; second, that the resident sub-samples in the study were similar to the main interview sample of 223 of young people in residential care; and third, that staff who returned the postal questionnaire were representative of the wider population of residential staff in the five participating authorities.

REPRESENTATIVENESS OF THE RESIDENT SAMPLE

Table A1 sets out details for the basic characteristics of the residents in the York study, set alongside comparable information from the report, *Corporate Parents* (Social Services Inspectorate 1994) and provisional figures for England in March 1992 (Department of Health 1993), about the time when the main study started.

As can be seen, the two York samples (the first derived from the Resident Log, completed by 44 of the 48 homes in the study, and the second based on the main resident interview sample) are very similar to each other and to the national samples in their age and sex distribution. Where there are small differences, this may represent sampling error or the later date at which the York material was gathered. The SSI figures on legal status are, for example, intermediate between the national data and our own, and this may reflect the fact that they were gathered later than the national data, whereas our data are later still.

We have estimated some of the SSI data from diagrams in their report (*Corporate Parents*) and are not sure that we have interpreted their intervals correctly. Nevertheless, the figures are encouraging in that they suggest that both the homes and the interview sample are reasonably representative of the national picture.

Table A1   Comparison of resident characteristics in national and York studies

	National 1992 (%)	SSI 1992 (%)	York 1994 resident log (%)	York 1994 resident sample (%)
Sex				
Females	42.3	41.8	41.2	43.6
Males	57.7	58.2	58.8	56.5
Age				
Under 10	4.6	10.0	1.8	(Excluded)
10–15	64.4	58.8	71.3	72.2
16–17	26.8	30.0	26.2	26.9
Over 17	3.8	1.2	0.7	0.9

Length of stay	SSI current	SSI past	York current	York past
Under 1 month	16.3	52.6	10.8	50.5
1–2 months	22.4	18.0	21.1	22.3
3–5 months	24.5	12.9	17.2	13.5
6–12 months	16.3	8.3	22.2	8.2
Over 1 year	20.4	8.3	28.7	5.5

Legal status	National 1992	SSI 1992	York 1994 current resident	York 1994 past residents
Accommodated	55.3	62.4	66.3	61.7
Order	41.7	31.6	26.5	12.7
Remanded	3.0	6.0	7.2	25.6

Nature of admission	SSI 1992	York 1994
Emergency	45.0	57.0
Planned respite	13.0	12.9
Planned assessment	12.0	6.1
Planned long-term	25.0	21.5
Other	5.0	2.5

SSI = Social Services Inspectorate.
Sources: Resident Log; interview with residents; Fraser 1993; Department of Health 1993.

REPRESENTATIVENESS OF THE DIFFERENT SUB-SAMPLES

We have demonstrated in Table A1 that the young people interviewed were reasonably representative of the wider population of young people in residential care. In Table A2 we compare the characteristics of the residents in the main interview sample (n = 223) with their characteristics as reflected in the different sub-samples. So, for example, were social workers prompted to respond for only certain types of young people who had been interviewed by us? Inspection of Table A2 suggests that this was not the case. In addition to a high response rate (176 out of 223— 78.9% response), social workers provided information on a representative range of young people.

The same can also be said of the Resident and Social Worker Follow-up Questionnaires and, apart from one exception, the Parent Interview. The one exception is that the parent(s) of girls and young women are under-represented. We certainly experienced considerable difficulty in

Table A2   Representativeness of the samples within the study

	Basic characteristics of different samples				
	Resident interview n = 223 (%)	Social worker 1 n = 176 (%)	Resident follow-up n = 141 (%)	Social worker 2 n = 141 (%)	Parents n = 99 (%)
Sex					
Females	43.5	40.0	44.0	44.7	31.6
Males	56.5	59.1	56.0	55.3	68.4
Age					
12 and under	13.0	12.5	13.5	12.1	13.3
13–15	59.2	58.5	61.0	58.2	62.2
16 and over	27.8	29.0	25.5	29.8	24.5
Family type					
Lone parent	38.6	36.9	38.3	34.0	40.8
Birth parents	15.7	15.9	17.0	14.2	14.3
1 Birth : 1 other	33.6	35.2	31.9	36.9	33.7
Other	12.1	11.9	12.8	14.9	11.2
Reason for care					
Relationship breakdown	39.0	39.8	40.4	41.1	35.7
Delinquency	23.3	25.0	19.1	24.1	30.6
Victim	31.4	32.4	34.8	29.8	30.6
Other	6.3	2.8	5.7	5.0	3.1
Attitude to care					
Good idea	40.9	38.2	45.4	41.4	45.4
Bad idea	33.2	35.3	29.8	31.4	32.0
Mixed	25.9	26.5	24.8	27.2	22.6

Sources: Interview with residents; questionnaire to social workers; follow-up questionnaire to residents; follow-up questionnaire to social workers.

obtaining interviews with parents and it is possible that those of girls and young women where sexual abuse was involved may have been particularly reticent to be interviewed. By cross-checking with the accounts from social workers there was some, but not overwhelming, evidence to support this conclusion.

Apart from the under-representation of parents of girls and young women, we believe that the composition of the main interview sample of young people, and the different sub-samples, were reasonably representative of the national picture and not an undue cause for concern.

THE STAFF LOG AND STAFF QUESTIONNAIRE

The Staff Log was completed by the head of home and provided basic biographic details on each member of staff in the home, including age, sex, length of time in post and qualifications. The log was completed by 44 of the 48 homes in the study.

Table A3 sets out the results from the Staff Log in the 44 homes, covering 540 members of staff. The majority of staff are female and their average (mean) age is 38.5 years (men = 36.9; women = 39.4). The census indicated that about one in ten staff and one in two heads of home, held a social work qualification. The majority of staff (75), though, were unqualified according to the census. The table also provides comparable figures based on returns from the Staff Questionnaire.

A slightly different picture emerges from the Staff Questionnaire; while the proportion with a social work qualification is about the same as in the census, the proportion of unqualified staff falls from 75% in the census to under 40% in the staff questionnaire. There are two possible explanations for this discrepancy. First, the census covers all staff in the home, including cooks and other domestic staff, while the staff questionnaire was completed only by care staff. Second, it is possible that unqualified staff were less motivated to complete the questionnaire and therefore underrepresented in this questionnaire sample. The main point remains, though that few staff hold relevant qualifications, a finding broadly in line with that of the Social Services Inspectorate's (1994) report, *Corporate Parents*.

The majority of staff work full-time and, perhaps surprisingly, a large proportion (66%) of all staff have been in their current post for at least three years. Indeed, 40% have been in post for at least five years. The finding may be a reflection of the stability in the home or, conversely, a lack of job mobility and opportunities among the large proportion of unqualified staff.

Table A3 Characteristics of staff in Staff Log and Staff Questionnaire returns

	York census of staff $n = 540$ (%)	York questionnaire to staff $n = 303$ (%)	SSI Corporate parents
Sex			
Males	37.0	35.7	A majority
Females	63.0	64.3	are female
Age			
Under 30	22.6	28.2	
30–39	30.8	28.9	
40–49	28.5	30.2	
50 and over	18.1	12.7	
Mean	38.5	37.6	40.0
Main qualification			
Dip.SW/CQSW/CSS	9.6	10.2	About 15%
Certificate In Child Care/			with social
Nursery Nurse	4.9	19.5	work quals;
Teacher training	0.8	2.6	58%
Other (unspecified)	9.4	28.4	unqualified
None	75.3	39.3	
Hours			
Under 20	6.7	4.3	
20–29	20.1	8.9	
30–38	10.4	12.3	
39 and over	63.6	74.5	
Time in home			
1 Year	18.0	26.3	
2 Years	16.3	17.0	
3/4 Years	25.8	21.4	
5 Years and over	39.9	35.3	
Mean	—	4.7	4.8
Post			
Manager/supervisor	21.0	Questionnaire	
Care staff	55.7	completed by	
Domestic and other staff	23.3	care staff only	
Ethnicity			
White British/White other	93.5		
African-Caribbean	4.5	Question not	Non-white
Asian	0.7	asked	= 10%
Mixed African-Caribbean: White	0.7		
Mixed Asian: White	0.6		

Sources: Staff Log; questionnaire to staff; Fraser 1993.

APPENDIX B

RELATIVE ROLES OF SOCIAL WORKERS AND HOMES

The social workers were asked about the main steps taken to remedy any of the developmental problems identified in Chapter 2. The main foci of work were, as expected, 'family and friends' (in around four out of ten cases), 'education and work' (in around half the cases), and social and emotional development (again in around half the cases). For example:

Family work being undertaken to enable communication between young person and adult; planned programme towards rehabilitation.

Young person receives a lot of input re: schooling to encourage him to attend and to support him whilst at school.

Referral to adolescent psychiatrist re: self-harming behaviour.

Now buying and cooking for self, eats less. Staff have attempted to take her shopping and give encouragement and advice on diet/preparing a meal but she doesn't co-operate.

The social workers mentioned a variety of techniques (for example, family therapy and skills training) but they rarely referred to the residential environment. Occasionally, mention was made of the need to a transfer to a more 'therapeutic' establishment. The current home seemed essentially to be seen as a base for treatment, rather than a treatment in itself.

Work was mainly shared between social worker and keyworker, with some division of labour and some overlap. The social worker was most likely to take the lead in issues involving the young person's legal status, in arrangements for new placements, and in work with the family. Social workers and the keyworker or the home both had substantial roles to play in relation to the young person's behaviour and identity, long-term future, schooling and jobs. Keyworkers or the home were more likely than social-workers to be involved in issues around contraception and leisure.

Table B1 Professionals' involvement with young people for different activities

	Social worker (%)	Key-worker/ home (%)	Other profes-sional (%)
Finding/arranging/introducing:			
Foster parents	25.0	7.4	11.4
Visits home	56.3	39.8	4.0
Other residential care	20.5	9.1	4.0
Lodgings/supported care	18.8	10.8	8.0
Counselling/individual work with young person over:			
Identity/care career	60.2	52.3	19.4
Behaviour	72.8	72.7	26.7
Family relationships	81.3	54.0	15.3
School/job	62.5	60.2	31.8
Return home	35.8	26.1	5.7
Long-term future	87.5	60.2	18.8
Practical arrangements over:			
Medical treatment/contraception	34.1	76.7	9.1
School issues/subject choice	40.9	43.2	33.5
Leisure	25.6	75.0	11.4
Job/YT	21.0	29.0	13.1
Contact with siblings	59.7	31.8	3.4
Changing legal status	31.8	4.0	2.8
Work with family over:			
Rehousing/housing problems	22.2	3.4	6.3
Debt	17.0	2.3	3.4
Other sources of stress	46.6	9.7	6.8
Alcohol/drugs	14.2	7.4	5.1
Family/marital relationships	35.2	8.5	7.4
Helping/managing young person	49.4	33.0	8.8
Young person's return	35.8	18.2	3.4
Young person's long-term future	71.0	30.1	7.4
Supportive visiting/monitoring	72.2	25.6	5.7

Source: Questionnaire to social workers.

The sheer amount of work undertaken by both groups of workers looks impressive. On average, social workers reported 11 activities for themselves, just under eight for the keyworker and nearly three (2.7) for other workers, an average of 21 activities per case. Overall they reported visiting the young person weekly in a quarter of the cases and at least monthly in nearly nine out of 10. The corresponding figures for the family were that one in eight saw the families weekly and half monthly. As would have been predicted from previous research (Millham *et al.* 1986), the level of visiting was lower among those who had been in the home for some time.

APPENDIX C

ETHNICITY

This Appendix brings together findings relevant to ethnicity—some repeated elsewhere in the book and others not. In analysing the data we have usually had to combine all ethnic categories into one large category of 'black and ethnic minority'. This grouping puts together Asian, dual-heritage and African-Caribbean young people in one group, and then combines young people and staff whose cultures and experience were extremely diverse. However, black and ethnic minority and Asian people do share a common experience arising from racism and this provides a justification for treating them as a group.

Seven per cent of the staff were said by the heads of home to be black and ethnic minority, a higher proportion than the census would suggest for the authorities as a whole. More than two-thirds of the black and ethnic minority staff were said to be African-Caribbean, with the next largest group being 'dual-heritage' and a very small proportion Asian. The proportion of black and ethnic minority staff varied sharply between authorities (0–13%). Compared with white staff they had been in the homes a relatively short time—a consequence, possibly, of the increasing awareness of the need to recruit staff from ethnic minorities, although it could also arise for other reasons. Only 4.7% of staff who had been in post for five years or more came from these minorities. The comparable figure for those who had been there for two years or less was 16%. A possible consequence of this relatively recent recruitment was that black and ethnic minority staff were on average younger (33 years as against 39).

As noted in Chapter 6, there were wide variations between homes in the proportions of black and ethnic minority staff, and two in particular had relatively high proportions (in one case 64%), presumably with the intention that the home would admit black and ethnic minority residents if possible. In practice, however, there was almost no correspondence between the proportion of black and ethnic minority young people in the home and the proportion of black and ethnic minority staff.

The proportion of residents over the past year who were black and ethnic minority was at 7.5% comparable to the proportion of staff. This was again higher than the census would suggest for the authorities. However, we did not know the districts within the authorities from which the young people came and if we had the figures they would probably have seemed less disproportionate. The proportions of black and ethnic minority residents varied sharply by authority (2–15%). Generally, they had made up a small proportion of the residents in a home. Roughly a third of the homes had had no black and ethnic minority resident in the previous year, a third had had less than 11% and a further third had had between 11% and 27%.

These young people were varyingly described as African-Caribbean (19), Asian (13), mixed African-Caribbean white (35), mixed Asian white (11) and other (3). The striking preponderance of dual-heritage young people is in keeping with the findings of Rowe and her colleagues (1989) and Bebbington and Miles (1989). These residents were significantly more likely than their white counterparts to be in the homes on an order (36% vs. 19%), and to have been admitted as 'long-stay'.

We explored whether the black and ethnic minority residents in our interview sample saw the homes differently from their white counterparts. In interpreting the results it is important to remember that we did not have interviewers from ethnic minorities (although we did do exploratory work using a black interviewer). This means that we are more likely to under-represent than over-represent problems related to racism. We also had very few black and ethnic minority respondents (the following analyses are based on 18).

That said, the overriding impression was that the black and ethnic minority young people did not feel particularly victimised but did find the homes an uneasy and uncomfortable place in which to be. Approximately eight out of 10 agreed with the statement that 'black and Asian residents get a fair deal here' and the remainder said no more than that this was only 'sometimes true'. By contrast, nearly half said that the home was 'a better place for white residents than black' and ethnic minority and no more than half were prepared to say it was not.

This general impression of unease was backed by other analyses. The black and ethnic minority residents were no more likely than others to complain that others attempted to bully them and sexually harass them, and they gave very similar accounts to other young people of the behaviour in the home, the strictness of the staff and of their own relationships with them. However, they were significantly more likely to say that they had a problem with the food and more likely ($p = .08$) to say that they had a problem with the police checking on people with whom they might stay. They generally saw the home as much less friendly, being much less likely than others to agree that, 'There's always someone to have a laugh with', or that 'Home is a friendly place', or that 'Residents' families are made welcome here'. They were also more likely to agree that 'Families feel uneasy when they visit here'. They gave a positive account of their own relationship with the staff but, compared with other residents, they saw them as significantly less supportive on our Staff Support Scale.

These findings should not suggest that gross racism is never found in children's homes. Other research (Fletcher 1993) suggests that it does occur, but we found no direct evidence of it. What the research does illustrate is the considerable difficulty which homes have in dealing with black and ethnic minority children so that the latter are at ease. Attempts to match a high proportion of black and ethnic minority staff with a high proportion of black and ethnic minority young people fall foul—at least in these authorities—of logistics. So, although the overall proportions of black and ethnic minority staff and black and ethnic minority residents are similar, the proportions in any given home are likely to be far from aligned. The food may not be right (our pilot interviews suggested that similar problems may apply to dress). The residents' visits to friends are checked for the best of motives by police, whom they may have come to distrust. Any family is likely to find it difficult to approach a children's home with its connotations of parental failure and its potentially power-ful staff, but families who are wary of differences in culture and of racist responses may find such approaches particularly difficult. And even if staff and other young people act towards them in a correct and inten-tionally benign way, these residents may nevertheless not feel at home.

APPENDIX D

BEHAVIOUR AND DEVELOPMENT OF YOUNG PEOPLE

This Appendix contains a number of tables to which we referred in Chapter 2. Tables D2 and D3 contain the variables which we used to create our measures of Health (sum of all 'health' variables in D2), Adjustment (sum of all 'identity', 'presentation and social development' and 'behavioural and emotional development' variables, with the exception of 'effective treatment for problems'), Educational Involvement (sum of first three 'education and work' variables in D3) and Relationships (sum of the variables 'emotional ties with caregivers', 'acceptance by adults and children' and 'close friends').

Table D1 Behaviour before present placement

	(*n*)	None (%)	Occasional (%)	Persistent (%)
Running away from care	128	50.8	37.5	11.7
Running away from own home	123	55.3	32.5	12.2
Delinquency	126	37.3	42.1	20.6
Violence to parents/other adults	128	57.0	31.3	11.7
Violence to children	127	49.6	42.5	7.9
Suicide attempts/self-harm	130	67.7	27.7	4.6
Sexual behaviour—risk to others/self	129	52.7	31.8	15.5
Severe truancy/school exclusion	137	29.2	29.9	40.9
Other difficult behaviour	128	20.3	35.2	44.5

Source: Questionnaire to social workers.

Table D2 Areas of development: Health to Self-care

Area of development	(n)	Very low (%)	Low (%)	High (%)	Very high (%)
1. Health					
Growth and development	173	—	4.1	28.8	67.1
Preventive measures	169	6.5	8.9	34.9	49.7
Treatment	168	3.1	7.1	20.8	69.0
2. Identity					
Self-esteem	173	31.2	45.7	20.8	2.3
Understanding of current care situation	175	4.6	18.3	34.9	42.3
Knowledge of birth family	174	2.9	13.8	23.6	59.8
3. Presentation and social skills					
Appearance and behaviour	173	8.1	35.8	35.3	20.8
Communication	174	6.9	35.1	41.4	16.7
Adjustment of appearance and behaviour	170	7.1	40.6	38.8	13.5
4. Emotional and behavioural development					
Problems	174	4.6	25.9	36.2	33.3
Treatment of problems	149	20.8	26.8	45.0	7.4
5. Self-care					
Ability to care for self	174	6.3	17.8	36.8	39.1

Source: Questionnaire to social workers.

Table D3 Areas of development: education and family

Area of development	(n)	Very low (%)	Low (%)	High (%)	Very high (%)
1. Education and Work					
Attainments	165	25.5	41.2	24.8	8.5
Special skills and interests	167	24.0	41.5	24.0	9.5
Participation in school activities	137	46.0	23.4	19.0	11.7
Participation in work	66	34.8	16.7	31.8	16.7
2. Family and Friends					
Emotional ties with care giver	173	13.9	23.1	32.9	30.1
Acceptance by adults and children	173	10.4	32.9	38.7	17.9
Close friends	173	16.8	48.0	27.7	7.5
Contact with family of origin	172	14.0	30.2	25.0	30.8

Source: Questionnaire to social workers.

REFERENCES

Ackland J (1982) *Girls in Care.* Gower, Aldershot.

Aldgate J (1980) Identification of factors influencing children's length of stay in care. In Triseliotis J (ed) *New Developments in Foster Care and Adoption.* Routledge, London.

Aldgate J, Colton M, Ghate D and Heath A (1992) Educational attainment and stability in long-term foster care. *Children and Society,* **6**, 91–103.

Aldgate J, Heath A, Colton M and Simm M (1993) Social work and the education of children in foster care. *Adoption and Fostering,* **17**, 25–34.

Allen I (1983) *Short Stay Residential Care for the Elderly.* Policy Studies Institute, London.

Allerhand M, Weber, R and Haug M (1966) *Adaption and Adaptability.* Child Welfare League of America, New York.

Arnold A, Costello E, Pickles A and Winder F (1987) *The Development of a Questionnaire for Use in Epidemological Studies of Depression in Children and Adolescents.* Medical Research Council Child Psychiatry Unit, London.

Audit Commission (1994) *Seen but not Heard: Co-ordinating Community Child Health and Social Services for Children in Need.* HMSO, London.

Baldwin N (1990) *The Power to Care in Children's Homes.* Avebury, Aldershot.

Barr H (1987) *Perspectives on Training for Residential Work.* Central Council for Education and Training in Social Work (CCETSW), London.

Bartak L and Rutter M (1975) The measurement of staff–child interaction in three units for autistic children. In Tizard J, Sinclair I and Clarke R (eds) *Varieties of Residential Experience.* Routledge, London.

Bebbington A and Miles J (1989) Background of children who enter local authority care. *British Journal of Social Work,* **19**, 349–368.

Berridge D (1985) *Children's Homes.* Blackwell, Oxford.

Berridge D and Cleaver H (1987) *Foster Home Breakdown.* Blackwell, Oxford.

Berridge D and Brodie I (1996) Residential child care in England and Wales: the enquiries and after. In Hill M and Aldgate J (eds) *Child Welfare Services: Developments in Law, Policy and Practice.* Jessica Kingsley, London.

Berridge D and Brodie I (1998) *Children's Homes Revisited.* Jessica Kingsley, London.

Biehal N, Clayden J, Stein M and Wade J (1992) *Prepared for Living?* National Children's Bureau, London.

Biehal N, Clayden J, Stein M and Wade J (1995) *Moving On: Young People and Leaving Care Schemes.* National Children's Bureau, London.

Bowlby J (1953) *Child Care and the Growth of Love.* Penguin Books, London.

Brodie I and Berridge D (1996) *Exclusion from School: Research Themes and Issues.* University of Luton Press, Luton.

Brown E, Bullock R, Hobson C and Little M (1996) *Structure and Culture in Children's Homes.* Dartington Research Unit, University of Bristol.

Bullock R, Little M and Millham S (1993a) *Residential Care for Children: A Review of the Research.* HMSO, London.

Bullock R, Little M and Millham S (1993b) *Going Home: The Return of Children Separated from Their Families.* Dartmouth, Aldershot.

Carr-Hill R, Dixon P, Mannion R, Rice N, Rudat K, Sinclair R and Smith P (1997) *A Model of the Determinants of Expenditure on Children's Personal Social Services.* Centre for Health Economics, University of York.

CIPFA (1996) *Personal Social Services Statistics: 1993–94 actuals.* Chartered Institute of Public Finance and Accountancy, London.

Clarke R and Martin D (1971) *Absconding from Approved Schools.* HMSO, London.

Cliffe D with Berridge D (1991) *Closing Children's Homes: An End to Residential Childcare?* National Children's Bureau, London.

Coates R, Miller A and Ohlin L (1978) *Diversity in a Youth Correctional System.* Ballinger, Cambridge, MA.

Coles B (1995) *Youth and Social Policy: Youth Citizenship and Youth Careers.* UCL Press, London.

Colton M (1988) *Dimensions of Substitute Care and a Comparative Study of Foster and Residential Care Practice.* Avebury, Aldershot.

Colton M (1989) Foster and residential children's perceptions of their environments. *British Journal of Social Work,* **19**, 217–213.

Colton M and Hellinckx W (1994) Residential and foster care in the European Community: current trends in policy and practice. *British Journal of Social Work,* **24**, 559–576.

Department of Health (1991) . *Patterns and Outcomes in Child Placement—Messages from Current Research and Their Implications.* HMSO, London.

Department of Health and Welsh Office (1993) *Children Act 1992* (A Report by the Secretaries of State for Health and for Wales on the Children Act 1989). HMSO, London.

Department of Health (1995) *Child Protection: Messages from Research.* HMSO, London.

Department of Health (1997) *Children Looked After by Local Authorities. Year Ending March 31 1996.* Department of Health, London.

Dharamsi F, Edmonds G, Filkin E, Headley C, Jones P, Naish M, Scott I, Smith H and Williams J (1979) *Community Work and Caring for Children: A Community Project in an Inner City Local Authority.* Owen Wells, Ilkley.

Dunlop A (1974) *The Approved School Experience.* HMSO, London.

Evans B, Hughes B and Wilkin D with Jolley P (1981) *The Management of Mental and Physical Impairment in Non-specialist Residential Homes for the Elderly.* Department of Psychiatry and Community Medicine, University of Manchester.

Farmer E and Pollock S (1998) *Substitute Care for Sexually Abused and Abusing Children.* Wiley, Chichester.

Fisher M, Marsh P, Phillips D and Sainsbury E (1986) *In and Out of Care.* British Agencies for Adoption and Fostering, London.

Fletcher B (1993) *Not Just a Name: The Views of Young People in Foster and Residential Care.* National Consumer Council, London.

Fletcher-Campbell F and Hall C (1990) *Changing Schools? Changing People? The Education of Children in Care.* National Foundation for Educational Research, Slough.

Fraser C (1993) *Corporate Parents: Inspection of Residential Child Care Services in Local Authorities.* Department of Health, London.

Garnett L (1992) *Leaving Care and After.* National Children's Bureau, London.

Gibbs I and Sinclair I (1992) Consistency: a prerequisite for inspecting old people's homes? *British Journal of Social Work,* **22**, 535–550.

Gibbs I and Sinclair I (in press) Private and local authority children's homes: a comparison. *Journal of Adolescence.*

Godfrey A (1996) Staff Training in Homes for Elderly People. Who Wants It and What Does It Do? Unpublished D Phil Thesis, University of York.

Goffman E (1961) *Asylums.* Doubleday, New York.

Gooch D (1996) Home and away: the residential care, education and control of children in historical and political context. *Child and Family Social Work,* 1, 19–32.

Heal K and Cawson P (1975) Organisation and change in children's institutions. In Tizard J, Sinclair I and Clarke R (eds) *Varieties of Residential Experience.* Routledge, London.

Heal K, Sinclair I and Troop J (1973) The development of a social climate questionnaire for use in community homes and approved schools. *British Journal of Sociology,* 24, 222–231.

Heath A, Colton M and Aldgate J (1989) The educational progress of children in and out of care. *British Journal of Social Work,* 19, 447–460.

Heath A, Colton M and Aldgate J (1994) Failure to escape: a longitudinal study of foster children's educational attainment. *British Journal of Social Work,* 24, 241–260.

Hensey D, Williams J and Rosenbloom L (1983) Intervention child abuse: experience in Liverpool. *Developmental Medicine and Child Neurology,* 25, 606–611.

Hills D, Child C, Hills J and Blackburn V (1997) *Towards Qualified Leadership in Residential Care: The Evaluation of the Residential Child Care Initiative.* Final report to the Department of Health. Tavistock Institute, London.

Jackson S (1989) Residential care and education. *Children & Society,* 2(4), 335–350.

Kadushin A (1970) *Adopting Older Children.* Columbia University Press, New York.

Kahan B (1979) *Growing Up in Care.* Blackwell, Oxford.

Kendrick A and Fraser S (1992) *The Review of Residential Child Care in Scotland. A Literature Review.* Scottish Office, Central Research Unit Papers.

King R, Raynes N and Tizard J (1971) *Patterns of Residential Care.* Routledge, London.

King J and Taitz L (1985) Catch-up growth following abuse. *Archives of Disease in Childhood,* 60, 1152–1154.

Kirkwood A (1993) *The Leicestershire Inquiry 1992.* Leicestershire County Council, Leicester.

Knapp M and Smith J (1985) The costs of residential child care: explaining variations in the public sector. *Policy and Politics,* 13, 127–154.

Levy A and Kahan B (1991) *The 'Pindown' Experience and the Protection of Children. The Report of the Staffordshire Child Care Inquiry 1990.* Staffordshire County Council, Stafford.

Lewis W (1982) Ecological factors in successful residential treatment. *Behavioural Disorders,* 7, 149–156.

Madge N (1994) *Children and Residential Care in Europe.* National Children's Bureau, London.

Maughan B and Pickles A (1990) Adopted and illegitimate children grown up. In Robins L and Rutter M (eds) *Straight and Devious Pathways from Childhood to Adulthood.* Cambridge University Press, Cambridge, UK.

McConkey W, Balloch S, Andrew T, Davey B, Dolan L, Fisher M, Ginn J, McLean J and Pahl J (1997) *The Northern Ireland Social Services Workforce in Transition.* National Institute of Social Work, London.

Meadowcroft P, Thomlinson B and Chamberlain P (1994) Treatment foster-care services: a research agenda for child welfare. *Child Welfare,* 73, 565–581.

Millham S, Bullock R and Cherrett P (1975) *After Grace Teeth: A Comparative Study of the Residential Experience of Boys in Approved Schools.* Human Context Books, London.

Millham S, Bullock R, Hosie K and Haak M (1986) *Lost in Care—The Problem of Maintaining Links Between Children in Care and Their Families.* Gower, Altershot.
Minty B (1987) *Child Care and Adult Crime.* Manchester University Press, Manchester.
Moos R (1968) The assessment of the social climate of correctional institutions. *Journal of Research in Crime and Delinquency,* **5,** 174–188.
Moos R and Houts P (1968) Assessment of the social atmospheres of psychiatric wards. *Journal of Abnormal Psychology,* **73,** 595–604.
Newcombe R, Measham F and Parker H (1995) A survey of drinking and deviant behaviour among 14/15 year olds in north-west England. *Addiction Research,* **2,** 319–341.
Packman J, Randall J and Jacques N (1986) *Who Needs Care? Social Work Decisions About Children.* Blackwell, Oxford.
Parker R (1988) Children. In Sinclair I (ed.) *Residential Care: The Research Reviewed.* HMSO, London.
Parker R, Ward H, Jackson S, Aldgate J and Wedge P (1991) *Looking After Children: Assessing Outcomes in Child Care.* HMSO, London.
Petrie C (1980) *The Nowhere Boys.* Saxon House, Farnborough.
Polsky H (1965). *Cottage Six. The Social System of Delinquent Boys in Residential Treatment.* Wiley, New York.
Quinton D and Rutter M (1984) Parents with children in care: current circumstances and parenting. *Journal of Child Psychology and Psychiatry,* **25,** 211–229.
Ramsay M and Percy A (1997) A national household survey of drug misuse in Britain: a decade of development. *Addiction,* **92,** 931–937.
Rathburn C, Di Virgilio L and Waldfogel S (1958) The restitutive process in children following radical separation from family and culture. *American Journal of Orthopsychiatry,* **28,** 408–415.
Reddy L and Pfeiffer S (1997) Effectiveness of treatment foster care with children and adolescents: a review of outcome studies. *Journal of the American Academy of Child and Adolescent Psychiatry,* **36**(5), 581–588.
Reid W, Kagan R and Schlosberg S (1988) Prevention of placement: critical factors in program success. *Child Welfare,* **67,** 25–36.
Rowe J, Hundleby M and Garnett L (1989) Child care now: a survey of placement patterns. *British Agencies for Adoption and Fostering,* **6,** 188.
Sampson R and Laub J (1993) *Crime in the Making: Pathways and Turning Points Through Life.* Harvard University Press, Cambridge, MA.
Sinclair I (1971) *Hostels for Probationers.* HMSO, London.
Sinclair I (1975) The influence of wardens and matrons on probation hostels. In Tizard J, Sinclair I and Clarke R (eds) *Varieties of Residential Experience.* Routledge, London.
Sinclair I and Clarke R (1973) Acting out behaviour and its significance for the residential treatment for delinquents. *Journal of Child Psychology and Psychiatry,* **14,** 283–291.
Sinclair I and Heal K (1976) Diversity within the total institution: some evidence from boys' perceptions of community homes. *Policy and Politics,* **4,** 5–13.
Skinner A (1992) *Another Kind of Home: A Review of Residential Child Care.* Scottish Office. HMSO, Edinburgh.
Social Services Committee (1984) *First Report of the Social Services Committee 1983/84* (known as The 'Short Report'). HMSO, London.
Social Services Inspectorate (1985) *Inspection of Community Homes.* Department of Health and Social Security, London.
Social Services Inspectorate (1994) *Corporate Parents: Child Care Services in 11 Local Authorities.* Department of Health, London.

Social Services Inspectorate (1997) *Substance Misuse and Young People: The Social Services Response.* Department of Health, London.

Social Services Inspectorate for Wales (1991) *Accommodating Children—A Review of Children's Homes in Wales.* HMSO, London.

Soothill K (1995) Job satisfaction and dissatisfaction among residential care workers. *Social Care Research Findings*, No. 69. Joseph Rowntree Foundation, York.

Stein T J (1985) Projects to prevent out of home placement. *Children and Youth Services Review*, **7**, 109–122.

Stein M (1993) The abuses and uses of residential child care. In Ferguson H, Gilligan R and Torode R (eds) *Surviving Childhood Adversity. Issues for Policy and Practice.* Social Studies Press, Dublin.

Stein M (1994) Leaving care, education and career trajectories. *Oxford Review of Education*, **20**, 349–360.

Stein M (1997) *What Works in Leaving Care?* Barnados, Ilford.

Stein M and Carey K (1986) *Leaving Care.* Blackwell, Oxford.

Taylor D and Alpert S (1973) *Continuity and Support Following Residential Treatment.* Child Welfare League of America, New York.

Tizard B (1977) *Adoption: A Second Chance.* Routledge, London.

Tizard J (1975) The quality of residential care for retarded children. In Tizard J, Sinclair I and Clarke R (eds) *Varieties of Residential Experience.* Routledge, London.

Tizard J, Sinclair I and Clarke R (eds) (1975) *Varieties of Residential Experience.* Routledge, London.

Townsend P (1962) *The Last Refuge.* Routledge, London.

Triseliotis J, Borland M, Hill M and Lambert L (1995) *Teenagers and the Social Work Services.* HMSO, London.

Triseliotis J and Russell J (1984) *Hard to Place.* Heinemann, London.

Utting Sir William (1991) *Children in Public Care: A Review of Residential Care.* HMSO, London.

Utting Sir William (1997) *People Like Us: The Report of the Review of the Safeguards for Children Living Away from Home.* HMSO, London.

Vernon J and Fruin D (1986) *In Care: A Study of Social Work Decision Making.* National Children's Bureau, London.

Wagner, Lady Gillian (1988) *A Positive Choice.* HMSO, London.

Walter J (1977) *Sent Away: A Study of a Boys' Approved School.* Saxon House, Farnborough.

Warner N (1992) *Choosing with Care: The Report of the Committee of Inquiry into the Selection, Development and Management of Staff in Children's Homes.* HMSO, London.

Wells K and Biegel D (1992) Intensive family preservation services research: current status and future agenda. *Social Work Research and Abstracts*, **28**, 21–27.

Whitaker D, Archer L and Hicks L (1998) *Working in Children's Homes: Challenges and Complexities.* Wiley, Chichester.

Whitaker D, Cook J, Dunne C and Rockliffe S (1985) *The Experience of Residential Care from the Perspective of Children, Parents and Caregivers.* Unpublished report to the ESRC. University of York.

Wolins M (1974) *Successful Group Care: Explorations in the Powerful Environment.* Aldine, Chicago.

Zimmerman R (1982) Foster care in retrospect. *Tulane Studies in Social Welfare*, **14**, 1–119.

INDEX

Note: page numbers in *italic* refer to information in tables only.

Index compiled by Liz Granger

Related titles of interest from Wiley...

From Hearing to Healing
Working with the Aftermath of Child Sexual Abuse, 2nd Edition
Anne Bannister
Published in association with the NSPCC
0-471-98298-9   216pp   1998   Paperback

Making Sense of the Children Act
Third Edition
Nicholas Allen
0-471-97831-0   304pp   1998   Paperback

Women Who Sexually Abuse Children
From Research to Clinical Practice
Jacqui Saradjian in association with Helga Hanks
Wiley Series in Child Care & Protection
0-471-96072-1   336pp   1996   Paperback

The Emotionally Abused and Neglected Child
Identification, Assessment and Intervention
Dorota Iwaniec
Wiley Series in Child Care & Protection
0-471-95579-5   222pp   1995   Paperback

Cycles of Child Maltreatment
Facts, Fallacies and Interventions
Ann Buchanan
Wiley Series in Child Care & Protection
0-471-95889-1   328pp   1996   Paperback

 ## Child Abuse Review
ISSN: 0952-9136

 ## Children & Society
Published in association with the National Children's Bureau
ISSN: 0951-0605